(Mis)Representing Islam

The racism and rhetoric of
British broadsheet newspapers

John E. Richardson
Loughborough University

John Benjamins Publishing Company

Amsterdam / Philadelphia

The paper used in this publication meets the minimum requirements of American National Standard for Information Sciences – Permanence of Paper for Printed Library Materials, ANSI z39.48-1984.

Library of Congress Cataloging-in-Publication Data

John E. Richardson

(Mis)Representing Islam : The racism and rhetoric of British broadsheet newspapers / John E. Richardson.

p. cm. (Discourse Approaches to Politics, Society and Culture, ISSN 1569-9463 ; v. 9)

Includes bibliographical references and indexes.

1. Islam-Press coverage--Great Britain. I. Title: Misrepresenting Islam. II. Title. III. Series.

PN5124.I78R53   2004

070.4'49297'0941--dc22   2003062824

ISBN 978 90 272 2699 0 (EUR) / ISBN 978 1 58811 473 0 (US) (HB; alk. paper)

ISBN 978 90 272 0621 3 (PB; alk. paper)

ISBN 978 90 272 9580 4 (EB)

John Benjamins Publishing Co. · P.O. Box 36224 · 1020 ME Amsterdam · The Netherlands
John Benjamins North America · P.O. Box 27519 · Philadelphia PA 19118-0519 · USA

To Teun A. van Dijk

Contents

List of figures, graphs and tables

Acknowledgements

I am grateful to many people, in many capacities, for making this book possible.

First, I would like to thank my sister Amy for her financial support. Without her generous provision during my 'grant-less' first year of doctoral study, I simply would not have been able to start let alone finish my thesis: thank you very much Amy. In a similar vein, I would like to extend this gratitude to the ESRC for funding my research for the remaining three years of study (Postgraduate Award R00429834654). Without this financial support this research project would have been a great deal more difficult to complete, if it could have been completed at all.

I would like to thank the Department of Journalism Studies, University of Sheffield for their academic and institutional support — particularly Peter Cole who gave me the time and space necessary to redraft my thesis into the present volume.

My thanks to those colleagues and reviewers who have looked at, commented upon and at times criticised draft versions of this book. In particular I would like to thank the series editors Paul Chilton and Ruth Wodak, Bob Franklin (who supervised the thesis on which this book is based) and Roopa Ramaiya, whose advice and encouragement at a crucial juncture was particularly welcome. I would also like to thank my friends who have assisted in the completion of this book. In this regard I would like to thank Albert, Harps, Lee, Mike, Paul, Stephen and Vincent for their support, intelligent (though often infuriating) conversation and their friendship. Above all, I would like to thank my wife Kirsty for her encouragement, patience (at so many bundles of newspapers all over the house!) and love over years — the brevity of such an acknowledgement simply does not (and could not) do justice to the level of this support.

Finally, although it may embarrass him, this book is dedicated to Teun van Dijk. Teun's writings — both published and via personal emails — have contributed to the present volume at various stages of my research. For his informal support and advice during the early planning stages, and his helpful reviews and appraisal of my later work, I am personally particularly grateful. More generally, many of us who consider ourselves 'discourse analysts' owe him a larger intellectual debt for his pioneering research, particularly given the antipathy and sometimes outright hostility he received for his work on élite racism. This book is dedicated to him with thanks.

Preface to the paperback edition

In the 5 years since this book was first published, the need for a critical discourse study of anti-Muslim rhetoric in newspapers has arguably increased. When I started the primary data collection for this study, back in 1997, the press reporting of Muslims, derogatory or otherwise, was what could be described as a 'specialised interest'. When I talked to my colleagues and fellow PhD students about what I was researching, often the response was *'why?'* I doubt that such a response would be possible now, when we are presented, on an almost daily basis, with hyperbolic, over-lexicalised accounts of Muslim radicals, militants, Islamists, firebrand clerics, insurgents, *jihadiyoon*, *fedayeen*, *janjaweed* and terrorists (would-be and actual), all seemingly committed to the downfall of Western civilisation.

It is hardly an exaggeration to claim that the political and ideological significance of Islam and Muslims have never been higher. As Billig et al (2006) have demonstrated, the prominence of Islam in British political debate has increased dramatically since 1997, when many of the texts that this book examines were originally printed. Billig et al's (2006) analysis was limited to press reporting in the two weeks prior to successive UK General Elections – in 1997, 2001 and 2005 - but their findings are nevertheless revealing of the position that Muslims are perceived, by both press and politicians, to play in the daily life of the nation, and the way that this has shifted since 1997. During the 1997 and 2001 General Elections there were very few newspaper articles that mentioned Muslims — 13 in 1997 and 19 in 2001, and that was for all national newspapers combined. During the 2005 Election this rose to 141 articles — a rise from 1 per day across the two-week sample, to 10 per day. This rise is entirely a response to the war on terror in general, and the invasion of Iraq in particular, and how these events were thought to be playing out in the national (that is, domestic) political sphere. In many of these reports, the (non)issue of racial and religious difference was heightened, exaggerated or misrepresented for reactionary political reasons; the topoi that this book identifies played a key role in articulating these differences, and specifically the ways that 'Their' difference could (or should) be viewed as threatening to 'Us'. Broadsheets, specifically, were preoccupied with the largely phantom notion of 'the Muslim Vote' and the premise that the invasion of Iraq was an election issue which divided Muslim and non-Muslim Britons. Accordingly, Muslims were more preoccupied by the state of Iraq than the state of Britain, and more concerned with the troubles of foreigners than their fellow Britons. The 'Muslimness' of British Muslims was assumed, and argued, to be so powerful that there was never any question that their affiliation, or perhaps allegiance, to Iraqi Muslims would trump all other policy issues. More stridently argued articles came close to suggesting, again, that British Muslims represented a fifth column. In fact, news reports that claimed British Muslims would vote on the basis of a different set of concerns or priorities to non-Muslim Britons were repeatedly undermined by the actual views of British Muslims, frequently quoted in these same articles! In these cases then, the structuring influence of prejudicial ideas of 'Us' and 'Them' were such that difference was exclaimed even while staring sameness in the face.

The way that sameness/diversity is represented and understood has a crucial influence on social stability and social conflict. Journalism provides us with a window on the ways that social, ethnic and religious sameness/diversity are viewed. I say that 'a window' to avoid implying a unidirectional account of causal influence, since journalism doesn't simply *shape* people's beliefs nor does it simply *reflect* them; rather it does both. Hence, an examination of the ideas and arguments in journalism provides us with a way of examining social ideas and arguments, and specifically the key arguments and representations about who 'We' are and who 'They' that are circulating at any one time. Broadsheet newspaper representations, in particular, as an empowered discourse of middle and upper class producers and consumers, are especially important in this regard. They remain a key discursive site for the production and reproduction of anti-Muslim racisms, acting as a reflection and a cause of wider social discord and conflict, and therefore deserve to receive continued and detailed scholarly attention.

John E Richardson
Loughborough University
January 2009

Reference

Billig, Michael, Deacon, David, Downey, John, Richardson, John E. & Golding, Peter 2006. *Britishness in the last three General Elections: from ethnic nationalism to civic nationalism.* Commission for Racial Equality.

Introduction

Racism, xenophobia and anti-semitism are still widespread in Britain, perpetuating discrimination and disadvantage for the groups whom these (racist) discourses position as inferior and subordinate. Indeed a wealth of evidence, from academic studies of governmental or Parliamentary 'debate' on and around 'ethnic issues' (Martin-Rojo & van Dijk, 1997; van Dijk, 2000; Wodak & van Dijk, 2000) to the electoral successes of the Dutch List Fortuyn, the British BNP, the French FN and Austrian FPÖ, the Danish DPP and others, all points to the fact that racism is still very much a feature of everyday life across the European Union as a whole, and perhaps even on the increase. During the period of newspaper coverage sampled for this study (October 1997–January 1998) for example, the stark findings of a European Commission report on xenophobia and racism in the 15 member states were published (reported in both the *Daily Telegraph* and *Guardian*, 20 December 1997). In Britain, 32 percent of respondents openly admitted to being either "very racist" or "quite racist", a proportion which rose to a particularly disturbing 66 per cent when those respondents admitting to being "a little racist" were also included.[1] Further, given the general reticence to racism, it is by no means unthinkable that the level of racist prejudice in Britain is, in fact, much higher.

Racism, moreover, is not restricted to the 'minds' of men and women as prejudiced belief, attitudes and opinions. Rather, as Wieviorka (1995) has suggested, racism connotes

> two distinct logics, the one being a logic of inferiorisation, which aims to ensure the racialised group receives unequal treatment, the other a logic of differentiation, which tends to set it apart and, in extreme cases, expel or exterminate it. (p. xv)

Repeated studies indicate the high levels of discrimination and social exclusion suffered by Britain's black and 'Asian' communities. The Parekh Report (Runnymede Trust, 2000), for example, cites a Policy Studies Institute investigation from the mid-1990s which found

> overall about one in eight of the people it surveyed — Bangladeshi, Caribbean, Chinese, Indian, Pakistani — had experienced racist insults or abuse during the

previous 12 months. It estimated that about 20,000 people suffer a physical assault each year, 40,000 have items of property damaged and 230,000 experience abuse or insults. (from Modood et al, 1997; cited in Runnymede Trust, 2000: 57)

The widespread racism evidenced in the EC report (since supported by the Runnymede Trust, 2000), its implicit *acceptance* given the respondents' willingness to admit to being racist, and the injurious social conditions endured by 'racial' and ethnic minorities which emanate from such racism, demand immediate and vigorous critique and contestation.

This book assumes, and intends to illustrate, that racism, like all aspects of social life, is discursive: it is simultaneously a product of and a contributing factor in the continuation of hierarchical and unjust social relations. Put another way, racism simultaneously constructs social relations between individuals and groups in society — usually hierarchies of the sort mentioned above — and, at the same time, is constructed by these social relations. This is not to suggest that racisms are wholly constructed phenomena, that racist practices are assembled and reassembled "as social actors interact with each other and exchange interpretative meanings" (Manning, 2001: 21), or that racism can be collapsed into, and conceptualised wholly in relation to discourse. Rather, I suggest that racism, like all social phenomena, should be approached in relation to questions of structure and agency typical of critical social analysis. This critical perspective, "is centrally concerned with action and structure, in an attempt to discern the real constraints which shape the lives and opportunities of real actors in the real world" (Golding and Murdock, 2000: 72). Such a position focuses upon, and aims at illuminating, the subtle interplay between the economic, the political, the social and the personal, and in this sense, "critical theory is materialist, in its focus on the interaction of people with their material environment and its further preoccupation with the unequal command over material resources and the consequences of such inequality for the nature of the symbolic environment" (Ibid.).

Of course racism is not a fixed concept — to the degree that it may be more appropriate to talk of *racisms*. This point is illustrated by the manner in which racism has changed, shifted and re-emerged in different guises over the last 300 years or so, and the way it *continues* to re-emerge, creating new positions on racial hierarchies and warranting new forms of social control to police these new racisms. Most recently, an anti-refugee discourse has emerged in popular media culture, in which it has become common place and to a greater extent *accepted* for impoverished individuals and groups (who frequently are *white*) to be demonised, verbally and physically attacked and to be excluded — if not from Our shores entirely then at least from social resources, employment and therefore from an acceptable standard of living. As Fekete (2002a) argues, this newer form of racism — 'a xeno-racism', as she and the Institute of Race Relations call it — excludes "in the name of the preservation of economic prosperity" (p.1). "It is a racism", Sivanandan argues in this same article, "that is not just directed at those with darker skins from the former colonial territories, but at the newer categories of the displaced, the dispossessed and the uprooted, who are beating at western Europe's doors, the Europe that helped displace them in the first place. [...] It is racism that is meted out to impoverished strangers even if they are white. It is xeno-racism" (Ibid.). Thus, this racism is both a product of increasingly entrenched economic global inequalities and simultaneously (in the way in which, amongst other aspects, xeno-racists demand that refugees remain in 'the first safe country' they enter, thereby concentrating refugee camps in comparatively deprived African and Asian countries) a contributing factor in their reproduction. Thus, xeno-racism, like all racisms, can be approached and analysed as a material discourse: as a discursive process and a discursive practice, both born of and contributing to inequalities in opportunities and material resources.

Approaching racism in this way — as created and creative — begs a set of obvious questions: in what ways, and in what fora, is racist discourse expressed, reproduced and maintained? How are prejudicial ethnic attitudes, and the inequitable relations of dominance, discrimination and repression that follow from such attitudes, maintained? A great number of publications have illustrated that the news media is and has been culpable for the creation and maintenance of racist sentiment and social practice (Braham, 1992; Campbell, 1995; Cottle, 2000a; Entman, 1990; Ferguson, 1998; Halloran, 1977; Hartmann & Husband, 1974; Searle, 1987; van Dijk, 1987, 1991, 1993, 2000) and for the maintenance of anti-Muslim racisms specifically (Karim, 1997; Poole, 1999, 2000, 2002; Richardson, 2001a, 2001b; Runnymede Trust, 1997; Said, 1997). It is the task of this study to show *how* this occurs — how the reporting of élite (majority white) broadsheet journalists is implicated in the production and reproduction of (racist) attitudes, beliefs, sentiment and practices and the potential effects of this reporting on the lives of Muslims, both in Britain and in the rest of the world.

Background to the book

This book is a study of the discursive representation of Islam and Muslims in British broadsheet newspapers, analysing the ways in which they reproduce anti-Muslim racism. While the focus here is British newspapers, given the centripetal forces of political and economic globalisation, the greater standardisation of journalistic texts and the widespread and continuing influence of Orientalist scholarship (particularly in 'the West'), the conclusions offered may be useful to studies of broadsheet, or 'quality' newspaper reporting in other countries. There were three principal motivations for this study: First, by examining the reporting of a single identified theme within the British broadsheet press, this book fills a yawning gap in empirical literature. There are, to my knowledge, no other book-length studies of broadsheet (élite) newspaper coverage on *any* issue in *any* national or reporting context. This is quite a startling omission which reflects the more general under-theorisation of class power and privilege in contemporary society. In all fields of the social sciences, middle and upper class academics have persistently neglected to study their own social class(es), despite their obvious political influence and status. In the field of 'race relations' — and racism more specifically — this deficiency is particularly unfortunate. Given the well-known short-hand, that 'racism = prejudice + power', it seems wholly appropriate that the analysis and critique of racism should start with the (racist) discourse of society's more powerful groups: the middle and upper classes. The assumption here is that the occurrence of prejudice, rejectionist strategies and "everyday racism" in broadsheet newspapers will stand as an indication of the extent to which such racist practices have "become part of what is seen as 'normal' by the dominant group" (Essed, 1991: 288).

Second, only scant empirical research has been conducted on newspaper representation(s) of Muslims, with the majority of work completed to date relying largely on non-systematic anecdotal evidence to 'illustrate' biases in media coverage. The selectivity of such approaches has been unhelpful in demonstrating the extent to which the reporting of the broadsheet press is dominated by racist assumptions and outputs. In contrast this book is based on an interdisciplinary foundation, combining both quantitative and qualitative methods of data collection and analysis in order to highlight both manifest and latent meaning in the sampled items of reporting. I devised and operationalised a detailed coding instrument which recorded over 80 variables. This coding instrument was then applied to four months (October 1997–January 1998) of

British broadsheet newspapers (The *Financial Times*, the *Guardian*, the *Independent*, the *Daily Telegraph*, *The Times*, the *Independent on Sunday* and the *Sunday Times*), resulting in a data-set of 2,540 items of newspaper reporting. Following this detailed collection of quantitative data, I applied a more nuanced and reflexive research method based on the approach of critical discourse analysis. The combination of these two research methods is particularly useful in analysing patterns — both *between* and *within* texts — in the ways Muslims are represented and racism is marshalled in the élite broadsheet press.

After creating and developing (via small pilot studies) the my coding instrument, a set of criteria was needed to identify systematically *which* units of analysis — or *texts* — would come under the remit of the study. I decided that an article should be recorded, coded and analysed if its contents were 'Islam and/or Muslim related'. Clearly such a criterion was far too general and therefore a much more closely specified set of identifying criteria was developed. A text was identified as 'Islam and/or Muslim related' if it specifically mentioned:

- 'Islam'
- a Muslim individual
- an organisation, collective, pressure group, etc. identified as a Muslim organisation, collective, pressure group, etc.
- a nation wholly or predominantly populated by Muslims (e.g. Iraq, Indonesia)
- or a nation which, by virtue of history, culture, government or politics could be regarded as 'a Muslim country' (e.g. Lebanon)

in the text's:

- leader (headline, over-headline, lead-in or extended by-line)
- or either of its first two paragraphs
- or for the whole of a paragraph lower down the article.

This was intended to exclude passing references to Islam, Muslims, etc. (and thus concentrate on more specific, comprehensive, detailed or otherwise 'in-depth' newspaper coverage) but also to include texts in which Muslims (or countries like Nigeria) were reported but key words such as 'Muslim', 'Islam', 'Islamic' etc. were *not* used. During data analysis, this proved to be a productive approach, with the 'Muslim-ness' of certain countries persistently backgrounded or absent from reporting (Indonesia was a case in point, despite it being the most populous Muslim country in the world) while the 'Muslim-ness' of certain other countries was persistently foregrounded.

The third and most fundamental reason (and the ultimate goal) for this study was to contribute to a better understanding of not just the prevalence, but also the form and (potential) effects of anti-Muslim racism in élite discourse. Therefore, during the collection and (later) analysis of newspaper articles, I attempted to emulate the views and approach of Gerbner (1958) who argued for expanding media analysis from an exclusive focus on formal characteristics of content, towards regarding content "as expressive of social relationship[s] and institutional dynamics, and as formulative of social patterns" (p. 480). Rejecting both of the labels 'quantitative' and 'qualitative' in favour of the term 'critical' media research, Gerbner's contention was

> not so much that inherent physical characteristics of media as such, or that elements of style, vocabulary, syntax, are themselves of profound and direct significance. Rather [...] that the nature and consequences of these elements and characteristics can be understood best if content is viewed as bearing the imprint of social needs and uses. (p. 481)

From this perspective, the consequential meanings of newspaper texts are "the property of a specific event or system of events" (Ibid.) which surround the production of media communication. From this starting point, further questions also need to be asked of the studied texts:

> In what ways does this material reflect physical and social qualities of communicating agencies (publishers) and their relationships to other systems such as markets, advertisers, audiences and their world of events? What points of view about life and the world as [the communicator] sees them are implied and facilitated? What social arrangements of ownership and control of communicative means and facilities are revealed by the prevalence of this material? [...] What might be the consequences [...] of social relationships and points of view mediated through this content as a social event system? (Gerbner, 1958: 488)

These are indeed ambitious goals. But (to add a proverb to the mix) 'there is not much point shooting rabbits while locusts are feasting on your crops' — to eradicate racism we need to set our sights high.

The book in outline

Chapters 1 and 2 introduce the theoretical and empirical body of work which will be drawn on throughout the remainder of the book. Central to these chapters are the theories and methods of Critical Discourse Analysis, and the chapters are structured across three sections which discuss the three conceptual dimensions which should be foregrounded in a successful discourse analysis: social practices; discursive practices, including but not exclusively the practices of news gathering and news reporting; and the linguistic analysis of texts. During the discussion of each of these three levels of analysis, emphasis is placed on both exploring their inter-related nature and, specifically, how texts — in this case the reporting of British broadsheet newspapers — may be involved in the production, reproduction and demolition of racialised social inequalities.

Chapter 1 provides an introduction to certain key social practices which form a backdrop to contemporary journalistic output. These social *forces* and *sources* frame the way(s) in which journalists interact with and report Islam and Muslims. I first outline the critique which Said (1978) offers of the (disciplinary) discourses of 'Orientalism' and the theoretical response which the thesis provoked, before focusing on the British social context, and the effects which 'Islamophobia' (Runnymede Trust 1997, 2000) and racism are having on the socio-economic position(s) of British Muslims.

Chapter 2 introduces the discursive practices of British journalism and the theories and methods employed in the discourse analysis of texts. I discuss the professional, organisational and financial characteristics of journalism and their relationships with the reporting of 'race' and racialised communities, before focusing on past research on journalistic outputs and reporters' representations of 'race' and ethnicity. Due to a shift from explicit racism in the news to more implicit 'coded' references to 'race', a more nuanced analytic approach to the study of news reporting is needed than the previous emphasis on 'coding and counting' in journalism studies. Such an approach has been developed in the field of discourse analysis. Therefore, the latter sections of this chapter introduce the principal contributions of discourse analysis to the (linguistic) study of news texts, focusing on lexicon, syntactic structures, semantic and argumentative structures, the pragmatic ability of texts to 'perform actions' and, thus, how meaning and action are related in language.

Following this discussion of the theoretical and methodological bases of this research, Chapters 3 to 7 present the resulting analysis of the recorded items of newspaper coverage. The choice and focus of these chapters are structured in order to reflect prominent patterns in broadsheet reporting of Islam and Muslims. Prominent reporting patterns were determined across two axes: the numeric frequency of reports on and about certain issues, topics, themes and countries and their (ideological) significance given the position and performative role of broadsheet newspapers in the(ir) social context(s).

Chapter 3 is the first of two chapters illustrating the centrality of the 'ideo-logical square' (van Dijk) to the reporting of Islam and Muslims. An 'ideologi-cal square' of prejudiced talk and text frames the presuppositions, themes and arguments of news reporting around a negative 'Other' presentation and a simultaneous positive 'Self' presentation and is dominated by a twin process of 'division and rejection' of Muslims ('Them') from 'Us'. First I explore the pres-ence and frequency of the negative 'Muslim Other' in broadsheet reporting. I investigate how 'Their' negativity is constructed and maintained, focusing on four stereotypical *topoi* used in derogatory representations of Muslims: the 'military threat of Muslim countries'; the 'threat of Muslim extremism'; the (internal) 'threat to democracy' posed by Muslim political leaders and parties; and the 'social threat of Muslim gender inequality'.

Following from the previous chapter, Chapter 4 explores the simultaneous contraposition of the ideological square — the presence and frequency of the positive 'Self' in broadsheet reporting — and analyses how 'Our' positivity is assumed, constructed and maintained in broadsheet reporting. The chapter examines two case studies in which 'Our' civilising influence *on* or *over* Muslims is either implicitly assumed or else explicitly stated. The first critiques the report-ing of Iranian internal politics, which is so dominated by an 'Islam vs. the West' reporting homology, that President Khatami and his supporters are recreated as the personification of 'Western' progress, battling the assumedly regressive forces of Islamic government. This 'two party split' is a gross simplification based on a 'good guy/bad guy dialectic' which precludes an understanding of Iran. The second case analyses the normalisation of Israeli aggression in broadsheet newspapers, and shows how the position 'We' is mutable and can be expanded to include individuals, groups and even other nations which in other contexts are represented as 'foreign'.

Chapter 5 discusses and analyses the reporting of British Islam and British Muslims in broadsheet newspapers. The chapter is structured across five major sections, each of which analyse significant aspects of the domestic reporting of Islam and Muslims. The first two of these sections discuss the broad character-istic features of domestic coverage: the tendency of the press to divide 'Islam' and 'the West', even in domestic reporting; and an analysis of articles which move from such 'strategies of division' to 'strategies of rejection'. The third sec-tion develops the negative representation of British Muslims further, through a more extended analysis of the domestic reporting of 'Muslim terrorism' in broadsheet newspapers. Fourth, the chapter analyses how the sampled newspa-pers represented 'Muslim education' and Muslim schools, focusing specifically on the coverage generated by the granting of Voluntary Aided status to two Muslim schools. The fifth section discusses items of recorded coverage which, whilst constituting a very small minority, present a much valued 'positive', or 'open' representation (Runnymede Trust, 1997) of British Islam and Muslims.

Chapter 6 explores the broadsheet reporting of Iraq, which over the sampled four months was dominated by the issues and activities of UNSCOM weapons inspections. I argue that a single discursive strategy, directed at justifying military attacks on Iraq and the removal of President Saddam Hussein from power, predominates across the sampled Iraq articles. This strategy is, in essence, an argument for 'Western intervention' in Iraq which arises from the claims, themes, implications and a number of presuppositions present in the reports. Analysis is divided into seven sub-sections, the first five of which examine, in detail, the prominent elements of this discursive strategy. The sixth section analyses the minority of dissenting articles and the arguments they employ in undermining the dominant discursive strategy. The seventh section discusses articles which, although at first glance appear to be unconnected to the issues of the UNSCOM inspections, on closer inspection are highly functional to the dominant discursive argument for war. The chapter concludes with an analysis of two examples of 'travel' writing, in order to illustrate that even journalistic formats conventionally directed at presenting the most attractive aspects of a country were subverted and written from a position in which the 'threat of Iraq' — militarily, civilly and socially — was emphasised.

Chapter 7 demonstrates that the reporting of Algeria during the sample period was linked, seemingly inexorably, to violence and terrorism, to the extent that an increase in the number of Algerian reports resulted in a corresponding rise in reported (Muslim) 'terrorist violence'. This, combined with a thoroughly myopic vision (which restricted reporting of the Algerian conflict to an almost exclusively 'Algerian' focus thus ignoring the influences and agenda of not just other nations but also the several international oil companies currently active in 'prospecting' for Algerian oil and gas) led to an especially impoverished account of the conflict in the broadsheet press. The chapter shows that ascribed agency for Algerian civilians' deaths varied substantially across the sample period, with journalists mirroring each other's frequent shifts in apportioning blame. The exception to this pattern was the exemplary reporting of Roula Khalaf, writing for the *Financial Times*, whose perspective on the conflict exposed the complicity of 'the West' in the mass murder of Algerian civilians.

CHAPTER 1

Islam, Orientalism
and (racist) social exclusion

Discourses of 'race' and racism

Although the focus of this book corresponds closely with recent work on 'race', racism and prejudicial representation in general, and whilst I certainly regard my arguments and conclusions to be located within a critical anti-racist paradigm, I will only present the briefest of introductions to the complicated and highly contested field of research on and around 'race' in order to concentrate on research which focuses specifically on 'anti-Muslim' prejudice, exclusion and rejection.

Hage (1998) argues that whilst 'racism' is generally erroneously considered to be

> a system of beliefs, a mode of clarification or a way of thinking [...] this general and dominant tendency to define racism as a mental phenomenon has continually led to an under-theorisation of the relationship between the mental classification involved and the practices in which they are inserted, between what racists are thinking and what racists are doing. (p. 29)

Zubaida (1970) similarly argues that "social psychological and micro-sociological" studies which study "prejudice and discrimination in interpersonal and community contexts [...] do not concern themselves with the social-structural location of groups" and therefore fail to acknowledge how place, space and time "crucially affect the nature of discrimination and prejudice" (p. 2). Billig (1991: 122–141), equally drawing on this critique of the cognitivist focus of much social-psychological research on prejudice, suggests that the commonly held definition of the word 'prejudice' *in itself* supports implications of essentialised, simplified, false, or else irrational conclusions. In this way, by focusing research on the 'mental origins' of racism there is the added danger that the very *practical* functions of racism will be sidelined. Donald and Rattansi (1992) have made a similar point, arguing that racism ought to be approached from a position which assumes that it is "rooted in broader economic structures and material interests" (p.3). From such a position:

> Meanings and beliefs do not become irrelevant, but the coherence and falsity of racist ideas [are] now ascribed to the function they serve in legitimating social practices that reinforce an unequal distribution of power between groups differentiated in racial and/or ethnic terms. (Ibid.)

Explicit in this critique of racism is not just an acknowledgement of the differentiation and stratification of 'racialised' individuals and groups, but also the very *practical* functions of racism in maintaining: first, inequitable systems of social power; and second, behavioural manifestations of racism such as verbal rejection, avoidance, discrimination, physical attack and extermination (see Allport (1954) for further discussion). The definitional account of racism offered by Anthias (1995) is particularly useful in drawing together the ideational and practical elements of racism(s). First, Anthias (1995) notes that it is important to acknowledge that

> Racisms come in different guises. All are, however, underpinned by a notion of a natural relation between an essence attributed to a human population, whether biological or cultural, and social outcomes that do, will or should flow from this. (p.288)

Central to the above quote is racism's 'fixity' of social action, or the idea that social phenomena — by which I refer not just to social activity but also to human *potential*, be that personal or collective — are irrevocably and indelibly directed, arrested or advanced by a population's identified ethnic or racial essence. Further, and in a similar vein to the previous quote taken from Hage (1998), Anthias (1995) acknowledges "what are referred to as racist practices and outcomes cannot be understood exclusively as outcomes of race categorisation" (Ibid.) since:

> Racism is not just about beliefs or statements (discourse in this narrow sense). Racism also involves the ability to impose those beliefs or world views as hegemonic, and as a basis for the denial of rights or equality. Racism is thus embedded in power relations of different types. (p.291)

The strength of this particular account of racism, particularly for the current research, is that it is not restricted to 'biological' racism. Racism's 'biological' heritage has often been a sticking point in past discussion of anti-Muslim racism, necessitating the use of neologisms such as 'Islamophobia' (see discussion below) to account for such practices. Anthias (1995) suggests a more inclusive definition: that racism is "a discourse and a practice whereby ethnic groups are inferiorised" (p.294). Therefore:

> Undesirable groups need not be conceptualised in explicit racial terms, but as Others more generally. [...] For example, anti-Muslim racism in Britain relies on notions of the 'non-civilised', and supposedly inferior and undesirable, character of Islamic religion and way of life, rather than an explicit notion of biological inferiority. However, what allows us to refer to all these discourses and practices as racist is to be found in the attribution of collective features to a given population. This population is endowed with fixed, unchanging and negative characteristics, and subjected to relations of inferiorisation and exclusion. (Ibid)

I have two partial objections to Anthias' position above. First, I regard her proposed division of racism into "discourse and practice" as definitionally inadequate. Discourse analysts — 'critical' and otherwise — define discourse as "language in use" (Brown & Yule, 1983: 1; also see Fairclough, 1989; Schiffrin, 1987, 1994; and others) and discourse analysis as the analysis of what people *do* with talk and text. Such an approach views discourse *as* practice, not separate from it, and therefore regards racist discourse as constitutive of racist practice. Second, the disadvantage and exclusion suffered by British Muslims is more aggregated and entangled with (more traditionally) racist notions of biological inferiority than Anthias' above quotation suggests.[1] "The essential point to stress", the Runnymede Trust (2000) argues,

> is that over the centuries all racisms have had — and continue to have — two separate but intertwining strands. One uses physical or biologically derived signs as a way of recognising difference — skin colour, hair, features, body type, and so on. The other uses cultural features, such as ways of life, customs, language, religion and dress. [...] Most Muslims are recognised by physical features as well as by their culture and religion, and the biological and cultural strands in anti-Muslim racism are often impossible to disentangle. (p.62)

Therefore, racism involves "discriminatory practices, as well as a system of prejudiced ethnic attitudes and ideologies supporting and monitoring such discrimination. It may include discrimination and prejudice against 'racial' minorities as well as other forms of ethnocentrism and xenophobia, such as anti-semitism" (van Dijk et al., 1997: 165). 'Discourse', here defined as language in use,

> [...] plays a crucial role in the enactment as well as in the reproduction of this system. Thus, racist talk and text themselves are discriminatory practices, which at the same time influence the acquisition and confirmation of racist prejudices and ideologies. This is especially the case for white élite groups and institutions, such as politics, the media, scholarship and corporate business, whose prestige, power and influence have played a prominent role in the 'preformation' of racism at large. (van Dijk et al., 1997: 165)

Thus discourse both constitutes social relations between individuals and groups in society and, at the same time, is constituted by these social relations. The representation of, for example, Muslims in broadsheet newspapers is similarly simultaneously socially constitutive and socially determined — assumptions which are developed and operationalised further in the Critical Discourse Analysis of Norman Fairclough (1989; 1992; 1995a; 1995b; 2000; Fairclough & Wodak, 1997). The model which Fairclough proposes, is founded upon the recognition of the discursive dialectical relationship of "structure" and "event" ('agency' in traditional sociological terminology) present in all communicative action. This communicative act can be further defined as "a complex of three elements: social practice, discursive practice (text production, distribution and consumption), and text, and the analysis of a specific discourse calls for analysis in each of these three dimensions and their interrelations" (Fairclough, 1995b: 74). Accordingly Fairclough (1995b) claims

> language use [is] imbricated in social relations and processes which systematically determine variations in its properties, including the linguistic forms which appear in texts. One aspect of this imbrication in the social which is inherent to the notion of discourse is that language is a material form of ideology, and language is invested by ideology. Also inherent to discourse is the dialectical relation of structure/event [...] : discourse is shaped by structures, but also contributes to shaping and reshaping them, to reproducing and transforming them. (p. 73)

Fairclough's account of a theoretical tension in language use is clearly visible in the above excerpt through his uniting of "structure/event" — aspects of discourse which Fairclough regards as inseparable. Language use is "shaped by structures, but also contributes to shaping and reshaping them" — a constitutive characteristic of language which Fairclough regards to be not just 'conventional' but also 'creative', "denoting social change in accordance with the flexibility of prevailing social circumstances" (Titscher et al., 2000: 149). Hence even in its most creative, 'radical' moments, language use cannot be viewed outside of the context of the communicative event — a context which both enables and restricts its (creative) articulation.

For analytic reasons however, it is useful to introduce and discuss separately the three "elements" of (racist) discourse — social practice, discursive practice and text — before their (re)unification in this book's analysis of results. There will, of course, be a certain degree of 'bleed' between the discussions of the three elements given their manifest interrelations, but despite these convergences, three distinct theoretical sections are identifiable:

- *Social Practice*: the social phenomena existing prior to, and hence shaping, impinging upon and accessible to journalistic practice. That is, the social and economic disadvantage suffered by Muslims in Britain, the histories of empire and imperial domination, and the relationships between these historic and socio-political contexts and 'Orientalist' (and other prejudicial *re*presentative) accounts of Islam.
- *Discursive Practice*: the Sociology of Journalism in general, the newsroom production of news-text in the UK in particular, moving to a more detailed account of previous work studying the representation of 'race', racism and 'Othering' in the news.
- *The (critical) analysis of Text*: the analysis of linguistic and discursive strategies (in the more limited sense of discourse as 'structures above the level of sentences') influential in the reproduction of racism.

The social practices surrounding and underpinning the reporting of Islam and Muslims form the focus of the remainder of this chapter.

Orientalism

In contrast to the vast diversity in Muslim practice across the globe (Asad, 1993; al-Azmeh, 1993; Barakat, 1990; Beinin & Stork, 1997; Esposito, 1998; Haddad & Esposito, 1998; Rodinson, 1978; Said, 1978, 1997), "[t]he orientalist approach to Islam can be summarised as essentialist, empiricist and historicist; it impoverishes the rich diversity of Islam by producing an essentialising caricature" (Sayyid, 1997: 32). From a critical perspective, Orientalism and orientalist scholarship are systems of representation framed by the hegemonic political forces of colonialism, post-colonialism and neo-colonialism, which act towards bringing 'the Orient' into 'Western' consciousness, Western dispensation and under Western dominion. In a less than wholly sympathetic summary, Macfie (2002: 4) argues that Orientalism is presently approached as

> [...] a corporate institution, designed for dealing with the orient, a partial view of Islam, as instrument of Western imperialism, a style of thought, based on an ontological and epistemological distinction between Orient and Occident, and even an ideology, justifying and accounting for the subjugation of blacks, Palestinian Arabs, women and many other supposedly deprived groups and peoples.

According to an orientalist ontological schema, 'the Orient' is separate, different, conservative or archaic or barbarian (depending on the vehemence of the critique), sensual and passive. Accordingly, 'the Orient' tends towards despotism and away from development; further, its 'progress' is measured in terms of, and in comparison to 'the West', which implicitly and occasionally *explicitly* maintains its position of the 'inferior Other'. That said, the field of Orientalism and the meaning associated with being 'an Orientalist' have not been fixed, even over the past 40 years. Originally, Orientalism had a positive or agreeable meaning, referring to "the study of languages, literature, religions, thought, arts and social life of the East in order to make them available to the West" (MacKenzie, 1995: xii). The growing opposition to colonialism, particularly in the Indian subcontinent, brought with it growing scepticism that orientalists were ever truly benign in their intensions towards 'the East', and more specifically, that 'the West' was by no means benevolent with what it *did* with the information made available to it through orientalist scholarship. The critique of Orientalism — both as scholarship and as economic-political hegemonic practice — grew tentatively following the Second World War and the gradual de-colonisation of the East, developing on four fronts:

> [...] on orientalism as an instrument of imperialism designed to secure the colonisation and enslavement of parts of the so-called third world (Abdel-Malik [...] 1963); on orientalism as a mode of understanding and interpreting Islam and Arab nationalism (Tibawi [...] 1964 and 1979); on orientalism as a "cumulative and corporate identity" and a "saturating hegemonic system" (Said [...] 1978); and on orientalism as the justification for a syndrome of beliefs, attitudes and theories affecting the geography, economics and sociology of the Orient (Turner [...] 1978). (Macfie, 2002: 5–6)

In the most influential of these four seminal critiques, Said suggests that one of the most significant accomplishments of Orientalism is the construction of '*an* Orient'. The depiction of a single 'Orient', or a single Muslim 'Middle East' which can be studied as a cohesive whole, works to essentialise an image of an archetypal (and usually male) 'Oriental', unchanging in 'His' primitive, culturally specific beliefs and practices. More specifically,

> Said argued that orientalism provides accounts of Islam (and the Orient) which are organised around four main themes: first, there is an 'absolute and systematic difference' between the West and the Orient. Secondly, the representations of the Orient are based on textual exegesis rather than 'modern Oriental realities'. Thirdly, the Orient is unchanging, uniform and incapable of describing itself. Fourthly, the Orient is to be feared or to be mastered. [...] All these narratives rest upon the assumption that Islam is ontologically distinct from the West. (Sayyid, 1997: 32)

However, *Orientalism* is still a vigorously discussed text, producing widely diverging assessment of the contents and implications of Said's arguments (for example, see Gellner, 1993; Lewis, 1993; MacKenzie, 1995; Turner, 1994, 2002). In an account of Said's thesis which is supportive, but one which nevertheless contrasts with Sayyid's (1997) focus on the (*re*)presentative account of Islam 'provided' by Orientalism, Sardar (1999: 13) suggests that

> The history of Orientalism shows that it is not an outward gaze of the West toward a fixed, definite object that is to the east, the Orient. Orientalism is a form of inward reflection, preoccupied with the intellectual concerns, problems, fears and desires of the West that are visited on a fabulated, constructed object by convention called the Orient.

Similarly, Yeğenoğlu (1998), adopting a distinctively Hegelian position, suggests that Orientalism concerns "the cultural representation of the West to *itself* by way of a detour through the other" (p.1), in which "the [Western] subject is constructed by a mediation through the [Eastern] other" (p.6). In this way,

> The subject represents itself to itself through the other and constitutes itself as universal, abstract subject (the I or ego) by signifying the other as a categorical opposite, a radical denial or negation of itself. (Ibid.)

Thus, this signification of categorical opposites simultaneously *supposes* and *sustains* the epistemological and ontological distinctions between 'the West' and 'the East', between 'the West' and 'the Muslim World', strategies by which "the Oriental or non-Western societies are pushed back in time and constructed as primitive or backward" (Ibid.) in contrast to the socio-cultural properties which 'the West' is (indubitably) assumed to possess.

Orientalism and Empire

A discussion of *Orientalism* would not be complete without a brief summary of Said's use of Foucault's power/knowledge nexus, given Orientalism's construction of a particular form of negativised 'Otherness' intended to subordinate and (dis-)possess. Sayyid (1997) suggests that, for Said, Orientalism constitutes "an exercise in power/knowledge by which the 'non-western' world is domesticated. [...] He contended that orientalism was made possible by the imperialist expansion into the Muslim world, and, simultaneously, it made such an expansion possible" (p. 31). A great amount of academic ink has been spilt drawing out the implications of this *discursive* (in the Foucauldian sense of the word) nature of 'Orientalism', in much the same way as the 'origins' of racism have been and are still regularly discussed. Broadly expressed, this debate centres on a 'which came first' question: did colonialism *create* these racisms in order to justify the theft of lands and the subjugation of peoples? Or was colonialism a *product of* these racisms (in as much as the theft of lands and the subjugation of peoples is encouraged, or perhaps only possible, following the assumption of 'Their' inferiority)? The positions taken in this debate are, of course, essentially contestable, but understanding is hampered by a lack of distinction drawn between medieval orientalism, imperialism, racism and imperial Orientalism. The view adopted throughout this book is that medieval orientalism promoted imperialism; racisms — by which I refer not only to essentialised difference and essentialised hierarchies but also to the *disciplinary* and *repressive use* of power — are the product of colonial and imperial incursions into lands occupied by ('racial' and/or ethnic) 'Others'; and modern Orientalism nurtured, reproduced and, in some cases, is now attempting to *restore* such racist practices.

Thus, knowledge of orientalist scholarship — past and present — is *key* to understanding the context and significance of contemporary representations of Islam and Muslims across a wide range of social/political discourse, including journalism and other mass-communicated media as well as more 'academic' research. To be clear, I am not suggesting that racial prejudice did not occur prior to colonial conquest(s) and territorial acquisition; nor do I suggest that modern racism(s) are solely directed against (previously) colonised peoples. However, prior to Western imperialism and (later) colonisation, such prejudice existed to a much greater extent as *belief* rather than *practice* — that is, in the minds and writings of (white) people, as 'phobias' and as 'anxieties' rather than racism(s) as defined above.[2]

To some, it may seem inappropriate that I consider the work of medieval Christian polemicists as inaugurating orientalist discourse. The conventional view, seemingly derived from the work of Martino (1906), has been that "the rise of orientalism as a profession may be dated from the fourth quarter of the eighteenth century" (cited in Macfie, 2002: 25), coinciding with the growth in translation of Hindu and Sanskrit texts. In fact western 'studies' of Islam, and of the Qur'an in particular, have a much longer history. The intellectual debt which even the early 'Arabic orientalists' — who had been institutionally recognised with a lectureship (later a chair) in Arabic at Cambridge from 1636 and a chair in Arabic at Oxford from 1640–owed to these medieval polemicists cannot be denied, with clear continuities observable in the focus and the aims of their work. A brief discussion of precolonial prejudicial writing on Islam will illustrate this.

As early as the twelfth century, although many European writers "had acquired a sufficient knowledge of Islam to understand its principal features [...] their understanding was vitiated by a polemical desire to distort the religion" (Macfie, 2002: 42). Daniel (1960) has shown that prior to the Christian Crusades and the occupation of the 'Holy Lands', Christian polemics were firmly rooted in attacking Muslim *belief* rather than Muslim *people*. Such polemics attempted to illustrate the heretical, immoral and irrational nature of *Islam*, usually in the form of attacks on the structure and style of the Qur'an, as opposed to arguing for the subjugation of Muslims. The prominent argumentative line taken by these polemics in attacking the Qur'an was often quite simply that "it was too badly written to be of God" (Daniel, 1960: 58). The polemicists' evasion of the living practices of Muslims was *essential* to the 'success' of their argumentative intentions to derogate Islam:

> [...] it was the number of wives allowed that was the focus of interest, rather than the number Muslims mostly had; it was generally implied, rather naively, that they would always enjoy in practice as many as they could by law. It was the permission for divorce which was given attention, rather than its actual frequency; it was the very idea of [...] *coitus interruptus*, or, in Spain, of unnatural relations between spouses [e.g. the marriage of divorcees] rather than any knowledge of the actual occurrence of these things, which gave scandal. (Daniel, 1960: 160–1)

Over time, and drawing strength from the way in which successive authors shared both prejudices and conclusions, the "Christian scholars and polemicists created an accepted canon, a constituted body of belief about Islam, which identified a 'real truth', substantially different from what Muslims actually believed" (Macfie, 2002: 42–43).

While the early Professors of Arabic at Oxford do not seem to have shared the intensity of these medieval scholars' fear and dread of Islam, three of the first five holders of the chair at Oxford — Thomas Hyde, Thomas Hunt and James White — combined it with "the regius professorship of Hebrew, [and] were first and foremost biblical scholars" (Macfie, 2002: 27). Meanwhile, the first chair of Arabic at Cambridge — Abraham Weelock — "attempted a refutation of the Koran [*sic.*] and translated the Gospels into Persian" (Macfie, 2002: 28) during his professorship. Furthermore, the relationship between the study of these academics and imperialism should also be mentioned: the Arabic lectureship at Cambridge, for example, was intended to support the "good service of the King and State in our commerce with those Eastern nations, and in God's good time to the enlarging of the borders of the Church, and the propagation of Christian religion to them who now sitt in darknesse" (Arberry, 1948, cited in Macfie, 2002: 44–45). The combined and *conflicting* interests of these scholars raises interesting and difficult questions regarding the status and adequacy of their critiques of Islam — not least whether their services to King and commerce and their Christian ardour were sufficiently intense to have prevented due contemplation and clouded their understanding. More will be said on the difficulties involved in distinguishing between justifiable and prejudicial critiques of religion in a later section of this chapter.

In the latter part of the seventeenth and into the eighteenth centuries, despite yet *more* authentic information regarding the practices of Muslims becoming available, writers on Islam still laboured under the weight of their predecessors' influence. With the increased incursion into 'the Orient' there now were political and economic as well as religious reasons why Islam (and other 'native' religions) should be thought defective, and orientalist scholars marched hand-in-hand with the commercial interests of 'companies' like the East India Company (effectively governing Bengal from the eighteenth century) and the imperial interests of countries like Britain, France, the Netherlands and (to a lesser extent) Germany:

> [...] European trade enclaves began to develop on a more systematic colonising basis in the East, and territorial sovereignty was gradually established over substantial parts of India and south-east Asia. At both scholarly and popular levels, a set of stereotyped views of how and why the peoples of the Orient were different and inferior developed. [...] Scholars contrasted the development of modern civilisation in the West with the backward and tradition-dominated East, an opposition that persists today. (Runnymede Trust, 2000: 65)

Of course, prejudicial polemics directed towards *Islam* (as opposed to supporting the subjugation, domination or exclusion of *Muslims*) have continued to be written and published during and since this time. In 1742, for example, Voltaire "frankly preferred to invent his own legends rather than use those already circulating, which were apparently not scurrilous for his purposes" (Daniel, 1960: 289). Amongst other more directly personal attacks on the Prophet in his '*Fanatisme ou Mahomet le prophete*', Voltaire wrote that Islam is based upon Mohammed's boasting "of being rapt to heaven and of having received there part of this unintelligible book which affronts common sense on every page" (cited in Daniel, 1960: 290).

Fixity and (comparative) regress in 'Arab society'

One of the key interpretative assumptions of orientalist writing during, and indeed since, this imperial period of scholarship, has been the *static* nature of Arab-Muslim society. Contributing in part to this view of Arab-Muslim society was the (inter-) textual and citational nature of Orientalism (Barakat, 1990) — a method whereby specific historic examples are drawn upon to make hasty, overly strong or 'part for whole' generalisations about contemporary Muslim individuals and societies. When approaching 'the Orient', every writer consciously or unconsciously

> assumes some Oriental precedent, some previous knowledge of the Orient, to which he refers and on which he relies. Additionally, each work on the Orient affiliates itself with other works, with audiences, with institutions, with the Orient itself [...constituting] an analysable formation [...] whose presence in time, in discourse, in institutions (schools libraries, foreign services) gives it strength and authority. Said (1978: 20)

Barakat (1990: 146) argues that by following such a static approach to the study of Arab-Muslim politics, society and cultures

> [...] some Western and Arab scholars have tended to rely on texts, proverbs and anecdotes rather than field studies of actual behaviour; to focus on traditional culture, overlooking counter trends to it and cultural struggle within it; to examine texts outside their historical and social contexts; and to stick to the explicit and mechanical rather than the implicit and situational or symbolic meanings of cultural concepts.

In contrast, a dynamic approach to the study of Arab-Muslims "would demonstrate that an intense struggle has been taking place within Arab culture itself. This struggle is not merely between the dominant culture, the subcultures and the counter-cultures [...as] struggle and contradictions exist within each of these three" (Barakat, 1990: 147). Such a dynamic critical approach would raise the discussion of Islam and Muslims away from the unqualified and often ahistoric talk of 'the always and the never', between 'Islam and the West' and the conflict (often erroneously) presupposed to be taking place between 'tradition and modernity', towards one focused on the *interpretation* of terms such as 'tradition', 'modernity', 'the West' and 'Islam'. Egypt, for example, "is not simply witnessing a struggle between tradition and modernity, between rural and urban environments, or between uneducated peasants and educated elites, but rather between competing definitions of modernity — secularist and Islamist — often aimed at the new middle class" (Esposito, 1998: xxi).

In contrast, working within a context of Western imperialism and colonialism, Western scholarship historically "served to naturalise, in the most literal
sense of the term, oppressive social relations. In doing so they sought to
legitimise systems of power and domination" (Cottle, 2000a: 4). Gabriel (194:
16) suggests that "[d]ifferent discourses varyingly articulated this. In the 'science' of anthropology, Arabs were held to be inferior, whilst in political
discourse, texts were woven around the paternalistic idea that colonial subjugation would not only benefit the West (notably Britain and France) but also
the Orient itself." So too in sociology, where Weber used "an inversion to
define his ideal-typical concept of (European) legal-rationality, contrasting it
with what he called 'kadi-justice' [...] Weber tells his readers that Muslim
justice is the antonym of modern Western practice" — an assumed antithesis
which remains in contemporary discourse (Carapico, 1997: 29).

Crashing forward to the present, Barakat's desired 'critical dynamism' has
yet to rise to anything more than a diminutive squeak in contemporary Western scholarship, where grand narratives undercut by presumed Western superiority continue to be highlighted in preference to an interpretative frame of
research which foregrounds the lived perspectives of ordinary people. Many
recent studies of 'political Islam' for example, adopt such an orientalist frame
of reference, attributing "political struggles in the Middle East to [religious]
culture, not social, economic or individual factors" (Carapico, 1997: 30). It is
on such a basis that 'traditional' Orientalists like Lewis (1964) can claim that
"Islamic history shows no councils or communes, no synods or parliaments,
nor any other kind of elective or representative assembly" and thus conclude
that Muslims are (forever) incompatible with democracy. Later Lewis (1990)
wrote: "the Muslim world is again seized by an intense — and violent —
resentment of the West. Suddenly America has become the arch-enemy, the
incarnation of evil, the diabolic opponent of all that is good, and specifically,
for Muslims, of Islam." Similarly, the influential neo-Orientalist Daniel Pipes
(1990) claimed that "Muslim countries have the most terrorists and the fewest
democracies in the world", and related such startling generalisations to the
Muslim-ness of these nations above all other characteristics. As a final example,
Miller (1993: 33) argued: "in Islam's war against the West and the struggle to
build Islamic states at home, the end justifies the means [...Muslims] are, and
are likely to remain, anti-western, anti-American and anti-Israeli." According
to Milton-Edwards (2002), such neo-orientalism "associates Islamic politics
exclusively with violence, authoritarianism, terrorism, fundamentalism, cleri-
cal domination and hostility to modern, 'western', secular democratic govern-

ment, a constellation of negatives that the 'radical' in 'radical Islam' then signifies and invokes" (cited in Donnan & Stokes, 2002: 9). From this perspective, 'Muslim extremists' are repositioned as simply 'extremely Muslim'.

The naturalisation, indeed the proposed *entrenchment*, of Western domination and socio-political hegemony reaches its zenith in the 'clash of civilisations' thesis (Huntington, 1993; 1996). Although much has been made of this book since the terrorist attacks on America on September 11 2001, with journalists and assorted 'experts' dusting off their copies in frantic attempts to explain why this most recently acquired enemy 'hates Us', Huntington's central rather absurd argument — that the principal threat posed to 'the West' will come from a 'Confucian-Islamic alliance' — has been conveniently lost or forgotten. In explaining this conspiracy Huntington (1993) argues:

> In the post-Cold War world the primary objective of arms control is to prevent the development by non-Western societies of military capabilities that could threaten Western interests. [...] The flow of weapons and weapons technology is generally from East Asia to the Middle East. (pp. 46–47)

Such claims — both the general claim of a conspiracy between 'Confucian' and 'Islamic' civilisations and the specific one regarding the "flow" of weapons around the world — are clearly arrant nonsense, easily refutable by any semi-literate teenager. In 1993, the year of Huntington's first foray into a 'civilisational' explanation of international politics, for example, the USA accounted for 61% of *all* arms sales to 'third world' countries, with three quarters of these weapons — amounting to $11 billion in this one year alone — being sold and shipped to Middle Eastern countries (Beinin & Stork, 1997: 19). Second, the 'culturalist analysis' upon which Huntington bases his orientalist arguments not only dove-tails unpleasantly with racist stereotyping of Palestinians/Arabs/Muslims widespread in 'the West', it also lacks any empirical basis:

> It promotes a metaphysical concept of cultural unity and an ahistorical notion of fixed civilisational blocs. Such a vision cannot plausibly be sustained against recent scholarship offering a nuanced account of the interaction among the Christian, Muslim and Jewish traditions in the Mediterranean contact zone. (Beinin & Stork, 1997: 20)

Indeed Meyer (2001), using data previously collected by Geert Hofstede in a study originally intended to clarify *differences* between cultures in order that capitalists could develop nationally appropriate management strategies, argues that while the evidence illustrates some clear and basic differences between countries, 'civilisations' are "by no means distinguished from each other by sharp or even well-demarcated differences in the validity of core fundamental values" (p.79). Comparing results for the seven assumedly 'irreconcilable' civilisations suggested by Huntington (Western, Islamic, Confucian, Latin American, Japanese, African and Hindu) Meyer illustrates that the data showed *greater* divergence of social values between countries of supposedly *identical* civilisational affiliation than between countries of *differing* civilisational affiliation. Echoing the almost universally accepted evidence against 'race' as a biological category:

> the empirical data *do not validate* the ideology of a clash of civilisations on the grounds of irreconcilable differences among their basic social values. Rather, overarching similarities and overlaps may be identified among *all the cultures that were surveyed.* (pp. 79–80; emphasis in original)

However, should our analysis of Huntington's work stop here — illustrating that his assumptions are unsound and his data empirically unfounded — then other more monstrous implications of his work would be missed. In the words of Meyer (2001: 4): "Given the explosive nature of the situation [Huntington argues], the West is well-advised to arm and equip itself to the best of its ability, in order to assert itself through the use of force." The 'clash of civilisations' thesis is therefore not only an argument for American imperialism, but an argument for American imperialism motivated and fought on Social Darwinist grounds: to defend 'Our' (superior) cultural lineage.

In sum, 'Western' orientalist scholarship has helped *recreate* 'the West' as "the yardstick, as Christendom had earlier, by which Oriental cultures and civilisations were measured" (Sardar, 1999: 3). In doing so, contemporary scholarship has helped to crystallise the roles and relations of and between the 'uncivilised native' and the 'civilising coloniser', at the heart of which was (and *is*) "the western assumption that 'our present is your future'" (Gabriel, 1994: 25).

Contradictions and argumentative shifts: Sex and 'the Muslim Other'

If historic orientalist writings — particularly Christian polemics by Mark of Toledo, Robert of Ketton, San Pedro Pascual and the like — are examined and compared to contemporary criticism of Islam, the frequency with which certain themes are reproduced is quite startling. Thus, sex, violence, the cunning of Muslims and the irrationality of Islam continue to be key stereotypical argumentative themes — or *topoi* — useful in derogating Islam. Daniel (1960: 1) has attempted to explain this continuity:

> The points in which Islam and Christianity differ have not changed, so that Christians have always tended to make the same criticisms; and even when, in relatively modern times, some authors have self-consciously distanced themselves from Christian attitudes, they have not generally been as successful as they thought themselves.

Supporting the broadly Hegelian perspective of Sardar and Yeğenoğlu — in which orientalist discourse should be viewed as 'the West' constructing itself through 'the Other' — it is interesting to note that contemporary secular/atheist accounts arguing that 'Islam is unacceptable' tend to take the opposite position to that of past Christian polemicists. (In contrast, contemporary Christian polemics still maintain their focus on the nature of revelation, the irrational or repetitive structure of the Qur'an, Muhammad as a heretic or false prophet, etc.). This constancy of topic combined with a shift in argumentative position, can be demonstrated easily and with a variety of cases: take ideas of marriage, or of sexual relations more generally, for example, which Western writers have deliberated on frequently and "often with fascinated horror" for much of the last 1,400 years (Daniel, 1960: 135). Whereas Islam had previously caused much scandal (and was represented as condoning 'unnatural relations' between not just people of the same but also of the opposite sex, and encouraging immorality and depravity more generally) it is now the 'orthodoxies' of certain Puritan Muslims, and more specifically their sexual and social conservativism, which gives cause for criticism.

Taking marriage and divorce: previously, no Christian "was able to think of a divorced wife as no longer the property of her original husband; a second marriage was therefore a legalised adultery" (Daniel, 1960: 137). Currently, it is the idea of inequalities in marriage and divorce sanctioned by the Qur'an which cause most consternation, perhaps most readily illustrated in the possibility (it is important to note: *not* the frequency) of polygamous marriages. Thus a shift has taken place in arguments 'on Muslim marriage', from damning Islam for being too indulgent (or liberal?) to condemning Islam for being too repressive; this shift reflects, not a change in the religion, but a reversal in 'Western values'.

Regarding sexual intercourse: the belief that sexual licentiousness was particularly linked with Islam, and therefore Muslims, has been a ubiquitous orientalist preoccupation, particularly of the earlier Christian writers. Originally, it was the very idea that Islam commended sex *at all* — activities thought to be objectionable even within marriage — which drew such great indignation; later, the accusations became more developed. William of Adam, the Bishop of Sultaniyah, for example, accused Islam of the following:

> In the Muslim sect any sexual act at all is not only not forbidden, but allowed and praised. So, as well as the innumerable prostitutes that there are among them, there are many effeminate men who shave the beard, paint their own face, put on women's dress, wear bracelets on the arms and feet [...] The Muslims, therefore, forgetful of human dignity, are shamelessly attracted to those effeminates, and live together with them as, with us, husband and wife live together publicly. (cited in Daniel, 1960: 144).

Gerald of Wales maintained that this apparent proclivity towards 'sexual perversion' derived from the Prophet himself, who "taught whatever he thought would best please, and especially lust, which was the particular temptation of Orientals who live in a climate of great natural heat" (Daniel, 1960: 147). Often, the Qur'an itself was used as 'evidence' in proving the veracity of these and similar claims — a 'from the horse's mouth' argumentative strategy, if you will. The passage of the Qur'an which attracted much of the focus on 'unnatural intercourse' during this period was surah II, verse 223. Out of interest, and also to illustrate the rather elementary point that Qur'anic interpretation (which translation is part of) should always be relocated within the specific socio-economic and political context of its production (Stowasser, 1998), I include three translations of the relevant section of the verse:

> Yusuf Ali – *Your wives are as a tilth unto you; so approach your tilth when and how ye will* [...]
> Pickthall – *Your women are a tilth for you (to cultivate) so go to your tilth as ye will* [...]
> Maududi – *Your wives are your tilth: so you may go to your tilth as you please* [...]

The verse — described by Daniel (1960: 320) as "the [Qur'anic] verse most often translated in the whole Middle Ages" — was taken as proof of the lax morals of Muslims, since it was universally interpreted as authorising (any and all) sexual activities which Christians found offensive, including anal sex and sexual intercourse during menstruation (in doing so, deliberately ignoring the preceding verse which specifically prohibits this).

Predictably, the verse still preoccupies those wishing to denounce and condemn Islam; equally predictably perhaps, the meaning which they project onto the text has also shifted during the intervening years. A cursory, and admittedly hardly scientific, survey of the internet using the *Google* search engine (www.google.com) produced a wealth of websites using this verse (and their own, often perverse interpretation of it) as an argumentative resource in derogating Islam and Muslims. Some of these sites are 'Christian' and take an antagonistic position towards Islam in particular — for example, 'Truth and Grace', where s.II v.223 is quoted 'proving' that Muslim wives "are considered the sexual property of their husbands" (www.truthandgrace.com/muslimculture.htm); others are atheist, and adopt an antagonistic position towards all religions — for example, "Positive Atheism's big scary list of Holy Qur'an quotations" (www.positiveatheism.org/hist/quotes/quran.htm).

In fact, and perhaps ironically, it was the early Christian polemicists who were closest to the accepted interpretation of this verse: that sex (in marriage) is permitted in any sexual position. There are certain provisos however, and given that "a tilth" is fertile ground, or a place where something could grow, the verse is taken to only refer to vaginal intercourse thus prohibiting anal sex (which may, I imagine, be considered by some to constitute a 'repressive restriction'). Further, in contrast to some of the objections of contemporary 'atheist-humanist' orientalist attacks, the verse should be viewed as referring to only *one* of the basic aspects of marriage between men and women, rather than the relationship as a whole. Additional Qur'anic verses are easily available to counter the accusations above that s.II v.223 confirms upon women the status of sexual property. Surah II v.187 (only 36 verses prior to the 'offending verse') for example reads:

> Yusuf Ali – *Permitted to you, on the night of the fasts, is the approach to your wives. They are your garments and ye are their garments.* […]
> Pickthall – *It is made lawful for you to go unto your wives on the night of the fast. They are raiment for you and ye are raiment for them.* […]
> Maududi – *It has been made lawful for you to go to your wives during the nights of the fast days. They are (like) a garment to you and you are (like) a garment to them.* […]

While the verse's function is to permit sexual relations after sunset during Ramadan, the use of parallelism in the second sentence entails a sexual equality between husband and wife — that is, equality in terms of their desires, their sexual needs more generally and the support they should provide for one another. Thus, mirroring the developments which orientalist writing has passed through in academia (see Sadowski, 1997 for such a discussion of political theory), when 'polite society' held that sex was immoral, or at the very least something to be endured, orientalists argued that Islam promoted and celebrated such licentious activity. Now that 'polite society' valorises gender and sexual equality, neo-orientalists (and other assorted parties with some stake in vilifying Islam) argue that Islam promotes (or, sometimes *de-mands*) the opposite.

Patriarchy in Orientalism

Following from the above discussion, this final section discusses the relationships between orientalist scholarship and patriarchal power. In prejudiced 'Western' discussion of the 'racial' or ethnic other, the 'other' is always "a projection of an intra-European enemy consisting of a complex of features founded upon superstition and stereotypes of immoral and anti-social conduct" (Blommaert and Verschueren, 1998: 19). Thus:

> The perceived Arab tendency towards verbosity and antagonistic dispute is the opposite of the *self-ascribed* European norms of negotiation, consensus and rational dialogue. The more and more frequently emphasized Islamic inclination towards fundamentalism is supposed in contrast with Christian tolerance and democratic pluralism. (Ibid. emphasis added)

The ontological position which this projection produces and supports (an ontology which is, of course, based upon a 'higher order' ontological and epistemological distinction between 'the West' and 'the Orient') can be represented in the global signifying homology, integral to Orientalist discourse, and current Orientalist discourse in particular:

**'the West' is to civility and modernity
what 'the East' is to under-development and unenlightenment**

The power of this assumed connotative relationship is such that 'Oriental' symbols, metonymy and cultural artefacts are similarly imprinted with 'ignorance' and 'barbarism', as work carried out by scholars such as Leila Ahmad (1992) illustrates:

> [...] the reason for thinking that the veil was more repressive than, for example, Victorian corsets had more to do with *the way the veil was used as a marker* of [a] particular cultural formation. When white women of the nineteenth century saw veiled women, they understood it to be *a sign of cultural backwardness* and female subordination. They did not make the same assumptions about their own clothes, which for them did not signify female subordination — because they [themselves] did not signify subordination. (Ahmad (1992), cited in Sayyid, 1997: 10; emphases added)

The analysis above also illustrates the interconnected and reinforcing relationships between 'race', ethnicity and gender which are so frequently sidelined in academic research (see Anthias 1995, 1998; Anthias & Yuval-Davies, 1992). This connectedness between 'race' and gender is illustrated in the twin discourses of racism itself: one based on the *fear* of the 'ethnic other', primarily but not solely (see Daniels, 1997) the fear of the black male; the other based on the *fantasy* of an exoticised 'ethnic other', primarily but not solely (see critiques of Mapplethorpe's photography in Hall, 1997) the promiscuous, seductive and sexually pathological black female (Gilman, 1986). Lawrence (1982) shows that "common-sense" views of 'the Oriental woman' to be equally racist, wherein

> Her very 'passivity' is thought to be a reflection of her upbringing, geared to her learning to accommodate and please her future husband. This notion, working in conjunction with the absolute power of the male to elicit her compliance and mediated through the image of the lithe and sinewy gyrations of the 'belly dancer', works so as to produce a composite image of a smouldering sexuality — 'full of Eastern promise' — waiting only to be fanned into flames by the most potent masculinity. (p.73).

Such imaginings remain a regular feature of contemporary academic writing and contemporary culture.[3] Whilst these co-occurring essentialising discourses of racism — physical threat and sexual allure — may appear to be contradictory, they are, in fact, based on the same presupposition: that 'racial and ethnic others' are closer to nature and instinct than to rationality; more ruled by the urges of the body than the thoughts of the mind.

This does not mean, however, that either of these twin discourses, nor racism as a whole (both on a street level nor in more 'institutionalised' forms) affect women and men equally, and the issues and relevance of a gendered critique of Orientalism have been taken up most productively in the field of post-colonial feminisms (Alloula, 1986; Kabbani, 1988; Lewis, 1996; Mills, 1991; Mohanty, 1988; Spivak, 1988; Trinh, 1986–7). Yeğenoğlu (1998) for example, through her examination of the veil as a site of ('Western') fantasy, nationalism and discourses of gender identity, has illustrated the implicit imperialism of both traditional male Orientalism and Western feminism in their attempts to 'liberate' Muslim women in the name of progress. Yeğenoğlu (1998) suggests a "homology between the structures of patriarchal/sexist and colonial/imperial discourses" in which "the discourses of cultural and sexual difference are powerfully mapped onto each other" (p.10), in order to construct 'the Orient' as "a natural territory ready for the conquest of the 'rational' and 'civilised' European man" (p.11). The veil is positioned as a central trope in the articulation of this homology, representing

> a multi-layered signifier which refers at once to an attire which covers the Muslim woman's face, and to that which hides and conceals the Orient and Oriental women from apprehension; it hides the real Orient and keeps its truth from Western knowledge/apprehension. It is also a metaphor of membrane, serving as a screen around which Western fantasies of penetration revolve. It is this polysemous character of the veil which seems to play a crucial role in the unique articulation of the sexual with cultural difference in Orientalist discourse. (Yeğenoğlu, 1998: 47)

As such, an acknowledgement of this textual homology between patriarchal and colonial discourses should form a central feature of the analysis of Orientalist discourse.

Thus, through this discussion and these particular examples, the general analytic approach of Orientalism can be easily illustrated: that 'the Orient', its people and religions, "is constructed in Western ideology as a permanent and enduring object of knowledge in opposition to the Occident as its negative and alternative pole" (Turner, 2002: 20). The irony is that the exact form which this "permanent and enduring object" has taken, has shifted and changed in accordance with the aims, attitudes and objectives of (Western) writers. As a result of this interpellation,

> [...] Orientalism produces a balance sheet or an audit of negatives between West and East in which the Orient is defined by a series of lacunae: historical stasis, the missing middle class, the erosion or denial of active citizenship, [...] and the limitations of instrumental rationality as the critical culture of natural science, industrial capitalism and rational government. (Turner, 2002: 21)

"Islamophobia: A challenge for us all"

The publication of the Runnymede Trust's (1997) report on 'Islamophobia' marked a watershed in the United Kingdom, through it's allegation of a "pervasive hatred of Islam and Muslims across all sections of British society" (Nahdi, 1997: 18). Muslims living in Britain are exposed to prejudice and racism on such a frequent basis that it can be conceived of as an 'everyday practice'. Since Essed (1991), "everyday racism" can be defined as

> a process in which (a) socialised racist notions are integrated into meanings that make practices immediately definable and manageable, (b) practices with racist implications become in themselves familiar and repetitive, and (c) underlying racial and ethnic relations are actualised and reinforced through these routine or familiar practices in everyday situations. (Essed, 1991: 52)

In this way, "everyday racism can be characterised as the integration of racism into everyday situations through practices (cognitive and behavioural) that activate underlying power relations" (Reisigl & Wodak, 2001: 7). This current section presents evidence from two reports published by the Runnymede Trust (1997, 2000), illustrating how the (predominantly) discriminated and disempowered status of British Muslims is reinforced through frequent, and seemingly *routinised* anti-Muslim prejudice — defined, for the present, as 'Islamophobia'.

Although the Runnymede Trust did not coin the term 'Islamophobia' (they state that its first recorded usage in print was in the American periodical *Insight*, 4 February, 1991) they certainly popularised its usage in both academic and lay discussion. The term itself is defined in the report (1997: 4) as "unfounded hostility towards Islam. It also refers to the practical consequences of such hostility in unfair discrimination against Muslim individuals and communities, and to the exclusion of Muslims from mainstream political and social affairs." Whilst the Trust acknowledges that the term is not ideal, and that critics suggest "its use panders to what they call political correctness [and] that it stifles legitimate criticism of Islam" (Ibid.), the report chose to adopt the term 'Islamophobia' because "anti-Muslim prejudice has grown so considerably and rapidly in recent years that a new item in the vocabulary is needed so that it can be identified and acted against" (Ibid.). In order to by-pass this terminological difficulty, the Trust suggest eight binary argumentative positions characterising 'closed' and 'open' views of Islam and Muslims, which are available to protagonists to draw upon. These eight binaries are listed below in Table 1.1.

By this model, the more a protagonist draws upon 'closed' views of Islam, the more his/her position can be said to be 'Islamophobic' and therefore the more his/her opinion is likely to translate into racist action. Further, the last two binaries below suggest a direct move from 'mere' prejudice and into ("everyday") racism, wherein Islamophobic attitudes are "*used* to justify discriminatory practices towards Muslims" and this "anti-Muslim hostility [is] accepted as natural" (Ibid.; emphasis added).

As stated, the Trust's use of the term 'Islamophobia' has not gone uncriticised, not least for its seeming ability to conflate prejudicial, insensitive or bigoted representations of Islam with both the undifferentiated — and therefore not purely 'anti-*Islamic*' — criticisms of atheists, or the more general criticisms of the wrong-doing of (people who happen to be) Muslims. In one of the more sympathetic criticisms, Halliday (1999) offers a critique of selected writings on

Table 1.1. The Runnymede Trust's 'closed' and 'open' views of Islam

Distinctions	Closed Views	Open Views
Monolithic/Diverse	Islam seen as a single monolithic bloc, static and unresponsive	Islam seen as diverse and progressive, with internal differences
Separate/Interacting	Islam seen as separate and other	Islam seen as interdependent with other faiths and cultures
Inferior/Equal	Islam seen as inferior to the West	Islam seen as [...] not deficient, and as equally worthy of respect
Enemy/Partner	Islam seen as violent, aggressive, threatening, supportive of terrorism	Islam seen as an actual or potential partner in joint co-operative enterprises
Manipulative/Sincere	Islam seen as a political ideology, used for political or military advantage	Islam seen as a genuine religious faith, practiced sincerely by its adherents
Criticism of the West rejected/considered	Criticisms made by Islam of 'the West' rejected out of hand	Criticisms of 'the West' [...] are considered and debated
Discrimination defended/criticised	Hostility towards Islam used to justify discriminatory practices towards Muslims	Disagreements 'with' Islam do not diminish efforts to combat discrimination and exclusion
Islamophobia seen as natural/problematic	Anti-Muslim hostility accepted as natural	Critical views of Islam are themselves subjected to critique, lest they're inaccurate

from Runnymede Trust (1997: 5)

the concept of 'Islamophobia', which he feels does not sufficiently account for the derogation and prejudice experienced by Muslims.[4] At the outset, it should be stated that Halliday agrees with the Runnymede Trust in as much as "there is such a thing as denoted by the term 'Islamophobia' [...] Recent examples in the British press are not hard to find" (Halliday, 1999: 898). Thus, Halliday's objection is centred on the use of the neologism 'Islamophobia' when describing and/or accounting for the (racist) *exclusion* of Muslims, feeling that the term 'anti-Muslimism' should be used in preference. Four criticisms of the concept are offered: first, that 'Islamophobia' is somewhat of a misnomer, and that it

> misses the point about what it is that is being attacked: "Islam" as a religion *was* the enemy in the past: in the crusades or the *reconquista*. It is not the enemy now [...] The attack now is not against *Islam* as a faith but against *Muslims* as a people, the latter grouping together all, especially immigrants, who might be covered by the term (Ibid.).

This point is echoed by Reisigl and Wodak's (2001: 6) more general criticism of '-phobias': that they "neglect the active and aggressive part of discrimination" by focusing on racism as a collection of (pathological, pseudo-logical or illogical) beliefs. In contrast to the thrust of the 'Islamophobia' concept, Halliday (1999) argues that the stereotypical enemy "is not a faith or a culture, but a people" (p. 898) and therefore its use is misleading, shifting analysis away from the 'real' targets of prejudice: Muslims.

Second, Halliday argues that the concept 'Islamophobia' is undesirable on the grounds that it reproduces a particularly unhelpful distortion — "that there is *one* Islam: that there is something out there against which the phobia can be directed" (Ibid.). While "Islam, like all cultural systems, is a contested field of meaning" (Beinin & Stork, 1997: 21), Halliday argues the term 'Islamophobia' suggests otherwise, invoking a unified, singular and perhaps essentialised 'thing' at which such prejudice can be directed. This section of the essay is particularly strong, drawing heavily on Halliday's cogent critique of the constructed nature of the 'clash' between 'Islam' and 'the West'. The emergent, fluid and contestable nature of both 'Islam' and 'the West' are discussed (albeit with the stress upon the former) and, echoing the claims of Rodinson (1979), Said (1997), al-Azmeh (1993) and others, Halliday suggests that "what is presented as 'Islam' may well be one, but by no means the only possible interpretation" (1999: 897). What this focus does of course, is not only expose the discursive potential of 'Islam', but also the politically motivated actions of those who claim access to the *one true* Islam and therefore what is at stake in their maintaining such privilege.

Third, the combination of these two previous inadequacies with the concept 'Islamophobia' leads to "confusing" practical results. In particular Halliday claims, "issues of immigration, housing, employment, racial prejudice, anti-immigrant violence are not specifically religious" in either the UK or 'the West' as a whole (Halliday, 1999: 899). Here, my views differ from Halliday's. As I illustrate in a lower section, a great many British Muslims — predominantly women — report heightened discrimination and abuse when they appear 'conspicuously Muslim' than when they do not. Further, the increase in personal abuse and street racism since September 11 2001 in which the perceived 'Muslim-ness' of the victims was the central reason for abuse, regardless of veracity of this presumption (resulting in Sikhs and others being attacked for 'looking like bin Laden'), suggests that racial and religious bigotry and discrimination are more interlinked than Halliday suggests.

Fourth, in the criticism most pertinent to the current discussion, Halliday states that the use of the term 'Islamophobia'

> challenges the possibility of dialogue based on universal principles […since it] inevitably runs the risk of denying the right, or possibility, of criticisms of the practises of those with whom one is having the dialogue. Not only those who, on universal human rights grounds, object to elements in Islamic or other traditions and current rhetoric, but also those who challenge conservative readings from within, can more easily be classed as Islamophobes (Ibid.)

Halliday argues that this effect of 'Islamophobia' (curtailing dialogue on the basis that the "invocation of universal principles violates tradition") is felt at both the national and international levels. However it is abuse occurring "*within Muslim societies themselves*" (original emphasis) which receives the most attention, where "horrendous violations of human rights […] being committed, against Muslims, in the name of religion" are shielded from criticism (Halliday, 1999: 900). Few people would argue that human rights abuse or the inhumane or criminal activities of (people who happen to be) Muslims should be 'off limits' to criticism; and, for the record, I would disagree with anyone who suggested that they *should* be off limits. However, when does warranted criticism such as this slip into prejudiced, derogatory, and anti-Muslim discourse? To a certain extent this fourth problem with 'Islamophobia' arises out of the Runnymede Trust's own definition of the concept, wherein they suggest that Islamophobia is characterised by an "*unfounded* hostility towards Islam". This clearly entails an interpretative problem: in short, how do we establish that such hostility is unfounded, as opposed to justified? How do we differentiate between the defensible, the benign and the prejudicial (aside from simply adapting Justice Potter Stewart's now infamous phrase: *I know prejudice when I see it*)? While I do not claim to have anything close to a definitive or incontrovertible resolution to this question, I believe the answer must lie in the relationship(s) between *text* and *context*.

Looking at 'text' first: as suggested above, we may claim that a text is more or less prejudiced against Muslims by the extent to which it reproduces the Runnymede Trust's 'closed views' of Islam (i.e. that Islam is monolithic, Islam is separate, Islam is the enemy, Islam is a manipulative and ideological rather than a sincere faith, etc.). Each of these 'closed views' are undercut by key characteristic assumptions of racist discourse: first, they are founded on a belief in 'communities of descent', evidenced in the manner in which the actions Muslims are thought to be, and represented as, defined by their (almost) invariable, inflexible 'Muslim-ness' as opposed to a wide range of other explanatory referential or predicational categories (Reisigl & Wodak, 2001). Second, these closed views are based on a rhetorical *stratification* of groups in which Islam is presented as (in extreme cases) inherently undesirable or, to varying degrees, inferior to 'Us' and 'Our' value system. When these two features (or strategies) — essentialisation and stratification — appear in combination, the result will *necessarily* be prejudiced.

However, it is where argumentative discourse foregrounds *one* of these strategies and omits the other that the problematic issue of distinguishing between 'prejudiced' and 'defensible' opinion arises. In other words: when a text assumes an essentialised or 'timeless' Islam exists, but does not derogate or vilify Muslims; or when a text critiques Islam, and argues that an alternative religion/value system is superior, but does not misrepresent or stereotype Islamic beliefs or practices. The distinction between the acceptable and the discriminatory in these cases must lie in the *conduct* of the arguer. In other words: although the critique of Islam and the implicit stratification — or even the explicit judgment — of Islam are legitimate (just as they are for Muslim critiques of Christianity), this critique:

–   should be *temperate* and not descend into hostility or attack;
–   critical views should be *accurate* and relate to the actual beliefs, standpoints and practices of Islam rather than distorted or perverse interpretations;
–   argumentation should be *reasoned*, logical and non-fallacial;
–   and fundamentally, while individuals are free to disagree with Islam (provided they do not violate the above rules for interaction [also see van Eemeren & Grootendorst, 1992]), such disagreement should always be prefaced by the principle of *freedom of religion*, and the right of Muslims to practice the religion of their own choice.

Violation of these rules will produce discourse which is, to a greater or lesser extent, 'prejudiced against Muslims'.

Next, we need to consider the *context* in which such argumentative/textual representation of Islam takes place, since it is in social contexts that prejudicial arguments are endowed with racist effects. Despite each argumentative context being constituted by specific (and in some ways unique) complexes of social, political, historical and other extra-linguistic (e.g. institutional) discursive characteristics, for our purposes context may be considered in terms of three basic elements: the *arguer*, the *audience*; and the broader socio-political *locality*. Each of these contextual elements have a clear bearing on the opaque and transparent, implicit and explicit features of argumentation, and hence must be considered when distinguishing between unacceptable (racist) and acceptable (though debatable or contestable) argumentative representations of Islam.

Starting with the arguer, in the case of journalism we should ask ourselves: who is the journalist and for what purpose is s/he writing? The motivations of certain journalists writing about Islam are demonstrably questionable — take Peregrine Worsthorne for example, whose career (predominantly writing and editing the *Sunday Telegraph*) has been characterised by his base antipathy towards non-white immigration and non-white British communities. In one column (*Guardian*, 18 January 1997) he openly admitted to his dread and dislike of Black people, and apologised for the "shameful", "wicked nonsense" he'd written about Britain's African Caribbean communities over the last 35 years. However, he was *not* sorry for his treatment of Britain's Muslim communities who, he argued, still represent a problem because they fail to assimilate with White British values:

> " [...] they believe too much in family values rather than too little; take religion too seriously rather than not seriously enough and insist on defying the new mores of permissive society rather than caving in to them." (cited in Law, 2002: 82)

Weeks later, while he explicitly denied any dislike of Muslims, it still formed an implicit undercurrent to his 'anti-PC' column 'I believe in Islamophobia' (*Daily Telegraph*, 1 March 1997). Once Worsthorne's journalistic writing is viewed in relation to his admitted anti-Muslim prejudice, it makes little difference how many times he claims: "One can find in the Mohammedan religion [*sic!*] as many appeals for universal love and compassion as in the Christian religion"; or how many times he argues that blaming "Mohammedanism for Islam's militancy [...] makes no more sense than to blame the Sermon On The Mount for the atrocities of the IRA". — His claimed openness and goodwill is reduced to an apparent or 'show' concession by his unshakable loathing of Muslims. Similar accusations can be levelled at 'left-liberal' journalists such as Polly Toynbee, or more 'radical' journalists like Julie Burchill, who have regularly justified their open antipathy towards *Islam* using examples of *Muslim* wrong-doing — a 'whole for part' (*totum pro parte*) over-generalising argumentative schema characteristic of racist discourse.

Second, the audience or readers of a text should be considered. After all, argument is not simply text for its own sake, but is practical, even *political* discourse aimed at persuading an audience of the acceptability of a thesis and thereby provoking them into an immediate or future course of action. Echoing this perspective, Perelman points out that "it must not be forgotten that all argumentation aims somehow at modifying an existing state of affairs" (1979: 11), whether this be mental, social or political. Elsewhere, Perelman argues that "argumentation does not aim solely at gaining a purely intellectual adherence. Argumentation very often aims at inciting action, or at least creating a disposition to act" (1982: 12). Thus, the (potential) effects of argument on their audiences also need to be considered: what is the audience/readership being convinced of and, since people 'do things with words' beyond their immediate communicative context (Eliasoph, 1990), how are a text's argumentative conclusions likely to be *used*? For example: while we may agree that Israeli ex-Prime Minister Ariel Sharon is a war criminal, responsible for the murder of 2–3,000 men, women and children in Sabra and Shatila refugee camp massacres, I nonetheless feel uncomfortable reading arguments such as this on the website of the British National Party, given the well known anti-Semitism of the Party and its supporters. Would those reading this argument on the BNP's website (www.bnp.org.uk/news/2003_march/news_mar15) be motivated into campaigning for Palestinian rights, or is it more likely that they would see it as (more) evidence of 'the Zionist conspiracy' which they should fight against? This is particularly important to consider when analysing argumentation which an audience considers to be informed and authoritative — like the élite broadsheet press.

Finally (and related to the considerations given to the audience) we need to consider a text's "words, images and themes *in juxtaposition* to [...] the broader social, cultural and political context" (Daniels, 1997: 142). More specifically, we need to take into account the surrounding social and discursive locality — that is, to the "social/sociological variables and institutional frames of a specific 'context of situation'" (the occasion, the social, political and individual characteristics of participants and/or recipients) and to "the broader socio-political and historical context which the discursive practices are embedded in and relate to" (Reisigl & Wodak, 2001: 41). Although this level of analysis necessarily involves a certain degree of speculation and conjecture, I suggest that a text may be considered racist if it constructs, perpetuates or transforms racist social practices.[5] Contextual issues such as the values, routines and processes of journalism, the position of the audience with regard to such discursive practices and their relationship with racism and the broader socio-political locality, are discussed in much greater depth in Chapter 2.

In summary, the boundaries between racist anti-Muslim argumentation and legitimate critique of both Islamic beliefs and practices and the wrong doing of Muslims, are rather fuzzy and difficult to differentiate. Here I assume that critical discussion, or even arguments, about values and value systems are valid, providing, first, the argumentation does not overstep the boundaries of (textual) reasonableness listed above; and second, this discussion takes place in a social context in which the standpoint of one side or the other is not used (possibly by third parties) to derogate or discriminate. Specifically, a newspaper article may be considered *prejudiced* against *Islam* if it supports the essentialisation of Islam and the rigid stratification of religions and other belief systems. It may additionally be said to be *racist* if underlying racial or ethnicist inequalities "are actualised and reinforced" by the text (Essed, 1991: 52). In other words, we may consider a text to be racist if analysts can (plausibly) demonstrate that the text essentialises Muslims, supports the social stratification of (religious) communities and perpetuates discrimination against Muslims.

British Muslims and (racist) social exclusion

The demography and social background of the British Muslim communities deserves a brief introduction and contextualisation, given that their social status is an important factor in explaining the representation of Islam in British (élite) newspapers and why, more specifically, the coverage of such newspapers tends to ignore them. First, until very recently, no accepted statistics on the number of Muslims in Britain were available; only 'racial background' was recorded in official statistics, entailing problematic inaccuracies of predicting religion from ethnic/national origin. As such, previous figures quoted reflected "the fears and aspirations of interested parties" (Rex, 1996: 218) more than they did 'reality', with both 'Islamophobes' and 'Islamists' often inflating numbers in order to back their respective arguments of a 'Muslim threat' or 'substantial Muslim electorate'. The 2001 National Census data — which for the first time included an *optional* question on religion — revealed that there are now 1.5 million Muslims living in Britain, with a significant majority tracing their familial origins in Pakistan.

Within these British Muslim communities there are significant differences in religious and ideological belief and practice, the detail and sophistication of which are beyond the scope of the present book (see Halliday, 1997; Lewis, 1994, 1997). Looking solely at British Muslims of Pakistani origin, a number of divisions are observable: between denominations, with Sunni (Hanafi) Muslims in the majority and the Shia and 'Ahmadiyya' forming small minorities; within denominations, with (sometimes significant) doctrinal divisions existing in the Sunni majority between Barelvi and Deobandi Muslims; and within doctrines, for example between the Sufi (Barelvi) followers of the Qadriya and Naqshbandi orders. Such diversity in religious belief and identification suggests that the future "study of Islamic communities [...must] involve a sociology of how religion interacts with other ethnic, cultural and political forces" (Halliday, 1997: 76) in order to give productive insight into the lives of British Muslims.

The socio-economic status of these British Muslim communities is a subject which has become "a highly controversial subject of discussion" due to an alleged 'victim orientation' of the prevailing "deprivationist perspective" (Lewis, 1994: 22). British Muslims are, on the whole, "in a highly disadvantaged position in British society", with their socio-economic status displaying "a strong 'class' and to a certain extent 'underclass' dimension" (Statham, 1999: 622). The main exceptions to this socio-economic profile are East African Asians, a particularly successful group who enjoy a "higher educational and social status" (Lewis, 1994: 106; also see Alibhai-Brown, 2000). Economic deprivation is particularly prevalent in the majority Pakistani and Bangladeshi communities, where unemployment stood at 28.8 per cent at the time of the 1991 consensus (compared to 8.8 per cent for white communities), the underlying causes of which "include industrial restructuring and a range of discriminatory practices by employers" (Runnymede Trust, 2000: 193). By 1998 these rates of unemployment had increased across society, but appear to have affected Britain's 'non-white' communities most adversely. The Parekh Report (Runnymede Trust, 2000) shows that by 1998,

> the employment rate of white people of working age was 75.1 per cent. The average for all black and Asian people was only 57 per cent. […Whilst] for people of Bangladeshi and Pakistani backgrounds, the respective figures were 35 per cent and 41 per cent. Rates for women in these communities were lower still. (p.194)

In the UK, the outcome of such overwhelmingly high percentages of unemployment (or, perhaps more accurately '*non*-employment', given the creative and increasingly exclusive status of 'unemployment') must almost inevitably be a correspondingly high level of social exclusion and deprivation. Recent Department of Work and Pensions statistics show that 68% of Pakistani and Bangladeshi families are officially classified as 'low income households' — significantly higher than the 21% of white families classified.[6] The wealth and financial resources of British Muslim communities are not much improved by full time work, particularly in the British Pakistani and Bangladeshi communities, where economic deprivation is particularly striking. A recent TUC report (2002) shows that on average, Pakistani and Bangladeshi men earn £150 less per week than white men; for women the differences are less marked, with Pakistani and Bangladeshi women earning £34 less than white women per week.

An aggregating factor in this economic deprivation may, in the past, have been the educational disadvantage, particularly experienced by the (majority) Pakistani and Bangladeshi communities (see Modood, 1994: 2–3). However, whilst young people of Bangladeshi or Pakistani backgrounds are still "overrepresented among school pupils aged 16 with the poorest qualifications", these same communities are "well represented proportionately in terms of entry to university" (Runnymede Trust, 2000: 146). Students from both Indian and African backgrounds are represented in even higher proportions in university admissions. Further, even the suggested poor educational performance at GCSE level is partially misleading given that, although Bangladeshi and Pakistani pupils achieve results below the national average, they "steadily close the gap between themselves and others in the course of their education", and in "some authorities they perform at or above the national average at GCSE" (Ibid.). Therefore, contrary to suggesting that the (predominantly) highly disadvantaged economic position of British Muslims can be ascribed to poor educational qualifications,

> Labour force surveys have shown that Asian and black school leavers have less success in gaining employment than white people. That is the case even when all relevant variables, such as educational attainment, are held constant. (Runnymede Trust, 2000: 197)

Similar figures exist for university graduates, where

> [...] statistical analysis of census data has shown that Asian and black graduates, including those who appear to be doing well, have worse jobs than white graduates. People of Indian, African and Chinese backgrounds are generally better qualified than white people, but nevertheless have difficulty in gaining access to prestigious jobs. (Runnymede Trust, 2000: 193)

Long-term unemployment, partially attributable to such discrimination, is the most serious form of social deprivation, given that it is likely "to lead to low income, low standard of living, poor housing and poor health" (Runnymede Trust, 1997: 34). A wealth of research evidence demonstrates or implies that these 'racial' inequalities in employment, and hence the economic and social inequalities that blight Britain's Muslim communities, are attributable to discrimination (Commission for Racial Equality, 1996; DfEE, 1999; Modood, 1994; Modood & Berthoud et al., 1997; Runnymede Trust, 1997, 2000; Wrench & Modood, 2000).

In modern Britain, the manifestations of anti-Muslim racism are observable in a number of locations ranging from

> discrimination in recruitment and employment practices; [...]; bureaucratic obstruction or inertia in response to Muslim requests for greater cultural sensitivity in education and healthcare; objections and delays to planning permissions to build mosques; and non-recognition of Muslims by the law of the land, since discrimination on grounds of religion is not unlawful. (Runnymede Trust, 2000: 62)

The sites of anti-Muslim racism listed above represent predominantly material forms of exclusion from employment practices, from education and healthcare, and from protection under the law. The impact which such prejudice, discrimination and disadvantage may be having on Muslim social exclusion is quite disturbing — take the increasing percentage of Muslims in British prisons for example. The Runnymede Trust (1997: 37) show that between 1991 and 1995, the number of Muslims in British prisons increased by 40 percent, from 1,959 to 2,745 prisoners. Muslims now constitute 9 percent of the total prison population, a proportion over 3 times higher than the percentage of Muslims in the British population as a whole. Although the report stops short of suggesting that this rise is directly attributable to racism in the criminal justice system, given the recommendations of the Macpherson Report and the fact that 'black' suspects in general "are more likely than white suspects to be dealt with by arrest than summons [...] by prosecution rather than caution [and] are given longer sentences than white people" (Runnymede Trust, 2000: 130), 'institutional' racism in the criminal justice system is certainly a possibility (for further discussion see Runnymede Trust, 2000: 110–141).

In tandem with this increase in the incarceration of (predominantly male) Muslims, 'street racism' targeted against Muslims is also on the increase. Human Rights Watch (1997) concluded that Britain has one of the highest rates of racially motivated crime in Western Europe, attacks which "are not random but rather target particular ethnic groups in orchestrated campaigns" (cited in Runnymede Trust, 1997: 38). Recent racist attacks against asylum seekers serve as a reminder that such 'campaigns' are ongoing and successful ways through which racists intimidate and exclude already marginalised and disempowered individuals and groups.[7] Indeed, The Runnymede Trust (2000) has shown that the number of racist incidents reported to the police in (just) England and Wales "rose from 13,878 in 1997/98 to 23,049 in 1998/99, an increase of 66 per cent" (p.127). Attacks on Muslims living in the UK increased dramatically following the attacks on America on 11 September 2001. In the words of Human Rights Watch

> Although such attacks were condemned by the government — with a promise to toughen enforcement of hate crimes legislation — new government calls for anti-terrorist measures, more restrictive immigration and asylum controls, and for halting the flow of Afghan refugees into Europe contributed to an increasingly hostile climate toward refugees and migrants in the United Kingdom.[8]

There also appear to be clear relationships between such attacks and the activities of law enforcement agencies, or the public campaigns of the press. In Edinburgh, for example, there has been an increase in racially motivated attacks on Muslims following the arrest of 'terrorist' suspects in the city (*Edinburgh Evening News*, 3 March 2003). Thus, this racist social exclusion is due, in part, to the ready availability of anti-Muslim attitudes to justify discriminatory practices towards Muslims. The roles which the press and other news producers play in producing, reproducing or *resisting* such racism are examined in the following chapter.

CHAPTER 2

The discursive representation
of Islam and Muslims

Introduction

Islam and Muslims are represented and thereby 'made known' to us via, amongst other sites, the pages of newspapers. These writings are the product of filters, processes and discursive practices which differ across time, between genres and within organisations and it is critical therefore that we grasp the nature of these filters, what they emphasise and what they remove from view. Why are certain topics given so much (or so little) attention? How and *why* are certain individuals or groups given that opportunity to voice their opinions, and conversely why are others excluded? Here, in a wish to keep this section as brief as is commensurate with theoretical clarity, several different perspectives, suggestive of 'levels of analysis', are introduced and sketched in outline rather than drawn in detail. The theoretical approaches analysed below all assume news to be a product of a variety of social, economic and cultural factors and, while there is a 'range' of variation in both content and structure of news reporting, this variance is nonetheless confined within (organisational/ professional/ cultural/ economic) boundaries.

Race and reporting in British Newspapers:
Professional and organisational issues

Critical Discourse Analysis assumes that if racism is reproduced through discourse, then racism will be in evidence at all three 'levels' of discursive communication — social practices, discursive practices and the texts themselves — in ways which are integrated and mutually self-supporting (van Dijk, 2003). Prior to a discussion of racism in newspaper texts (their assumptions, their contents, their implications), we need to take account of the context in which such texts are produced, about the factors which enable and limit production and, specifically, the factors which shape the way in which British newspapers write about

Islam and Muslims. Unfortunately, a discussion of this form — looking at the way in which the organisational, financial and occupational conditions in British journalism intersect with the values, the norms and ideals of the profession to produce the news we read — is easier said than done, because compared to the number of studies on journalistic output and representation, little work has been published on newspaper production. As Cottle (2000a: 16) argues, "this imbalance threatens to underestimate, and under-theorise, the important forces that both condition and constrain, as well as facilitate and enable" the presence of ethnic minority voices, faces, opinions and journalists in the production of news. Furthermore, "production is not hermetically sealed behind institutional walls nor confined to organisational decision making and professional routines, and nor is it simply the expression of market forces. Production involves all of these forces in dynamic combination and much else besides." (Cottle, 2000a: 16). In this way, studies of newspaper production straddle most, if not all, of the significant forces which manufacture and shape the news — from editorial or proprietorial beliefs, through professional norms and news values, down to financial, organisational and structural forces at play.

In order for us to better understand some of the complexities of journalism and the forces which contribute to the (under- and mis-)representation of Muslim communities, we have to examine newspapers in relation to these different social, structural and professional processes. From a larger possible list, I have chosen to focus upon the following key areas of news organisations and news production and the (often negative) effects they have on the reporting of 'race', ethnicity and Muslims communities:

1. Finance, profit and advertising
2. Employment of Black journalists
3. White management and organisational discrimination
4. The 'burden of representation'
5. The professional norm of objectivity

Finance, profit and advertising

It is by no means a trivial point that newspaper publication is an industry and a business, and as such

> the activities and the output of the press will be partially determined by considerations related to this fact: by the need to make a profit; by the economic organisation of the industry; by its external relations with other industries; by conventional journalistic practices [...and] by production schedules. (Fowler, 1991: 20)

Indeed it has been argued that even news values themselves are, to an extent, negotiable in light of the need for a report to be 'profitable'. Supporting such an argument, Ettema, Whitney and Wackman (1987) illustrate that "when news occurs in places where its production and distribution is cheaper, it is more 'newsworthy' or at least more likely to be transmitted as news" (p. 35). The *Political Economy* models of news production offer the most developed and illuminating analyses of this economic orientation of news media. Under the current conditions of capitalism, the continued existence of a news producer relies upon it both selling its product (to its identified audience) and doing so in the most profitable manner possible. Political economic theorists suggest that this profit orientation does not merely *structure* but also *constrains* news production, in ways which are both reflexive and supportive of the wider class-based divisions of capitalist societies (see Bagdikian, 1987; Burton, 1990; Curran & Seaton, 1997; Golding & Murdock, 2000; Herman, 1992, 1995a, 1995b; Herman & Chomsky, 1994; Huffschmid, 1983; Murdock, 2000).

This profit orientation, seeking high audience penetration and the maximum receipts from advertising revenue, has two principal global effects on the objectives and outputs of newspapers. First, when news is viewed as a commercial product, the corollary is that the audience is conceptualised as 'the market', as the *consumer* of news. This capitalist logic dictates that if there is more money to be earned by supplying a newspaper that is desired by a section (ideally the majority) of the population, editors and executives will attempt to satisfy this demand and supply such a newspaper. Audiences are segmented into groups with broadly similar tastes and preferences, and sales/circulations are judged in terms of the penetration into a chosen audience demographic and also in comparison with other titles competing for this audience. Thus, the profit-orientated forces of a capitalist news media will overly emphasise stories that are amusing, pleasurable and engaging to this already identified readership, since stories which achieve 'audience appeal' form the basic, most fundamental gauge of what to put in the paper. On the subject of audience segmentation, Worcester (1998) has claimed: "Hardly anything so divides the British by class as does their newspaper reading habits. [...] in 1993, of the middle class households, eight in ten (79 per cent) read the so-called 'quality' papers and only one in five (21 per cent) working class adults did" (p. 41). The readership profiles of the seven British broadsheet newspapers chosen for this study are all heavily skewed in favour society's more powerful middle and upper classes, and this predominance is illustrated by the table below:

Table 2.1. Class composition (%) of British broadsheet newspapers' readerships

		Class				
		A/B	C1	C2	D/E	Total
Newspaper	Financial Times	57	28	9	6	100
	The Times	55	27	9	9	100
	Telegraph	47	31	12	10	100
	Independent	45	32	13	10	100
	Guardian	39	33	13	15	100
	IoS	44	32	14	10	100
	Sunday Times	50	31	12	7	100
All		18	23	28	31	100

Source: MORI, from Worcester (1998: 42)

The figures in Table 1 above are well established, with similar proportions given in a number of studies of British media (Fradgley & Niebauer, 1995; Jucker, 1992; Negrine, 1994; Sparks, 1999). The audiences of broadsheet newspapers, therefore, are predominantly educated, professional, economically and politically powerful individuals and groups, and the content and agenda of broadsheet newspapers reflects the preferences and politics of this predominantly middle and upper class audience.

The corollary of this audience segmentation, of course, is that within a predominantly white society, where 93% of the audience are white, this playing to "the middle ground of white opinion and interests" can result in minority ethnic voices, opinions and interests becoming marginalised (Cottle, 1999: 196). Thus, "content of interest to smaller, or minority, audiences will not be produced in amounts that will satisfy the preferences of that minority" (Gandy, 2000: 47). British Muslim communities are over-represented in the poorer, less well educated, disempowered sections of British society. Consequently, the reporting resources of élite British broadsheet newspapers will not be 'wasted' by attempting to appeal to such an audience. Furthermore, because this is framed as a 'ratings issue', the racialised (racist?) outcomes of profit orientated audience segmentation are not problematised let alone interrogated.

Second, we need to examine the influence which advertising revenue exercises upon the production of newspapers. The significant links between newspaper titles (and types), capital generated from advertising revenue and the audience cannot be overlooked. To slightly adapt Owen and Wildman's (1992: 3; cited in Gandy, 2000: 48) comments on broadcasting, newspapers "are in the business of producing *audiences*. These audiences, or means of access to them, are sold to advertisers." When journalism is viewed in such a way, the audience shift from being the *consumers* of a product, to being the *product themselves*, particularly within news organisations in which advertising is the primary source of income. In doing so, newspapers which conform to the "marketing requirements of advertisers" obtain large external subsidies which they "can then spend on increased editorial outlay and promotion in order to attract new readers" (Curran & Seaton 1997: 37).

Of course, advertisers are not interested in audiences *per se*, but in audiences who are willing and able to (over-)consume. Therefore the value of these (audience) products, and the corresponding amount of money that advertisers are willing to pay, varies greatly between media. Franklin (1997) for example shows that the near identical price of full page adverts in the (tabloid, populist) *Sun* and the (broadsheet, élite) *Financial Times*, at £28,000 and £29,568 respectively, hide significant divergences in the costs of speaking to their respective readers. Once the *Sun's* considerably higher circulation is taken into account, the amount "advertisers are prepared to pay to reach the highly influential and affluent *Financial Times* reader would buy access to no less that 14 *Sun* readers" (Franklin, 1997: 92). This rationale has organised newspaper publishing for over 150 years. Quoting an advertising handbook from 1851, Curran and Seaton (1997: 35) show that, when it comes to audiences, "'Character is of more importance than number' [...] adding that 'a journal that circulates a thousand among the upper or middle classes is a better medium than would be one circulating a hundred thousand among the lower classes.'" Indeed history has shown that once "newspapers became identified with the poor, they found it difficult to attract advertising" (Ibid.), sometimes to the extent that they're forced to close down (the *News Chronicle* and the *Daily Herald* being two frequently cited British examples of this). Conversely, successful broadsheet newspapers are 'forced' to keep their coverage 'up market' in order to serve up wealthy readers to advertisers (Negrine, 1994: 67). In short:

> What is crucial to understanding a media system governed by capitalist logic, is that not all audiences are equally valued in the market. If particular audience segments that are attracted (produced) by particular content are undervalued in the market, advertisers will be unwilling to pay the same 'cost per thousand' they would be willing to pay for more 'desirable' audiences. (Gandy, 2000: 48–9).

The cost of this to disproportionately poor British Muslim readers hardly needs spelling out.

This profit orientation is further complicated when we consider that a great many mainstream news media are owned by media corporations or other conglomerates, and are managed by executives with profit concerns in other, often wholly unrelated fields of industry. On this subject, Graham Murdoch's research has shown that "in 1976–7 two-thirds of the chairmen and vice-chairmen of the ten largest press groups were educated at public school and/or Oxbridge, from where many of Britain's financial and industrial élite were also recruited" (cited in Curran & Seaton 1997: 83). Political economic theorists claim that these shared points of contact — including "similar social origins, shared educational experiences, overlapping social networks, close working relationships" etc. (Ibid.) — all conspire to encourage a shared outlook between media managers and financial/business élites. From such a perspective it comes as little surprise that Max Hastings — who recently described the 'Wapping Revolution' as "Rupert Murdoch's most brilliant achievement", enabling him "to produce his newspapers with non-union labour and to break the tyranny of the old print workers"" (Hastings, 2002: 20) — would rise to be the editor of the (right-wing) *Daily Telegraph* and later the editor of the (still more right-wing) London *Evening Standard*. We do well to remember that Murdoch's 'brilliant achievement' resulted directly in the forced redundancy of 5,000 print workers and indirectly in the redundancy of many more as other newspapers were 'forced' to follow Murdoch's example.

In addition to this more unreflective alignment of journalism to the interests of capital, the purchase and management of news outlets has historically been an explicit "strategy by which large business organisations sought to influence the environment in which they operated" (Curran & Seaton, 1997: 85). For example, the willingness of American broadcaster NBC to use the oil crisis threatened at the start of the 1990–1 conflict with Iraq, as an opportunity to re-promote the 'option of American nuclear power' — thus reflecting the interests of its parent company *General Electric* — illustrates the potential influence which corporations may wield on the output of (Their) news media. A more personal vendetta against the (Al) Fayed brothers in the *Observer* Sunday broadsheet was initiated by the newspaper's parent company, Lonrho, and owner Tiny Rowland. For four years the paper published a series of articles criticising the take-over of the House of Fraser retail group by the (Al) Fayeds, at the expense of the Lonrho offer, culminating "in the publication of an unprecedented mid-week issue, dedicated to attacking the 'Phoney Pharaoh' Mohamed al Fayed, to coincide with Lonrho's AGM" (Curran & Seaton, 1997: 82–3).

This relationship also moves 'the other way': 'fact' and opinion are not only put *into* news but are also taken *out* through censorial and occasionally authoritarian policing of news companies by either their parent companies or other corporations providing financial support. Herman and Chomsky (1994) illustrate several examples where programme sponsorship has been removed when the interests of corporate funders were threatened, most notably when *Gulf + Western* removed funding for WNET, following their broadcast of a documentary questioning multinational interference in 'Third world' countries ('Hungry for Profit'). At the time, the programme was described by *G + W* officials as being "anti-corporate" and even "anti-American", inducing the *Economist* to remark that "most people believe that WNET would not make the same mistake again" (Herman & Chomsky 1994: 17). Similarly with British broadsheet newspapers: the purge of 'wet' and 'lefty' stories — and eventually journalists — from the *Sunday Times* following the appointment of Andrew Neil as editor in 1983, are still the stuff of legend (Curran & Seaton, 1997).

A defining assumption of political economic theories of news production is therefore that "[m]oney and power will penetrate the media by direct control or indirect influence and will filter out the news thought unfit for most of us to consider" (Herman, 1995a: 81–2). This certainly no less true in the case of newspapers produced and read by élites.

Employment of Black journalists

It is difficult to comment accurately on the number of Black journalists working in the UK because British newspapers, as private companies, do not have to publish statistics about the racial/ethnic backgrounds of the journalists they employ. In addition, most newspapers don't *have* figures on the racial/ethnic status of their employees anyway, due to the wilful ignorance enshrined in their 'colour-blind' employment practices (Hodgson, 2002). However, this much we do know: In the mid to late 1990s, there were usually between 15 and 25 Black journalists working for national newspapers — roughly corresponding to 2 or 3 per paper out of a total of about 3,000 national press journalists (Ainley, 1998). If Black journalists were proportionally represented on national newspapers, this figure would be around 200. Alternatively, if we base our calculation on the 28% Black population of London where the UK national press is based, the number would be around 840.

The reasons given for having so few Black journalists are varied. Editors of national newspapers usually react uncomfortably when they are asked why there are so few Black journalists on their paper, resenting the idea that this under-employment has anything to do with 'race' or racism and certainly not (in post-Macpherson Report Britain) *institutional* racism. As Peter Preston has said, "[w]henever charges of institutional racism start flying around, editors of national newspapers tend to study their boots or glance over their shoulders" (quoted in Hodgson, 2002). However, the system of employment which national papers generally use to recruit journalists *is* discriminatory because papers very rarely advertise vacancies: candidates either get to know about a vacancy via word of mouth, over the table of a dinner party or through contacts already in the paper. Even the more meritocratic approach where gifted journalists are head-hunted from the local or regional press is flawed since, as Ainley (1998) illustrates, only 15 out of 8,000 journalists working in the local and provincial press were Black (again, proportionate representation would return a number close to 800). Consequently, this system of patronage, where jobs are given to 'the right people', means that white middle class men continue to dominate the national press (Delano & Henningham, 1995), to the detriment of not just Black journalists but also working class and female journalists.

Of course, the question running through this discussion about the number of Black journalists is: would reporting improve with more Black journalists? Would a Black editor on a national Broadsheet newspaper act in a manner strikingly different to the current cohort? The situation is a great deal more complex than to simply suggest that 'Black journalists write Black news copy', as discussed in more detail lower down.

White management and institutional discrimination

There is a great deal of evidence, unfortunately mostly anecdotal, to suggest that when Black journalists manage to get jobs in mainstream news organisations, they are treated differently to their colleagues. This discrimination can occur in three principal forms, each of which is important to outline because of what they illustrate about the occupational culture of journalism. First, outright discrimination resulting in unfair dismissal, lack of promotion and the 'glass ceiling' effect. Looking to broadcast news for a moment, the BBC (which has attained its goal of 8% Black employment, albeit concentrated in poorer paid jobs) was hit in 2002 by two high profile race discrimination cases in its World Service division. The broadcaster Sharan Sadhu, who subsequently withdrew her complaint after the BBC agreed to an undisclosed settlement, cited a "colonial culture" in operation in the World Service, while Perry Gambas has claimed that he was discriminated against and unfairly dismissed (cited in Francis, 2002). Returning to print, Gary Younge has argued that the high profile which the British broadsheet newspaper the *Guardian* gives to him is unrepresentative of the organisation as a whole. He says: "There's definitely been an acceleration in giving black journalists picture bylines and higher profiles. But it's really not what this is about. What they don't tackle are subeditors, photographers, reporters." Thus, simply citing the paltry number of Black journalists without a more detailed account of their status and position can hide a multitude of sins, covering up the fact that news "really is controlled by a bunch of white boys" (Heider, 2000: 22)

Second, 'ethnic diversity' in the UK has historically been interpreted in a simplistically tokenistic manner, with Black staff expecting to fit into a news room culture dominated by the values of white, middle class, Oxbridge educated men. Francis (2002) quotes a black female journalist working in the BBC who claims: "There is this unspoken reality that, although I look different to you, I must act, think and speak the same as you, which is then promoted as diversity". Similarly in print journalism, one black American reporter working for the Washington Post, has claimed that the paper "frequently seems to interpret equal opportunity as meaning that if minorities and women work hard and follow directions, they too can become white men" (Coleman, 1986, citied in Wilson, 2000: 97).

Third, the pressure to pursue and 'create' diversity — particularly in broadcasters with a public service remit like the BBC and Channel 4–can result in more subtle forms of discrimination. For example, Black journalists may have been employed to improve newsroom racial diversity — essentially, they were employed 'for their blackness' — but are subsequently expected to act, and write, *as* 'Black journalists'. One award winning broadcaster for example (cited in Francis 2002), describes her experiences "as an Asian woman" working in journalism:

> At my appraisal I was criticised for not bringing in enough black and ethnic minority stories. I challenged them on this, as when I was appointed I was up against white colleagues and there was no mention of this in my job description.

Furthermore, given the lack of an economic rationale for writing for or about British Muslims — or indeed about any of Britain's Black communities — in a critical or judicious manner and the correspondingly low 'news value' in such stories, this drive for 'diversity' must also be viewed in relation to the capitalist logic of much British journalistic culture. In one of the only academic studies of the professional experiences of Black journalists, Ainley (1998) includes the testimonies of reporters to indicate how this journalistic professional culture can operate in practice:

> I worked for this paper for two years and left frustrated. Firstly I was not treated like white journalists. I was a general reporter yet they wanted me to only report on race stories because I am black. The editor thought that I couldn't report on white stories. In other words I was not good enough. When there was a race story I received no editorial backup. There was no paper coverage and this leads to no contact and no stories means you are soon left with no confidence. In two years I had just three front page stories. Basically, *they did not want a black reporter unless they covered black stories yet when they had black stories they did not consider them important.* (Black reporter for a Liverpool newspaper, from Ainley, 1998: 59; emphasis added)

Another, more openly prejudicial example:

> I am qualified with provincial newspaper experience but when I went for a job [in a national] they wanted me only to report on race stories covering muggings, rapes and immigration. I didn't take the job. (from Ainley, 1998: 63)

But there are journalists who don't feel uncomfortable writing such stories, believing that news is truth and the truth is more important. Ainley (1998: 63) again, quotes a journalist on a national Sunday newspaper, who had written a lengthy investigative piece on medical friends of his parents who were allegedly selling NHS drugs to India. In recalling this story, he explained:

> I don't care who it is, I just report what happens. My parent's friends were crooks so I exposed them. I had to move out of my community and my parents don't talk to me any more but writing the truth is more important.

Implicit in these examples is a longstanding dilemma which journalism forces upon Black journalists (also disproportionately forced on female and working class journalists). Broadly speaking: "Am I a journalist who happens to be Black, or am I a Black journalist?" Should one's responsibility be towards objective reporting — which, as in the above case, may result in writing stories which implicitly associate 'race' and crime, or 'race' and social threat? Or should responsibility lie in positive or campaigning journalism, which may not be that popular with the organisation one works for, or that helpful in advancing one's career? Where should loyalties lie?

The 'burden of representation'

This dilemma has become referred to as the 'burden of representation'. Clearly, the basis of the dilemma and the cause of the problem is that the values of journalism are themselves *'white'*. Specifically, "the perspectives, values and direction of journalistic information and commentary are culturally exclusive of non-White vantage points" (Wilson, 2000: 97). Hence, some journalists (some of whom are white themselves) feel torn between seeking to reconcile their desire to gain the respect of their peers with the responsibility to help rectify the sometimes distorted or misrepresentative portrayal of 'race' and racialised communities. Implicit in this position, and in the sort of questions cited at the end of the above section, is the dilemma that journalists face

> [...] in seeking to reconcile their desire to fulfil personal professional ambitions by gaining acceptance of peers and superiors with the responsibility to fill a void in the informational needs of society. While many may assume that the two objectives are compatible and complementary, history and tradition have shown that they are not. (Ibid.)

In the case of television production, Cottle (2000b) illustrates that the burden of responsibility is now "used to describe the situation of black film makers who, confronted with so few opportunities to produce films, feel that they must use each and every opportunity to 'represent' black interests and viewpoints and counter dominant mainstream images" (p.106). However, in making programmes which expressly challenge dominant, negative cultural representations of race, journalists are also *constrained* by these negative representations — which, in the end, can not only be counter productive, but also quite offensive. Take the recent debates in both broadcast and print news on the 'relationship' between Islam and terrorism, or Islam and *jihad*, for example. To engage with the argument, even to argue that 'Islam condemns terrorism, Islam condemns murder and the killing of innocents, etc.' not only contributes to the general relationship between Islam and terror via their collocation, it also grants a certain credibility to the racist argument: it suggests, albeit implicitly, that both sides are 'debatable positions'. Clearly, to still be having such a debate is offensive: it is offensive because it is part of this "relentless insistence — even if it is put in the form of a debate — that [the Muslim] faith, culture[s] and people[s] are seen as a source of threat" (Said, 1997: xxi).

Equally with articles or television programmes about racism — for example, about the anger of British black youth, excluded, or disenfranchised due to white racism — it is extraordinarily difficult for journalists to accurately represent this anger without implicitly advancing popular misconceptions about 'Black youth'. As one executive producer for the BBC, who Cottle quotes, puts it:

> I think you have to be careful because there's a lot of ignorance. You don't want to compound the ignorance. You don't want to confirm people's worst suspicions. So you've got to do something to say 'here's a problem' and find a way of contextualising which doesn't make all the old ladies in middle England buy another bolt for the door because they think black people are coming to get them. (in Cottle, 2000b: 106)

Exercises in campaigning, or pro-active journalism such as this are not only difficult in themselves, they are also bound to come up against significant resistance from colleagues, both black and white, in the newsroom. 'Race', and openly anti-racist articles are discussed and included very warily by mainstream news organisations (Wilson, 2000). Sig Gissler, a former editor of the *Milwaukee Journal*, for example, argues that Black mainstream journalists are often reluctant to speak up about racism — both within and outside the newsroom — for fear of being labelled a whiner or, as suggested above, for fear of appearing unbalanced, partial or lacking in emotional distance. Therefore, by this account, underlying some of this reluctance to write campaigning, anti-racist journalism seems to be a commitment to the professional norm of objective reporting.

The professional norm of objectivity

In essence, to be 'objective' a journalist need to distance herself from the truth-claims of the text. However, as suggested above, while the journalist's opinions may indeed be taken out of an objective report, this by no means results in the processes and products of reporting being value-less or unbiased — quite the reverse in fact. Campbell for example argues:

> Those who demand that the news media achieve 'balance' — if not objectivity — must acknowledge that balance is a code word for [white] values. These values are encoded into mainstream journalism. (R. Campbell, 1991: 75; cited in C. Campbell, 1995: 17).

Going further, Santos argues that "The long-hallowed cult of journalistic objectivity has too often been a veneer for what is essentially a predominantly white male point of view in our news culture" (cited in Keeble, 2001: 72). Is there any weight to these accusations? For the purposes of this discussion, I will employ a widely accepted definition of 'objectivity' outlined in Tuchman (1972). Tuchman argues that journalists adopt four "strategic rituals" in realising the goal of objectivity in reporting: first, the use of sources giving competing truth-claims; second, the presentation of supporting evidence; third, the use of quotation marks to distance themselves from (very often *their own*) truth claims and assumptions; and finally, the structuring of information to present conflicting or alternative 'facts' (taken from Tuchman, 1972).

Each of these strategies for achieving objectivity is infused, to a greater or lesser extent, with support for dominant, stratified (racialised) power relations. First, the approach of *quoting sources* and conflicting truth-claims is the most visible capitulation to power, since access to any particular medium of discourse is a power resource *in itself*. Access to the news media is something to which "members of more powerful social groups and institutions, and especially their leaders (the elites) have more or less exclusive access" (van Dijk, 1998a: 5). The effect of this hardly needs stating: 'objective' news reporting reproduces "an imbalance between the representation of the already privileged on the one hand, and the already unprivileged on the other" (Fowler, 1991: 22).

Secondly, the use of *supporting evidence* results in a similar support for dominant power relations, since the primary method of presenting evidence is through quoting influential or 'expert' sources. Another approach is to offer supporting 'facts', which are themselves a product of social discourse and hence an index of power. The third strategic ritual — the *use of quotation marks* around words and phrases — is particularly interesting from a discourse analytic perspective, because it demonstrates not only the constructive role of the reporter in the story but also the ideological stake which journalists have in *disavowing* such a role. This constructive role of the reporter clearly needs to be acknowledged and interrogated because journalists, like the rest of us, are shaped by a powerful bedrock of social principles. Most citizens of Western societies hold a number of deep convictions, most notably "that their society represents the very apex of civilisation" (Schudson, 1978, p. 184, cited in van Ginneken, 1998, p.63). The journalist's preconceptions of 'the world', its nations and peoples, inform not only the manner in which articles are written, but also the *gaze* and *selection* of articles. Van Ginneken has illustrated this through the example of the 'tragic death' as reported in the press. Every day around 137,907 people die across the world, of which between only 1 in 1,000 and 1 in 10,000 are ever reported in the news.[1] Taking children's deaths as an example:

> Of all these tragic deaths every day, 34,676 are under five years of age. Most die from preventable elementary diseases resulting from under nourishment and vitamin deficiencies, from lack of clean water and hygienic conditions. [...] The major media do not paint this as an acute disaster which warrants immediate foregrounding. (van Ginneken, 1998: 25)

Van Ginneken argues this shows that "the 'tragic death' is a highly 'social' construction: certain tragic deaths are systematically under-reported, others are systematically over reported" (van Ginneken, 1998: 25), and that such disparities occur according to encultured (ethnocentric) norms and values. Thus (adopting a more 'culturological' position), journalists may not be "obliged to endorse the dominant ideological accounts of reality because of direct pressure from proprietors or others, but because they have internalised the dominant societal values" (Franklin, 1997: 46). These principles and others shape that which is included in so-called 'scare quotes' and that which is not.

The fourth strategic ritual controls the *context* in which information is communicated, which is particularly relevant in the case of newspapers, where the importance of any particular actor, statement, argument (etc.) is implied by its location in the text. News text is structured like an inverted pyramid, whereby the facts/points deemed to be most important are located at the top in the headline, leading down in importance through the story lead, the first paragraph and so on to the bottom. From a CDA perspective, Fairclough (1995) has discussed this discourse structure in terms of "a scale of presence" in news texts, "running from 'absent' to 'foregrounded': absent – presupposed – backgrounded – foregrounded" (p. 106). In this way inclusion in 'the news' may important, but equally (if not more) important is the *location* of the actor, statement, argument (etc.) in the story and in the paper as a whole. Therefore, a piece could be 'objective', because it has included competing facts or perspectives, and yet still privilege a white male point of view because of the way news journalism places more importance on certain facts and people because of where they appear.

However, Tuchman (1972) points out that these four strategic rituals "can be bent sufficiently to be oppositional, as well as acquiescent, to the dominant ideological framing of questions" (Eliasoph, 1988: 232). Eliasoph supports this 'radicalisation of strategic rituals' and, by using data collected over almost two years of participant observation, she demonstrates that any news organisation could produce such "oppositional news", even while following the (conventional) norms and routines of news production. Thus, the 'event-centric' nature of news can, for example, accommodate the reporting of public anti-government demonstrations, or the publication of Human Rights Reports, or, in the case of the radio station studied, use the Iran-Contra scandal "as a peg for an interview with John Stockwell [...] about CIA covert tactics in all parts of the globe" (Eliasoph, 1988: 236). Similarly, journalists' reliance on 'official' or 'expert' sources can accommodate the quoting and *foregrounding* of an Muslim Imam, or a Trade Union official, Naomi Klein, or a host of others, depending on the subject of the report. Other news routines (such as regular production schedule, or the need for balance) are shown to hold a similar potential for "oppositional news".

Eliasoph thus illustrates that it is not necessarily the routines *on their own* which produce ideologically conformist news reports which support the racist status quo. Rather, the alignment of journalism with the interests of the powerful is a combination of the (mainstream) media's corporate bureaucracy, the reliance on other corporations for funding (through advertising revenue), the institutional conservativism of white management and editorial staff, and apathetic, or self-serving and career-hungry, journalists.

Race and reporting in British newspapers: Output and representations

Given the above discussion of organisational and professional constraints on the production of news, it should come as little surprise that research literature on the way British journalism represents minority ethnic communities shows that the press "selectively repeat, rework and reinvent a simple pattern of key racist messages which have 'helped to build a respectable coherent common-sense whiteness'" (Law, 2002: 77). Across the years, and as a matter of routine, domestic and international reporting has predominantly depicted 'black and brown' people in terms of a restricted repertoire of representations and in reporting contexts which foreground three features: conflict; controversy; and deviance. In their study of the *Guardian, The Times,* the *Daily Express* and the *Daily Mirror* between 1963 and 1970 for example, Hartmann et al. (1974) found that 'race' was frequently combined with 'conflict' or 'violent' words in the headlines of press reports, resulting in an association between 'race' — treated in the press as a synonym for Britain's black communities — and threat, hostility and violence (p.158). Further, Hartmann et al. (1974) showed that this 'problematisation' of Britain's 'racial' minorities (which, of course assumes the existence and suitability of 'race' as a conceptual category) also guides reporting at a thematic level, concluding that

> there was a quantitative similarity in the handling of race by the four newspapers
> and that a number of themes emerge as the most salient. These were: immigration
> (in particular control of coloured [*sic*] immigration); relations between black and
> white (in particular inter-group hostility and discrimination); legislation to con-
> trol immigration and counter discrimination; and the politician Enoch Powell.
> (Braham, 1982: 271–2)

Indeed, as Braham (1982) suggests, most academic analyses of press representation of 'race' and 'ethnicity', particularly journalistic output up to and including the 1980s, conclude that

> the media have concentrated on the threat perceived by the white majority to be
> implicit in black immigration and in the black presence; and that they have
> neglected the extent of discrimination and disadvantage experienced by blacks
> except in so far as these key conditions seem to contribute towards the supposed
> threat, for example, by fostering anti-social behaviour. (p.279)

Halloran (1977) indicates that research carried out during the 1970s at Leices-
ter University's Centre for Mass Communications Research, yielded similar
results:

> [...] as the number of coloured people [*sic*] and the social concern over race
> relations has increased, so [press] attention has moved away from the relation of
> coloured people to the major social resources of housing, education and employ-
> ment [...] towards the hostility itself and its manifestations, including the concern
> to keep coloured people out of the country and the concern to regulate hostility by
> the various laws and machinery set up to these ends. (p.12)

Aside from the outmoded language, Halloran's above quotation is important in
the way in which it highlights an erroneous presupposition of both the press
and successive governments since the 1950s: the 'problem' is the *presence* of
black communities 'here' *causing* racist hostility, rather than prevailing racist
hostility which problematises the presence of black communities. Similarly, as
Troyna (1987) has shown, when the press reported violence between racist
supporters of the National Front on a march through Southall and anti-racist
counter demonstrators, it was "the aggressive resistance of anti-NF demonstrators to the provocative actions of that racist party, [...] the *protesters* rather than
the *cause* of the protest, the NF, which [were] defined as the more immediate
threat to the political stability of the nation" (p.286–6; emphasis added). This
(*re*)presentation of 'racial disturbances' was made possible via the press

> consistently underplay[ing] the question of why the NF decides to hold its dem-
> onstrations in areas where local residents are likely to feel threatened by its

presence, and focus[ing] its attention instead on the manifest consequences of those decisions: namely, violence between what are seen as two opposing, extremist groups. (Troyna, 1987: 285)

This emphasis on the violence of the demonstrations, without the contextualisation necessary for understanding, enabled *The Daily Telegraph* to conclude: "The disturbances that took place in the streets of Southall this afternoon were unprovoked acts of violence against police and property by groups of people determined to create an atmosphere of tension and hostility" (Ibid.). Significantly, as Troyna (1987) points out, *The Daily Telegraph* did not include the NF as one of these "groups" creating "tension and hostility". In this way, "the news framework is constructed around the *problem* of the black presence and within it news values revolve around *conflict* and tension" (Braham, 1982: 285; emphases added). A similar approach — focusing on the event rather than the causes for the event — is also clearly observable in international reporting, particularly reports covering clashes between Palestinian stone throwing youths and the Israeli army. In such reports, any contextualising information regarding the impoverished, segregated and *ghettoised* status of the Palestinians is subordinate, and to a large degree *deleted*, in favour of an almost exclusive concern with reporting the 'violence' between two protagonists. This, of course, draws an equivalence between the 'two sides', whitewashing over the inestimable disparity between the resources, not least the *weaponry*, at the disposal of each.

Journalism and the (racial) stereotype problematic

Moving on slightly, a considerable body of research illustrates that journalists recurrently use prejudicial stereotypes to represent and characterise Britain's minority communities (Cottle, 2000a; Gabriel, 1994; Hartmann & Husband, 1974; Lawrence, 1982; Twitchen, 1992; van Dijk, 1987, 1991). Fowler (1991) argues that the formation of news events is "a reciprocal, dialectical process in which stereotypes are the currency of exchange" (p. 17). By his definition a stereotype "is a socially-constructed mental pigeon-hole into which events and individuals can be sorted, thereby making such events and individuals comprehensible: 'mother', 'patriot', 'business man', 'neighbour', [for example] on the one hand, versus 'hooligan', 'terrorist', 'foreigner' on the other" (Ibid.). Developing this argument, Fowler shows that in news discourse, stereotypes and their equally stereotypical antitheses are both constituted and constitutive of the news value of 'meaningfulness', as proposed by Galtung and Ruge (1965):

> 'Meaningfulness', with its subsections 'cultural proximity' and 'relevance', is founded on an ideology of ethnocentrism, or […] more inclusively, homocentrism: a preoccupation with countries, societies and individuals perceived to be like oneself; […and] with defining groups felt to be *unlike* oneself. (Fowler, 1991: 16, emphasis added)

In this way, the stereotypical representation of 'Others' may be one (negative) feature of news discourse facilitated and maintained through the very values upon which news is constructed.

Further to 'first order' issues of media representation, the salience of 'racial' stereotypes in everyday speech, interaction and argument is well established (Essed, 1991; van Dijk 1987), since, as van Dijk (1999) suggests, "[s]peakers routinely refer to television or the newspaper as their sources (and authority) of knowledge or opinions about ethnic minorities" (p.11). The discursive potential of such 'racialised' — and often rac*ist* — knowledge to modify power relations in other social fields is similarly acknowledged (Bourdieu, 1991), the "most benign effect" of which is "to separate people of colour from the white mainstream. The more malignant, lasting effect — in the media and beyond — has been an unfounded but unshakable connection between people of colour and social pathology" (Woods, 2000: 41). Omi (1989: 114) makes a similar point:

> Popular culture has been an important realm within which racial ideologies have been created, reproduced and sustained. Such ideologies provide a framework of symbols, concepts and images through which we understand, interpret and represent aspects of our 'racial' existence. (cited in Orbe et al., 2001: 119)

The reproduction of "racial ideologies" in broadsheet newspapers is particularly consequential given the educated, empowered and economically successful status of broadsheet readers (Jucker, 1992; Worcester, 1998).

The above points regarding 'racial' stereotyping are all important factors to consider when analysing journalistic representation of 'race' and 'ethnicity', and undoubtedly deserve recognition. However, analysing 'stereotypes' without giving equal, or perhaps even *greater* emphasis on societal complexes of power, knowledge and ideology, is at best imprudent and at worse myopic. Entman (1990), Campbell (1995) and Lule (1995) have each separately argued that the attempts of American news producers to portray African-Americans in more positive ways "create an impression of black social advance [that] undermine claims on white resources" (Cottle, 2000a: 11). Brian Kleiner (1998), in his discussion of 'racist pseudo-argumentation' for example, shows how (racist?) protagonists support their arguments for reducing or abolishing American affirmative action scholarships for African-American students, by referring to the black communities' apparent economic success. Similarly, Jhally and Lewis (1992) have suggested that the successful black characters in programmes such as 'The Cosby Show' may promote "enlightened racism" since they "tell us nothing about the structures behind success or failure", and thereby open the way for "white viewers to assume that black people who do not measure up to their television counterparts have only themselves to blame" (p. 138). Thus, media theorists are increasingly showing that the active contestation of prejudicial stereotypes, or the substitution of 'negative' with 'positive' minority ethnic characters in the entertainment and news media, may result in unintended negative outcomes for those represented.

On the other hand, should the predominantly deprived status endured by Britain's 'racial' and ethnic communities be represented then the potential for racists to gain evidential material supporting their 'naturalised' hierarchies, based on inherent 'racial' differences, may be increased. This inherently problematic status of 'stereotypes' to analytic work has been addressed in Cottle (2000a: 9–13), in which a series of pertinent critiques of research on 'stereotypes' are listed and discussed. In the critique perhaps most significant to the current discussion, Cottle suggests that the concept of a 'stereotype' is limited due to

> its competing realist and idealist political premises — should representations portray the 'negative' realities of 'raced' lives and therefore seemingly endorse wider cultural typifications, or portray a more 'positive' imaginary but then be accused of distorting reality? (Cottle, 2000a: 12)

Further, Cottle (2000a) argues that the concept of 'stereotypes' assume "that meanings are 'contained' within its terms and are not dependent on (differentiated) audience interpretations" and that meanings "are assumed to be confined to, embodied within, and 'read off', depicted characters" (Ibid.). Rather, textual meaning cannot be divorced from the context of social and discursive practice. At a metatheoretical level, this accords with the Wittgensteinian position that "the meaning of an utterance rests in its usage in a specific situation" (Titscher et al., 2000: 146) — a communicative context in which 'decoding', and specifically the potential for *racist* 'decoding', represents an indivisible constituent part. On this subject, the 'Parekh Report' (2000) makes the following observation:

> Any one news story is interpreted by the reader or viewer within the context of a larger narrative, acting as a kind of filter or template. If the larger narrative is racist

> — or, more benignly, representative of a 95/5 society — then the story is likely to
> be interpreted in a racist or majority-biased way, regardless of the conscious
> intentions of reporters, journalists and headline writers. (p.169)

Given this position, and the insight that "ideological representation is never merely reflective, since objects of knowledge are always culturally constituted within complexes that intertwine meaning and power" (Parker, 1992; Burman & Parker, 1993, cited in Henwood & Phoenix, 1999), any discussion of 'stereotypes' — 'racial' or otherwise — needs to be explicitly drawn from a systematic analysis of the "relationship[s] between the text and its social conditions, ideologies and power-relations" (Titscher et al., 2000: 146).

The open expression of explicitly racist opinions in Britain, is now likely to be received with at least disdain and public reproach. While overt racism, a regular feature of (particularly tabloid) newspaper reporting in the 1970s and 80s, is therefore seen far less regularly in the contemporary press (Allan, 1999; Searle, 1989; van Dijk, 1991), "the force of representations which draw upon concepts of 'normality' in order to give strength to negative representations", so prevalent in 'up market' reporting, remain unscathed (Ferguson, 1998: 130). Hammond and Stirner (1997) argue that it is through such notions of 'normality' and 'cultural difference', that prejudicial (racist) discourses are given a more acceptable gloss. Similarly, Malik (1996) argues that the notion of genetic lineage previously encoded as 'race' has been *re*coded as primordial ethnicity and invariant cultural difference — "natural terms", which ensure that "culture acquires an immutable character, and hence becomes a homologue for race" (p.150). Racism occurring in this way — as 'inferential racism' — is "in many ways more insidious [than overt racism] because it is largely invisible even to those who formulate the world in its terms" (Hall, 1990: 13). Such inferential racism, also present in newspapers' banal discussions of 'nation' and 'nationalism' (Billig, 1995), has

> provided a language which has allowed for a coded vicarious discussion of race:
> what Reeves (1983) has called discursive deracialisation [...] Thus the new racism
> has acquired a theory and a range of styles of argumentation which are enveloped
> in a self-evident reasonableness. (Husband, 1987: 321)

Broadsheet newspapers' argumentative structures tend to be based on such "standards of reasonableness" (van Eemeren et al., 1997), and as such are particularly adept at providing support for the "expression of delicate or controversial social opinions" whilst simultaneously "protecting the speaker against unwanted [*negative*] inferences about his or her ethnic attitudes" (van

Dijk, 1987: 76). This is due, in part, to the style policies of broadsheet newspapers, with news items written in a "moderate, emotionally controlled language, close to the standard register" and using "more sophisticated and less explicit mechanisms [...] to control and bias the information given" (Martín-Rojo, 1995: 51). In order to gain the fullest understanding of how broadsheet newspapers achieve this "discursive deracialisation", a theoretical research framework aimed at "analysing opaque as well as transparent structural relationships of dominance, discrimination, power and control" (Wodak, 1995: 204), is needed.

(Critical) Textual analysis of newspaper reporting

> Excellent journalism starts with an understanding that language has power.
> (Woods, 2000: 41)

Language use, in the form of text and talk, forms the third aspect of Fairclough's notion of discourse, and is approached, as was suggested above, as being both a direct result of and a formative influence upon social beliefs, values, ideology and power formations. This position is also taken by Fowler (1991), who argues:

> Anything that is said or written about the world is articulated from a particular ideological position: language is not a clear window, but a refracting, structuring medium. If we can acknowledge this as a positive, productive principle, we can go on to show by analysis how it operates in texts. (p.10)

Evident from Fowler's position above is the non-pejorative definition of 'ideology' adopted by many critical linguists. By this definition, the notion of ideology as 'false consciousness' is rejected in favour of

> something more neutral: a society's implicit theory of what types of object exist in their world (categorisation); of the way that world works (causation); and of the values to be assigned to objects and processes (general propositions or paradigms). These implicit beliefs constitute 'common sense' which provides a normative base to discourse. (Fowler, 1996: 10–11)

This neutral definition is by no means shared by all CDA theorists.[2] Fairclough (1995b) for example, building on the work of Althusser (1971) and Pêcheux (1982), maintains a more traditionally Marxist understanding of ideology and the ideological work which discourse does through the mediation of "political and economic structures, relationships in the market, gender relations [and] relations within the state", and "the creation and constant recreation of relations, subjects (as recognised in the Althusserian concept of *interpellation*) and objects which populate the social world" (p.73). In this way, Fairclough (1995b) suggests that, in contrast to Fowler's (1996) neutral conception above: "Ideologies [*only*] arise in class societies characterised by relations of domination" and therefore discourse is ideological only in so far as it contributes "to sustaining or undermining power relations" (p.82).

However, the notions of 'ideology as common sense' and 'ideology as a vestige of class power/knowledge' are not as antithetical as the above passage suggests. Stuart Hall for example, drawing on Gramsci's definition of 'common sense' and its inter-relation with ideology (see Simon, 1982: 63–4) has suggested that

> [Ideologies] work most effectively when we are not aware that how we formulate and construct a statement about the world is underpinned by ideological premises: when our formulations seem to be simply descriptive statements about how things are (i.e. must be), or what we can 'take-for-granted'. (cited in Lawrence, 1982: 47)

These simple "descriptive statements about *how things are*" are particularly important to consider in relation to racist 'common sense' given the fixity of human potential which racism assumes. In order to gain a fuller understanding of the ideological work, maintaining and/or resisting (inequitable, deleterious) power relations, that such 'common sense' (racist) representations manage, we must take a step back and discuss discourse and discrimination in much greater depth, and specifically if and how ideological meaning may (or may not) be 'read off' the representations of Muslims in text and talk. On this point Fairclough (1995b) suggests:

> There are two major aspects of representation in text [...] In logical terminology, the first has to do with the structuring of propositions, the second with the combination and sequencing of propositions. (p.104)

Central to this theoretical position, is the notion of *levels* of textual construction and analysis. Thus, the first aspect of representation concerns the construction of *clauses*, and the representation of processes, events, actions and individuals in (for the most part) single propositions. The second aspect concerns the *organisation* of these single clauses into a coherently structured whole. This coherent whole can be loosely defined as the way the text presents a 'reality' to the audience and the manner in which the audience is positioned in relation to this same 'reality'.

It is therefore assumed that texts can, and perhaps *should*, be analysed at various levels and by focusing on different linguistic dimensions, each of which "may be involved directly or indirectly in discriminatory interaction against minority group members" (van Dijk, 1999: 4). Van Dijk, in a series of studies of the discursive representation of ethnic minorities (1984; 1987; 1991; 1992; 1993; 1996; 1997; 1998; 1999; 2000; van Dijk et al., 1997) has developed a conceptual tool called 'the ideological square' which he suggests dominates racist talk and text on and about 'racial' and ethnic others. This ideological square is characterised by a Positive Self-Presentation and a simultaneous Negative Other-Presentation and is observable across all linguistic dimensions of a text from the lexicon and syntactic structures, the meanings of sentences and the coherence relations between sentences, as well as the broader pragmatic — directed and functional — concerns of the text. Further, not only manifest words or other aspects of textual content are studied. Notions such as 'presupposition', 'implicature' (conversational and otherwise) and 'entailment' probe the hidden meanings of discourse, taking as their object of study the values, beliefs and ideological meanings which exist (occasionally necessarily) either 'before' or 'after' the manifest claims of the text. The remainder of this chapter is thus structured in accordance with the range of linguistic/discursive levels suggested above.

Reference, syntax and style

Taking lexicon first, the selection of words in a text may be more or less negative and hence 'frame' that which is represented — be it an individual, a group, an event, a process, an action, a state, or mental or verbal process — in a more or less negative way. Lexical choice becomes noticeably ideological when we consider:

- familiar noun-pairings such as 'thug vs. demonstrator', 'terrorist vs. freedom fighter', determiners (e.g. 'our Army vs. the Army') and in combination as noun phrases (e.g. 'the Army vs. our Boys');
- verb-pairings such as 'clash vs. debate' and 'attack vs. defend';
- and adjective-parings such as 'fanatical vs. devout' and 'ruthless vs. resolute' (also see Allan, 1999: 178–9).

Racist terms of derogation are well known and need no introduction here, particularly since such terms are very rarely used in any but the most virulently racist of publications (see Daniels, 1997). Internationally, newspapers — particularly élite, broadsheet or 'quality' newspapers — prefer to use either "negative words to describe the properties or actions of immigrants or minorities (for instance, 'illegal')" or else use special code words such as 'welfare mothers' or 'inner city youths' in negativised contexts (van Dijk, 2000: 39; also see Wykes, 2001: 30–60). *The Sunday Times* (3 December 2000) for example, reporting the tragic death of Damilola Taylor, referred to "a community used to violent crime" (Woods & Gadher, p.1), a **"Violent ghetto culture that claimed Damilola"** (– the headline to Woods et al., pp. 14–15), and "a moral, spiritual and emotional vacuum" arising "from rage, rooted in emotional chaos and neglect" which exists amongst "the squalor of the area where the Taylor family was living" (**Children learn to kill in a moral dead zone**, Phillips, p.19). In such instances it appears quite apparent that Britain's black youth — described by one article as dominated by "thugs" attracted to the "culture of violence and greed lauded by rap singers" (**Violent ghetto culture that claimed Damilola**, p.15) — are being blamed for this tragedy.

In one of the most detailed of recent publications on discourse and discrimination (Reisigl & Wodak, 2001) the ideological importance to racist discourse of 'naming' — "referential strategies" — and the attribution of traits, characteristics and qualities — "predicational strategies" — are discussed at great length (p. xiii; also pp. 44–69). Taking referential strategies first: Reisigl and Wodak (2001) show that in the act of 'naming',

> one constructs and represents social actors: for example, ingroups and outgroups. This is done is a number of ways, such as membership categorisation devices, including reference by tropes, biological, naturalising and depersonalising metaphors and metonymies, as well as by synecdoches in the form of a part standing for a whole (*pars pro toto*) or a whole standing for the part (*totum pro parte*). (p.45)

Adapting van Leeuwen's system network of the representation of social actors (1993; 1996), Reisigl and Wodak (2001) argue that analytical categories such as "'exclusion', 'inclusion', 'suppression', 'backgrounding', 'passivation', [...] 'collectivisation', 'aggregation', 'impersonalisation'" and others,[3] "are of great help for us in accurately describing some of the more subtle forms of discriminatorily, as well as positive-representatively, constructing, identifying or hiding social actors" (p.46).

Clearly referential strategies bear the imprint of *predication* — defined by Reisigl and Wodak (2001: 54) as "the very basic process and result of linguistically assigning qualities to persons, animals, objects, events, actions and social phenomena" — however, it is through predicational *strategies* that

> persons [etc...] are specified and characterised with respect to quality, quantity, space, time and so on. [...] Among other things, predicational strategies are mainly realised by specific forms of *reference* (based on explicit denotation as well

as on more or less implicit connotation), by *attributes* (in the form of adjectives, appositions, prepositional phrases, relative clauses, conjunctional clauses, infinitive clauses and participial clauses or groups), by *predicates* or *predicative nouns/adjectives/pronouns*, by *collocations* or explicit *comparisons, similes, metaphors* and other *rhetorical figures* [...] and by more or less implicit *allusions, evocations* and *presuppositions/implications*. (Ibid.)

Thus, the choice of words used in nomination and characterisation of social actors are of particular significance in analysing the positive self-presentation and negative other-presentation integral to the 'ideological square'.

Second, the syntactic structure of sentences is similarly shaped by the ideological square. Of particular relevance is the differential emphasis which can be placed on agency through active, passive or nominalised construction of transitive action processes (or 'transactive' processes by some theorists' terminology: see Hodge & Kress, 1993; Kress, 1994; Trew, 1979). For example, in the active construction 'a Jewish extremist killed Yitzhak Rabin', the agent (Jewish extremist) is placed in a foregrounded position which emphasises the role he played in the transitive ('transactive') action represented. In contrast, the passive construction 'Yitzhak Rabin was killed [by a Jewish extremist]' backgrounds the role of the extremist to a prepositional phrase. This phrase is placed within parentheses in order to show that it can be deleted (in a process called 'active agent deletion') leaving a passivised verb without agent: 'Yitzhak Rabin was killed'. Agents can be disavowed in this way "for various reasons — perhaps because they are obvious, but also perhaps as a way of obfuscating agency and responsibility" (Fairclough, 2000: 163). Patterns in such obfuscation are quite revealing of newspaper ideological codes. For example, van Dijk (2000) argues that 'racial' and ethnic minorities tend to be represented in the press "in a passive role (things are being decided or done, for or against them) unless they're agents of negative actions, such as illegal entry, crime, violence or drug abuse. In the latter case their responsible agency will be emphasised" (pp. 39–40). In one study of the Dutch press, van Dijk (1999) "found that of 1,500 headlines on ethnic issues, not a single one was positive when it involved minorities as active, responsible agents" (p.12).

The active agent deletion of passivised transitive verbs can be moved a stage further into nominalisation — the transformation of a process into a noun, a construction which characteristically involves further imprecision and ambiguity. Thus the passive 'Yitzhak Rabin was killed' can be represented as 'the death of Yitzhak Rabin', thus removing all sense of agency, time and location. Fairclough (2000) argues that nominalised constructions involve

> abstraction from the diversity of processes going on, no specification of who or what is changing, a backgrounding of the processes of change themselves, and a foregrounding of their effect. In backgrounding the processes themselves, nominalisation also backgrounds questions of agency and causality, of who or what causes change. (p.26)

The (selective) nominalisation of transitive verbs therefore holds enormous ideological potential, since it obfuscates responsibility by backgrounding (or often *deleting*) agency and causality. Hence, the *News on Sunday*, by suggesting that the disturbances on the Broadwater Farm estate were "sparked by *the death of Cynthia Jarrett* during a police raid on her home" (13 October 1985, cited in Wykes, 2001: 42; emphasis added) obscures the very active role which the police played in *killing* Ms Jarrett.

These two linguistic dimensions — lexicon and syntactic structures — are here combined and referred to as constituting the *style* of a text. Linguistic style is defined by Jucker (1992) as

> a comparative concept in that it describes some relevant differences between a text or a discourse and some other texts or discourses; or, in some methodological frameworks, with some kind of explicit or implicit norm. It generally applies to instances of real language, language that has been *produced* by speakers with their beliefs, aims and goals *in specific situations*, and *in particular physical, social and temporal environments*. (p.1, emphasis added)

Explicit in the above quotation, is the recognition that stylistic variation is by no means 'free' or 'arbitrary', but rather should be regarded as a contingent part of the role that context plays in the formation of text and talk (van Dijk, 1988: 27). Further, it is important not to be "misled by the language of 'choices' and 'options'; [stylistics] is a framework for analysing the variability of language and its social determinants and effects, and *self-conscious* linguistic choice is a relatively marginal aspect of the social processes of text production and interpretation" (Fairclough, 1995a: 18). In this way, stylistic variations should be analysed as an indicator of the

> relationship between participants in speech acts who, as individuals, negotiate speech acts and thereby create 'styles' strategically, but who are also exemplars of social roles and have relationships in larger social institutions beyond the frame of dyadic interaction. (Traugott & Romaine (1985: 29), cited in Jucker, 1992: 17)

Thus, through the dialectic — *constructed and constitutive* — relationship between language and context, texts may be used to "indicate personal or social factors of the communicative event" (van Dijk, 1988: 27).

It should also be remembered that "media institutions typically do have explicit policies on at least some aspects of language use. Rules about usage are commonly codified in a 'style sheet' or 'style book' [...] and there is also a more general notion of what constitutes 'good style' which is meant to inform reporting and editing practice" (Cameron, 1996: 315). This is an area of news analysis which has obvious relevance for critical linguistic analysis in general, and lexical/syntactic style in particular, for two principal reasons (Cameron, 1996). "First, when analysts look for ideological effects resulting from lexical and syntactic patterning in news discourse, it needs to be acknowledged that some textual regularities may be the outcome of explicit style rules rather than implicit assumptions about the matter in hand" (Cameron, 1996: 316). This point, quite obviously, cuts to the core of the approach which Critical Discourse Analysis takes with regard to language use: Given that patterns of stylistic variation in a text may not be attributable to its speaker/writer, but rather to the *prescribed* style of the organisation to which the speaker/writer is affiliated, to what extent can we suggest that such patterns are 'commonsensical' and hence ideological? However, Cameron, giving her second motive for analysing style guides, points out that

> style policies [...] *are ideological themselves.* Though they are framed as purely functional or aesthetic judgements, and the commonest criteria offered are 'apolitical' ones such as clarity, brevity, consistency, liveliness and vigour, [...] it turns out that these stylistic values are not timeless and neutral, but have a history and a politics. They play a role in constructing a relationship with a specific imagined audience, and also in sustaining a particular ideology of news reporting. (Ibid.; emphasis added)

Jucker (1992), in a study of stylistic variation in newspapers which broadly concurs with Cameron (1996), argues that linguistic style should "be seen as a correlate of the addressee(s). Thus, stylistic differences are caused not so much by different amounts of [the speaker's] attention, but by adapting to different audiences" (Jucker, 1992: 8). The corollary of this is, of course, that these lexical terms and syntactic structures do not possess a semantic equivalency with their alternate stylistic 'options', and therefore their use can be analysed as an indication of the ideological presuppositions of the text's producer: the newspaper.

In short, the study of linguistic style should attempt to relate patterns and features of linguistic variation to the larger non-linguistic (and ideological) context in which they occur. Such an approach to the study of language in use found a paradigmatic home in the form of Critical Linguistics, exemplified by the work of Gunther Kress (1983; 1994; Fowler, Hodge, Kress & Trew, 1979; Hodge & Kress, 1993). Kress (1983) argues that "[a]s ideological systems exist in and are articulated through language, the ideological system *in itself* can be reached via an analysis of language" (p.124; emphasis added). He illustrates this argument by showing the effect which specific syntactic processes can (and do) have upon textual meaning. In the sentence "*Telecom* employees are likely to reimpose work bans", taken from an Australian newspaper report, the reporter presents a specific *interpretation* of the reported action to the audience through the use of the verb/adjective pairing "are likely". Kress show that alternatives could have been:

Verb	Adjective complement
are (certainty)	*likely* (uncertainty)
seem (uncertainty)	*certain* (certainty)
are	*certain*
seem	*likely*

These alternatives "differ in that 'seems' establishes the relation as the judgement of some beholder (that is, *it seems to someone*) whereas 'are' establishes the relation as an existential fact" (Kress, 1983: 127). No doubt the reporter in question would then have provided evidence to back up the (implicit) claim of certitude, yet the choice and use of the verb 'are' is ideologically important in two ways: it stresses the *certainty* of industrial action by *Telecom* workers, and as such is a product of (and also a productive part of) the general discourse on 'industrial relations'. This is interesting in itself, and further investigation and analysis could perhaps reveal a consistency in the newspaper's portrayal of industrial disputes. The 'existential factuality' of the claim is also important in relation to the discourse on objectivity in journalism. Journalism necessarily makes truth claims through which, it is hoped, the audience will be convinced by the reporter that "his or her description and interpretation is the rational and appropriate one" (Kieran, 1998: 27). The conviction of the reporter (and in turn, *the report*) to the factuality of the particular interpretation presented is instrumental in the degree of reliability placed on the text upon reading. In this sense, the use of "are likely" as opposed to "seems certain" is highly significant.

Semantic and argumentative structures

The next aspects of news reporting which need to be examined are the semantic structures, at both micro (sentential) and macro (textual) levels. At the macro semantic level, van Dijk (1988) argues that the topic of a text "is part of a hierarchical, topical or thematic structure — the semantic macrostructure — which may be expressed by a summary and which defines what is subjectively the most important information, gist, upshot of the text" (p.34). Past content analysis of the representation of 'racial' and ethnic others (discussed earlier in this chapter) has shown that the topics of paragraphs or whole news items are limited to a restricted list of prejudicial images and issues and are presented in an overwhelmingly negative manner. Further, in accordance with the ideological square, there is a preference for topics which emphasise 'Our good actions' and de-emphasise 'Our bad ones' (van Dijk, 2000: 38). Equally, van Dijk (1999) illustrates the importance of developing a more local, micro semantic analysis of news texts, focusing on, amongst other features, the presence of *disclaimers*. These disclaimers are semantic manoeuvres — or "strategies" (Reisigl & Wodak, 2001) — "with a positive part about Us and a negative part about Them" (van Dijk, 1999: 9), and include moves such as:

> Apparent Denial: 'I have nothing against Muslims, but…'
> Apparent Concession: 'Of course *some* Muslims are tolerant, but generally…'
> Apparent Empathy: 'Of course asylum seekers endure hardships, but…'
> Apparent Ignorance: 'Now, I don't know all the facts, but…'
> Reversal: '*We* are the real victims in all this…'
> Transfer: 'Of course *I* have nothing against them; but my customers…'
> (adapted from van Dijk, 1999: 9)

These strategies are labelled 'apparent' disclaimers because the structure of their discourse is such that "the negative part of the sentence is spelled out throughout the discourse. The positive part thus especially has the function of avoiding a bad impression [of the protagonist] with the recipients" (van Dijk, 2000: 41).

The dividing line between semantic manoeuvres such as those introduced above and full argumentation is unclear. Indeed, Kleiner (1998) labels van Dijk's 'apparent disclaimers' as 'pseudo-arguments', which participants employ "in an effort to forestall negative inferences by others, and to project an image of rationality, objectivity and fairness" (p. 206). Traditionally, argumentative discourse has been divided into three ideal types: first logic, which concerns proof via deductively valid argumentation comprised by logical constants and internally verifying propositions. By this approach, if an argument has a valid form[4], and the propositions are true, the conclusion *cannot* be false. Second, dialectic argumentation, which by the Aristotelian definition "is best understood as the art of inquiry through critical discussion. Dialectic is a way of putting ideas to critical test by attempting to expose and eliminate contradictions in a position" (van Eemeren et al., 1997: 214). Dialectic forms the normative model of argumentation, and although it represents an ideal type, general definitions of argumentative discourse have a tendency to draw upon dialectic characteristics (see Kopperschmidt, 1985).

There are arguments however, "where the subject matter [does] not lend itself to certain demonstration", i.e. through using either logical or dialectic methods, hence a third argumentative discourse type: rhetoric. The classical definition of rhetoric "has to do with effective persuasion [...emphasising the] production of effective argumentation for an audience" (van Eemeren et al. 1997: 213). Contemporary analyses of rhetoric retain this theme, focusing on "the situated quality of argumentation and the importance of orientation to an audience" (van Eemeren et al. 1997: 215), and, in it's simplest form, occurs "when someone, who believes some statement, ...[presents] reasons which aim at persuading others to adopt this same point of view" (Thomson, 1996: 6). Here we see how rhetoric differs from the previously defined argument types, in that it appears as the *defence of opinion* as opposed to the pursuit of '*truth*'.

Of course, rhetorical argument is still based on the offering of factual reason in support of a conclusion, but rhetorical (persuasive) argumentation operates *through* valid forms of argumentative discourse, appropriating them in order to grant credibility, and hence persuasive weight, to the otherwise questionable propositions expressed in 'opinion'. In this way, argument represents "opinion statements [...] embedded in argumentation that makes them more or less defensible, reasonable, justifiable or legitimate as conclusions" (van Dijk, 1996: 24). This definition is not offered in any pejorative sense, but rather to acknowledge the 'laundering' function which dialectic argumentative forms play in rhetorical argument, lending the appearance of fairness, 'even-handedness' and objectivity, in order to ward off both negative inferences regarding the participants (Kleiner, 1998: 210), and the promotion of the argument in the eyes of the audience.

Thus, a fully formed critical model of argumentation should take account, not only of the form and content of argument, but also the functional and interactive aspects of argument within their discursive context, and their application and effect in the social field. The work of van Eemeren, collaborating with various other theorists (1992; 1993; 1996; 1997; 1999) is extremely useful in such a critical analysis of argumentative discourse, proposing a theoretical framework which attempts a unification of normative and rhetorical theories of argumentation: Pragma-Dialectical theory. This theory

> views argumentative discourse as an exchange of verbal moves ideally intended to resolve a difference of opinion. The dialectical angle of the theory is manifested in the maintenance of critical standards of reasonableness, the pragmatic angle in the definition of all argumentative moves as speech acts functioning in a context of disagreement. (van Eemeren and Houtlosser, 1999: 480).

Thus, although it is acknowledged that the principal function of argumentative discourse is to persuade or convince with "the aim of securing agreement in views" (van Eemeren et al., 1997: 208), this is achieved "according to appropriate procedures of reasonable dialogue" (Walton, 1989: 1). Such appropriate procedures, or 'standards of reasonableness', are manifest structurally (e.g. pertinency, turntaking), interactionally (e.g. rules of cooperativeness), semantically (e.g. avoiding ambiguity, equivocation and prejudicial language) and elsewhere across argumentative discourse. Semantic standards of reasonableness would, for example, include avoiding the expression of socially disapproved (anti-social) ideas, opinions and attitudes. This is not to say that such ideas are not still present in discourse, merely that they have found less obtrusive manifestations. The ideology of 'Modern' or 'New Racism' (Barker, 1981) is a case in point, wherein "modern racists are said to avoid expressing overtly anti-black opinions, instead preferring to express their views in more subtle, sophisticated ways which may be defended by appeal to seemingly universally accepted egalitarian values and principles" (Kleiner, 1998: 188).

Van Eemeren and Houtlosser (1999: 480) define the dialectic aspect of argumentation in terms of four stages, crucial to "establishing systematically whether the standpoint advanced by the protagonist of a viewpoint is defensible against doubt or criticism of an antagonist." These stages of argumentation are, in turn:

> the confrontation stage, where difference of opinion is defined; the opening stage, where the starting point of the discussion is established; the argumentation stage, where arguments and critical reactions are exchanged; and the concluding stage, where the result of the discussion is determined. (van Eemeren & Houtlosser, 1999: 480–1).

At each stage dialectic rules of argumentation are employed — by participant and analyst — the violation of which "can result in errors, faults and shortcomings of various kinds in argumentation" (Walton, 1989: 16).[5]

The rhetorical dimensions of the theory are defined as strategies "for influencing the result of a particular dialectical stage to one's own advantage, which manifest themselves in a systematic, co-ordinated and simultaneous exploitation of the opportunities afforded by that stage" (van Eemeren & Houtlosser, 1999: 485–6). This is accomplished, the theory suggests, through three strategic manoeuvres, exploiting: the *topical potential*, wherein "speakers or writers may choose the material they find easiest to handle"; adapting to *audience demand* by choosing "the perspective most agreeable to the audience"; and through *presentational devices* which frame "their contribution in the most effective wordings" (van Eemeren & Houtlosser, 1999: 484). Taking each in turn then: the rhetorical use of topical potential — which, in the case of text and talk on and about 'racial' and ethnic minorities, is dominated by discourses of difference, discord and threat — acts to imply an "importance and pertinence to the discussion" (Perelman & Olbrechts-Tyteca, 1969: 119), and therefore works to define the disagreement space to the benefit of the protagonist (van Eemeren et al., 1993). The use of topical resources in argumentation, in this case relying so heavily on negative other-presentations, thus provides interesting evidence about the ideological position of the (racist?) protagonist.

Regarding audience demand, Perelman and Olbrechts-Tyteca (1969) state that "since argumentation aims at securing the adherence of those to whom it is addressed, it is, in its entirety, relative to the audience to be influenced" (Perelman & Olbrechts-Tyteca, 1969: 19). Rhetorical argumentation attempts to create empathy or "communion" with an audience (van Eemeren & Houtlosser, 1999: 485), through appeal to the audience's beliefs or preferences. One manifestation of this, is the recourse to the 'common sense' of an audience, either though implicit or explicit assumption, since common sense is founded on "the existence of unquestioned and unquestionable truths" (Perelman & Olbrechts-Tyteca, 1969: 57). It is here that the model is most receptive to the definitions of ideology given above (Fowler, 1996; Gramsci, 1971).

Presentational devices, such as loaded definitions, figures of speech and rhetorical argumentative structures (e.g. analogy), should also be employed in rhetorical argument in order that "the phrasing of the words [...] be systematically attuned to their discursive and stylistic effectiveness" (van Eemeren & Houtlosser, 1999: 485). Since rhetorical figures of speech are one such presentational device, strategically employed as "a way of describing things which makes them present to our mind" (Perelman & Olbrechts-Tyteca, 1969: 167), their persuasive character in argumentation cannot be denied. Further, since rhetorical figures are non-obligatory structures in both argument and in text in general, their inclusion must be regarded pragmatically, showing "how and in what respects the use of particular figures is explained by the requirements of argumentation" (Perelman & Olbrechts-Tyteca, 1969: 168). The Pragma-dia-lectical model reflects such a concern for argumentation, analysing figures of speech "as part of the sequential environment to which they are tied, and [...paying] attention to their contribution to the local and global coherence of the text" (Ferrara, 1985: 140). For these reasons and others, the theory and methods of pragma-dialectics are particularly useful in opening up the (often implicit) argumentation of journalism to critique.

The functions of texts: Speech Act Theory

Finally, a linguistic analysis of news needs to take account of the pragmatic dimensions of media texts. Such a focus has already been touched upon in the preceding section, wherein I showed how the pragma-dialectical model of argumentation foregrounds the function which specific utterances play to the coherence and ultimately the success of an argument. However, pragmatic theory provides additional insights into the practical role(s) which, for exam-ple, an argument *in toto* may play at a more macro-pragmatic level, as well as suggesting *how* texts achieve such practical goals. This dimension of analysis therefore aims to not merely examine "the forms or the meaning (or reference) of verbal [and textual] utterances, but rather the social act we accomplish by using such an utterance in a specific situation" (van Dijk, 1988: 26). Beginning with Austin (1962) and later expanded and adapted by Searle (1969, 1979), we refer to such communicative acts as 'speech acts', archetypal examples of which being 'questions', 'assertions', 'promises', 'accusations', and 'threats'. The basic insight of the pragmatic approach to the study of language use is its focus on how meaning and action are related. The utterance itself is split into three 'speech acts' by both Austin (1962) and Searle (1969), although these taxonomies differ slightly in their terms of reference. For Searle (1969):

> The uttering of words (morphemes and sentences) is an *utterance act*. [...] Acts like stating, questioning, commanding, and promising are *illocutionary acts*. [...] The consequences of illocutionary acts (the effects on actions, thoughts, beliefs of hearers) are *perlocutionary acts*. (Schiffrin, 1994: 55–6)

Thus, in terms of newspaper reporting, the utterance is the sentential structure of the report itself: the arrangement of words in sentences and paragraphs. The propositional acts which this utterance achieves — primarily concerning "ref-erence and predication" (Schiffrin, 1994: 56) — are the most rooted in these textual structures. Thus, "the propositional content rule for promises, for example, is the prediction of a future act (A) by the speaker [S]" whilst "the preparatory condition for promises [...] concerns H's [the hearer's] preference about S's doing of an act (A)" (Ibid.). The perlocutionary act is realised in the change in H's belief which the utterance brings about: in other words, H's (new) belief that S will observe his/her commitment (also see Searle, 1969: 57–62).

The illocutionary act and its relation to the perlocutionary act are the most interesting aspects of an utterance for the current discussion, given the rules and constitutive conditions by which this relationship is created. Essentially, a speaker must have the ability, and moreover, be *perceived* to have the ability, to carry through on the illocutionary act of their utterance. For example, 'S' must be trusted (by 'H') for a promise, or any other commissive, to have any perlocutionary force; authoritative enough for assertions or declarations to have any force; and powerful enough for directives, such as requests or orders 'designed' to get 'H' to do 'A', to have any perlocutionary force. Therefore, in each communicative event — 'utterance' by Searle's terminology — the (differential) power of 'S' and 'H', and the complexes of societal power in general, are foremost concerns. Whilst it should be borne in mind that "[s]ince news discourse nearly exclusively consists of assertions (and not of promises or threats)", and as such "a pragmatic description in the strict sense would not yield much more than *the conditions necessary* for the appropriate *accomplishment* of assertions" (van Dijk, 1988: 26; emphasis added), these conditions are by no means insignificant. Broadsheet newspapers' tradition of respectable, quality journalism, their standard of writing and the overwhelmingly élite status of their readers, furnish broadsheet reporting with an authority absent from almost all other journalistic forms. Hence, the types of illocutionary acts which are intimately associated with (indeed are *reliant* upon) authority — for example, statements, descriptions, assertions, allegations, criticisms — are granted extra perlocutionary force in the mind(s) of the reader(s).

The work of Hage (1998) on Australian multiculturalism and Blommaert and Verschueren (1998) on the way ethnic diversity and tolerance in Belgium are discursively constructed, provide interesting and important applications of such a pragmatic approach to language study. Not only does their work illustrate the clearly disadvantageous effects which prejudicial discourse has on ethnic minority communities, the seeming distance (geographic, cultural and analytic) between the foci of these two studies provides proof, if proof be needed, that a discourse analytic perspective can be successfully applying in a variety of national and discursive settings. Blommaert and Verschueren (1998) for example, first show how an exclusive 'otherness' is created in public discourse, primarily by referential and predicational strategies (Reisigl & Wodak, 2001), and then *used* in discriminatory practices against Belgium's visible minority communities — particularly citizens of Moroccan or Turkish origin. Such an approach — which Blommaert and Verschueren (1998) label as an 'ethnic management paradigm' — views diversity as a problem, and as such, any "discourse on diversity is [used as] an instrument for the reproduction of social problems, forms of inequality and majority power" (p. 4). Similar results, in which the exclusion of ethnic minorities and 'foreigners' is legitimised through discourse, have been recognised as features of parliamentary discourse in Spain (Martín-Rojo and van Dijk, 1997) Austria (Sedlak, 1999), Britain, France and the USA (van Dijk, 1997).

Hage (1998), adopting a similar argument, suggests that racist talk and text about 'racial' and ethnic others are characterised by "discourses of spatial management" which, whilst they are undoubtedly

> 'informed' by racist modes of classification [...] are better conceived as nationalist practices: practices which assume, first, an image of a national space; secondly, an image of the nationalist himself or herself as master of this national space and, thirdly, an image of the 'ethnic/racial other' as a mere object within this space. (p. 28)

Accordingly, racist talk and text which draws on concepts such as 'too many' or 'go home', which are themselves "meaningless unless they assume the existence of a specific territorial space [and its 'ontological ethnic status'] against which the evaluation 'too many' is arrived at" (Hage, 1998: 37), are subordinate to the very practical function of maintaining (white) domination over a (territorial, cultural or symbolic) space. Such practices are recognisable in a wide variety of social settings, from the systems of exclusion and containment inherent in immigration policy, to readers' letters requesting Muslims prove their loyalty to the nation, to street racism and violent attacks against visible minorities, to the 'emancipatory' goal of certain liberals in their desire to unveil Muslim women: all emanate from an image of the national space and the agent's fantasy that they occupy a privileged position within this national space as "the enactors of the national will" (Hage, 1998: 47). Such assumed privilege is particularly important to consider in any analysis of élite discourse — of which the British broadsheet press is a clear example.

CHAPTER 3

The ideological square I

'Muslim negativity'

Introduction[1]

In the main, the reporting of Islam and Muslims is founded upon a structuring of presuppositions, themes and arguments indicative of van Dijk's ideological square, and dominated by a twin process of 'division and rejection' of Muslims (Martín-Rojo, 1995). The broadsheet approach to division and rejection suggests that its success is based upon a three part process: first the identification of a 'space' (which can be political, cultural, social, mental, physical or metaphorical) separate from 'Our own' space; second, explaining the workings or composition of this space in contrast to 'Our own'; and third, placing a (negative) social value on both this space and its composition. This third 'stage' in the process often occurs simultaneously with one or other of the preceding 'stages' given that value judgements are often achieved in reference and predication.

Division and rejection

Often the implicit assumptions of news reports, illustrate anti-Muslim prejudice. This prejudice is most clearly indicated in the referential strategies used to represent Islam and Muslims. An *Independent* editorial commenting on Iran's successful entry into the finals of football's World Cup 1998 (**All the world's a pitch; the fixture is friendly**, 6 December 1997) for example, argued:

> The idea of a nation peopled entirely by fundamentalist mullahs and women deep in purdah taking to the turf in studded boots, shorts and shirts covered in advertising logos is enough to give the popular imagination pause.

The prejudicial manner in which Muslim Iranians are referred to is clear in the above excerpt. Further, the newspaper *needs* to draw upon this prejudicial

identification of Iranians ("fundamentalist mullahs and women deep in purdah") in order to ensure the success of its argument. The idea of Iran "taking to
the turf" would not have appeared so discrepant without this representation of
'what Iranians are' and, therefore, 'what Iran is'.

Similarly, in a letter to the editor headed **Israeli peace with neighbours not
answer to Iraq/Iran threat** (Lord Stone of Blackheath, *Financial Times*, 25
November 1997), the author's negative perceptions of a homogenous 'political
Islam/Muslims' are illustrated throughout in his choice and description of
social actors, illustrated first in the above unification of Iraq/Iran in common
threat. The gist of Lord Stone's argument is: even if Israel "achieved peace with
all of its neighbours, the dictators in Iraq would not be transformed into liberal
democrats", and neither would "the religious zealots who rule Iran", nor "the
fundamentalists who oppose the reforms of Hosni Mubarek [...] by killing
tourists". Here, actors are rhetorically positioned in order to achieve the success of the letter's argument: that Israel's illegal occupation of Palestine and
other Arab nations is wholly unconnected with other regional power struggles.
He selects a highly functional "cast of villains"[2] who are: first, presupposedly
villainous, as illustrated in their being labelled "dictators", "fundamentalists"
and "zealots"; second, are homogenous — their equivalency implicitly suggested by their being offered in the form of a list (Fairclough, 2000: 161–2); and
third, intransigent, since their negativity is maintained despite "peace" being
"achieved". This "cast of villains" is then set against Israeli social action —
(re)presented here as an attempt to 'achieve peace'. This antithesis works to
further emphasise the (presupposed) intransigent threat to Israel posed by the
'Muslim world'.

This negative labelling of 'Muslim' social actors reaches its peak when
reporting countries in which the politics and 'policies' of the ruling regime are
almost universally decried. Afghanistan was one such country during this
period of time. One article printed in *The Times* (**A kingly gift lost in a war
zone**, Saturday Sports section, 29 November 1997) questioned the where-
abouts of a luxury Rolls Royce car "given to the King of Afghanistan by George
V", now lost in Afghanistan. Following general 'place-setting' rhetoric (Afghanistan as a war zone), the article cites "Taliban militia"; a "mad mujahidin
driver"; "black bearded Taliban zealots"; "reactionary mullahs"; "tribal revolt";
"fundamentalist"; "wild-eyed Mujahidin fighters"; "mud huts" and other
negative references drawn from the lexical style register of 'backwardness,
incivility and barbarity' which are then linked, via collocation, to Islam.

In other articles, the characteristics which individual Muslim actors are presupposed to possess draw upon similarly negative stereotypes. For example, a feature article written in response to the 50th anniversary of Israel's independence and profiling "the scholar-militant" Edward Said (**Spectre at the feast**, *Independent* Magazine, 24 January 1998), simultaneously disputes *and* draws upon stereotypical representations of 'the Arab' in the contrast it establishes between Said and Yasser Arafat. Following a complementary introduction and discussion of Said's contributions to both literary criticism and political activism, the author, Stephen Howe, argues that Said confounds "those who dislike [him] or his message", since "his very charm and urbanity are […] far too unlike their stereotypes of 'the Arab'". By contrast, Yasser Arafat — possibly the only "voice of Palestine […] better known" than Said — is given a far less complimentary appraisal:

> […] in many ways Said is the chairman's anathema — elegant as against Arafat's calculatedly bristly unkemptness, massively fluent as against Arafat's inarticulacy in English, a civilised aesthete in contrast to Arafat's bloody past and shifty present.

The contrasts which Howe establishes between Said and Arafat draw, in equal measure, on their faith and their residency: both men are Palestinian Arabs, but where Said is a Christian, Arafat is a Muslim; whereas Said lives, works and *resides* in 'the West', Arafat, with his "bloody past and shifty present", lives (and belongs?) in the 'Muslim world'. The two men therefore become the *embodiment* of their origins and beliefs: Said as the "elegant", "fluent" and "civilised" West; and Arafat as the 'unkempt', 'inarticulate', "bloody" and "shifty" 'Muslim world'. The articulation of such stereotypes in an article which aims at illustrating Said's academic and political influence — loosely defined as the realisation that "almost all contemporary writing about the Middle East, is deeply implicated in the histories of European and US racial arrogance" — is highly ironic.

The negative characteristics which Muslims are presupposed to possess can also be revealed through studying the national, geographical or 'cultural' spaces believed to best represent 'Them'. In one rather derisory article, for example (Her Majesty the Terminator, *Independent on Sunday* 12 October 1997), Robert Fisk argues that the "preposterous theory" that Princess Diana was intentionally killed — possibly by the Queen — in order to stop the Royal Family being infiltrated by Islam is directly attributable to its origins "in the Arab world, where the *moamarer* — the plot — is an essential part of all political discourse". Going further Fisk argued: "my banker friend had no right to transfer *this ruthless way of life* on to the tragedy of the Pont de l'Ama". Hence Fisk suggests a 'space' — "the Arab world" — where he believes such ruthlessness is more characteristic, and perhaps more appropriate.

In an article headlined **Pakistan TV bans the shampoo set** (*Sunday Times*, 9 November 1997), reporting censorship and "modesty requirements" on Pakistani television, 'Islamic values' are presented as culturally backward, illiberal and therefore inferior to 'the West'. In an introduction which suggests authoritarianism and the *imposition* of "Islamic values and culture", the article states that "images of women tossing their hair to promote shampoo and smiling seductively to sell toothpaste have been banned in Pakistan as politicians have bowed to pressure from the mullahs". Further, the article makes it quite clear that the newspaper views a move away from Pakistan's secular values (in place "since its foundation in 1947") "towards Islamic fundamentalism" as an undesirable shift:

> Some of Pakistan's more liberal thinkers have condemned the restrictions as draconian [...] Some critics have even likened the authorities' attempts to turn back the cultural clock to those of the Taliban regime in neighbouring Afghanistan, where women are banned from public life.

Here 'Islam' is contrasted with 'liberalism', and labelled 'backward' ("turn back the cultural clock"), repressive (from "regime") and sexist through the comparison with the Taliban's repressive (gendered) social practices. This (re)presentation — where 'Pakistani censorship is Islamic' and 'Islamic is repressive' — is expanded lower down the article:[3]

> [...] the limitations imposed in the media reflect a general increase in repression. While women in Pakistan's main cities face pressure to dress modestly, those in the countryside have been confronted by a rise in domestic violence which the authorities seem reluctant or unable to check.

The rise in domestic violence in Pakistan is unquestionable (see Rumsey, 2000); the link between this violence against women and 'Islamic values', which the article suggests, is unwarranted and prejudicial. In the final paragraph, the article finally quotes a source that draws attention to the questionable link which the journalist, Stephen Grey, is suggesting between the politically inspired actions of the Pakistani government, Islam and repression:

> Shehnaz Bokhari, leader of the Progressive Women's Association which campaigns against domestic violence, said [...]: "Islam says women should be covered but it never said anything about covering the face. In fact, during the pilgrimage to

> Mecca, women are actually prohibited from wearing the veil. I don't understand what this government is up to."

An argument based upon a schema of 'Islam vs. the West' in which 'the West' is civilised and 'Islam' is repressive, backward and barbaric, forms the gist of an article printed in the *Guardian* (**A deadly divide**, Saturday 'Weekend' supplement, 4 October 1997). This article is ostensibly about the social and ideological divisions between rich, "modernised" Egyptians and poor "Islamic extremists":

> [...] is Egypt in danger of losing it's identity? Is the schism that divides society — on the one side the Islamic extremists, on the other the modernised, Western-influenced Egyptians [...] now so wide that it cannot be repaired?

In discussing this split, the *Guardian* focuses on a district of Cairo called Imbaba, thereby following the first stage of the three part process suggested above — the identification of a 'space'. The journalist suggests that this location, "known as the Islamic Republic of Imbaba [is] a *breeding ground* for Islamic fundamentalists" (emphasis added on the metaphor: animals or germs). The article continues: Imbaba is so Islamic that "Everyone is robed, and all the women are veiled. According to the World Health Organisation, 85 per cent of the women are not only veiled they have undergone genital mutilation". By citing these two WHO pronouncements together, the article appears to be implying that genital mutilation is Islamic in the same way that being veiled is presupposed to be. In doing so, the journalist begins to demarcate the negative ('Muslim') values of the identified space. This negative representation continues throughout. The article suggests that the growing popularity of "Islamic fundamentalists" in Imbaba is due to the leniency which Egyptian ex-President Sadat originally showed the Muslim Brotherhood — an approach which, in a neat combination of orientalist imagery and the 'force of nature' metaphor, is described as "like opening a bottle and letting a genie out".

Lower down, the article quotes two rich "non-fanatical" Muslim girls who appear to have inadvertently provided the journalist with the metaphorical upshot of the whole article:

> "Our society is split. One has to choose which way to go — either ahead, forward, into the future and with the West, or backwards in time with the fundamentalists." Oddly she does not see the irony of her own situation [the ignorant native...]: that even though she is dressed in jeans and eating a hamburger, she, too, by entering into an arranged marriage is going backwards in time.

Here the Egyptian girl employs a common 'every day' metaphor (Lakoff and Johnson, 1980), in which time is treated as a spatial relation: forwards = the future; backwards = the past. This progression through time, in turn, forms a metaphor of *progress* from 'the traditional' — here rhetorically labelled 'the backward' — to 'the modern'. In the excerpt, this progression to 'the modern' is presupposed to entail choosing 'the West', which in turn places 'the non-West' in the pre- or perhaps sub-modern position of 'the backward'. The 'choices' which the quoted Egyptian girl is seen to have taken — "dressed in jeans and eating a hamburger" *yet* "entering into an arranged marriage" — are represented by the journalist as being so incongruous that her Western commodities appear to have been 'trumped' by her planned arranged marriage — an 'Islamic' and therefore backward social practice. The journalist's conclusion that her "going backwards in time" is "*ironic*" is purely the result of this string of metaphors and presuppositions.

Finally for this section is an article which attempted to contextualise and comment upon the mass murder of 60 tourists at Luxor on 17 November 1997. The article in question, a news feature entitled **In the name of Allah** (*The Sunday Times*, News Review section, 23 November 1997), was based upon a rhetorical question, posed in its by-line:

> Are the killers of Luxor a lunatic fringe, or a murderous symptom of the inability of Islam to live with the modern world, asks Walter Ellis.

It is interesting to note that the newspaper asks whether Islam can "live *with* the modern world", not even *in* the modern world. This suggests that Islam is first, not part of the modern world but rather exists *in parallel* with it (and 'Us') and second, that modernity is something which Islam is (unsuccessfully) attempting to come to terms with. By referring to "Islam" rather than 'Muslims', the question further implies that Muslims are similarly unitary in this "inability" to live with (cope with; reconcile themselves with) modernity.

In the last three paragraphs of the article, a lengthy quotation from the regularly drawn upon 'expert' David Pryce-Jones fully articulates the implications of the argument which Walter Ellis forwards throughout the article, and in doing so provides the rhetorical upshot of the text:

> "The Arab world — indeed the Muslim world generally — is unable to form pluralist societies" he says. "They claim they are in favour of democracy but the reality is an endless power struggle between competing absolutisms. [...] What does it mean to be Muslim and to be modern? That's what it comes down to. It must be possible but at the moment they have got their wires all crossed. [...] If they do not solve the problem of living with themselves and their neighbours, someone else is going to have to do it for them."

Here we see a single terrorist incident blamed on 'Muslim extremists'; placed within an "endless" historic continuum of Arab-Muslim violence, terror and extremism; (re)presented as *the* history of the 'Arab world'; expanded concentrically to include the 'Muslim world'; and applied as an argumentative warrant to the conclusion that Muslims are "unable to form pluralist societies". The possibility (however unlikely according to Pryce-Jones) of Muslims reconciling themselves with modernity is acknowledged, but only in order to suggest that this is a "problem" which "at the moment" they are unable to solve themselves: "someone else" — i.e. 'not-them', or 'Us' — "is going to have to do it for them." The similarities between this argument and Orientalist paternalism, so characteristic of historic justifications for imperialist incursion and colonial rule, are quite striking (see Said, 1978: 33–4).

Their negativity

Articles such as those analysed above are premised on *presupposed* 'Differences' between Muslim and non-Muslim, Islam and the West. Such presuppositions are both prejudicial and creative, and are translated into reports of Muslims which are marked by 'Their' inferiority, negativity and threat. Given the frequency with which certain of these negative representations of Islam and Muslims appear, the remainder of this chapter discusses four archetypal argumentative strategies — or *topoi* — which journalists use to depict 'negative Muslim social space'. First, the military threat of Muslim countries; second, the threat of 'Muslim political violence' and extremism; third, the (internal) threat to democracy assumedly posed by authoritarian Muslim political leaders and parties; and finally, the social threat of Muslim gender inequality.

Military threat

The military threat posed by 'Muslim' countries is an argumentative strategy which the broadsheet press frequently uses in order to convey a sense of 'Their' negativity. Often, articles employing such arguments are based on barely concealed prejudices, offering two premises — 'They are Muslim' and 'They have weapons' — and on the basis of these premises, concluding 'They are dangerous and threatening to us'. This argumentative structure is an *enthymeme* — a kind of truncated syllogism, with a premise omitted or missing which the audience are themselves required to supply "out of [their] stock of opinion and knowledge" (Bitzer, 1959: 407). Another way of explaining this type of argument is offered by Conley (1984): in an enthymematic argument, "the rhetor [arguer] argues A, so C, with the audience filling in the missing B to understand how the connection between A and C could be asserted" (p.170). In the case of this enthymeme, the missing premise (which is 'C' rather than 'B') could be 'Muslims don't like us', or 'Muslims always want to attack us', or 'Muslims want to kill us', or a number of other variations on this basic theme. Thus, the reconstructed argument is something on the lines of:

> **'They are Muslim' 'They have weapons'**
> [*'Muslims always want to attack us'*]
> **'They are dangerous and threatening to us'**

A series of items presenting the (alleged) non-conventional weapons programme of Iran (the archetypal 'Muslim country') as inherently threatening are sufficient to demonstrate the content and application of this topic. The first article, printed in the *Sunday Times*, flags the newspaper's negative assessment of Iran's weapons programme in the sub-editor's choice of metaphor in the headline: **Britain at heart of Iran nuclear web** (18 January 1998). The presupposed threat of Iran developing such weapons is also illustrated by the manner in which the gist of the article is presented: "Some Foreign Office officials have *warned* that Iran is becoming a *daunting* military force in the region" (emphasis added). Here, the verb phrase "have warned" is highly ideological, placing a negative frame on the remainder of the predicate in a way which alternative verbs ('have revealed'; 'have suggested'; 'believe') would not. This negativity is continued in the suggestion that Iran's military prowess is "daunting" as opposed to (for example) 'consequential' or 'significant'. The presupposed military threat posed by Iran is continued lower down, where the article suggests that

> Experts fear that with the new technology, Iran may be less than two years from building the first Islamic nuclear bomb.

Here, by labelling Iran's (potential, suspected and unconfirmed) nuclear ordnance an "*Islamic* nuclear bomb", the journalist imbues the device with a (Muslim) ideological agenda. And, in case the reader does not automatically associate this 'Muslim nuclear bomb' with 'threat', "a Whitehall official" is quoted as saying that Iran "has become a far bigger threat" to 'the West' than even Iraq. Missing throughout is the premise which explicitly links Iran's (alleged) weapons with the threat they pose to the region, or to 'Us', or 'the West', or to the world.

Returning to the previously discussed reader's letter entitled **Israeli peace with neighbours not answer to Iraq/Iran threat** (*Financial Times*, 25 November 1997), in addition to his prejudicial representation of social actors, Lord Stone argues that even if Israel "achieved peace with all of its neighbours":

> [...] Regional problems would remain the same. Powerful states, driven by hegemonic ambitions, would continue to threaten their weaker neighbours and build up their non-conventional arsenals, while the international community dithered over appeasement.

Exactly which "Powerful states" Lord Stone is referring to here is unclear, but, given the letter's conclusion (the "arming of Iran and Iraq with nuclear, chemical and biological weapons under any circumstances does not bare thinking about") we can safely assume that Iran and Iraq are two of them. The ongoing negativity of these (unnamed) states is made clear by Lord Stone asserting that they both "*continue* to threaten" and "*continue* [...] to *build up* their non-conventional *arsenals*" — note these are not 'weapons' but "arsenals", suggesting a variety of non-conventional weapons. Finally "appeasement" is mentioned in order to allude to Britain's initial approach to Nazi Germany and Chamberlain's guarantees of Hitler's benign intentions — 'and we all know what happened there...'

The growing threat which Iran, and specifically Iranian *weaponry* represents, formed the central argument of a column headlined **Time to untangle from containment** (*Guardian*, 3 January 1998). As the headline suggests, this column essentially argued that America should discontinue its economic and political "containment" of Iran — a policy which the column argues is both illogical and unworkable. In such a context, it is possible that a reader may not perceive Iran as threatening, and therefore, with little reference to evidence, David Hirst declares:

> As well as international terrorism and a violent opposition to the peace process [Iran] is taxed with developing the same kind of non-conventional weapons that have earned Iraq its international quarantine.

These presumed crimes of the Iranian regime go unsupported, and rely solely on (prejudicial) 'common-sense' knowledge of Iran to remain coherent: the references to "international terrorism" and "violent [not 'vocal' or 'obstinate'] opposition to the peace process" are cases in point. There is, after all, a significant difference between supporting a defensive guerrilla group (which is what Hizb Allah, presumably the terrorists which Hirst has in mind, are) however 'violent' they are, and supporting international terrorism. Secondly, although

Iran does oppose the 'peace process' (and this is their right as a sovereign state) there is little evidence to suggest that such opposition is 'violent' in the way suggested.

In contrast to the claims of the three items discussed above, an editorial printed in the *Financial Times* (**Iran comes in from the cold**, 9 December 1997) quite rightly pointed out:

> Tehran is signed up to international treaties on nuclear and chemical weapons proliferation while Israel — possessor of the region's sole nuclear arsenal — is not. As for the peace process, Iran's criticisms are beginning to sound moderate in comparison to those now heard in Egypt and Jordan, which have signed treaties with Israel.

Similarly, a second *Financial Times* editorial (**Talking to Iran**, 12 January 1998) argued that *of course*

> […] Iran must be dissuaded from supporting terrorism and from acquiring weapons of mass destruction. But terrorism should be distinguished from resistance to Israeli occupation in South Lebanon, and regional arms control efforts cannot ignore Israel's own nuclear weapons. Likewise, Iran should not obstruct the Arab-Israeli peace process, but should not be blamed for echoing the same criticisms as Washington's Arab allies.

Such balanced assessment of Iranian foreign policy was notably infrequent: indeed the two editorials quoted above were two of only a handful of recorded items based on such argumentation.

Therefore, when viewing the 'military threat' which Iran allegedly represents to the region and to the (Western?) world, these British broadsheets presume their readers to hold prejudiced (racist?) opinions of Muslims, and *require* them to use this 'knowledge' to fill in any implicit or missing premises, in order that their argumentative conclusions remain plausible. Without the essentialising and prejudiced 'missing' premises of these enthymematic arguments, the information offered simply does not support the conclusions of these reports.

Extremism and terrorism

References to violence, religious extremism and acts of terrorism committed by individuals and groups calling themselves 'Muslim' are legion when the broadsheet press 'cover' Islam, as Table 3.1 illustrates below:

Table 3.1. The 'Islamic-ness' of reported negative actions

		Is Islam cited as a factor?				Total	
		Yes		No			
		Count	col %	Count	col %	Count	col %
Violence included?	Yes	930	79.0%	611	56.2%	1541	68.1%
	No	247	21.0%	476	43.8%	723	31.9%
Peace included?	Yes	318	27.0%	225	20.7%	543	24.0%
	No	859	73.0%	862	79.3%	1721	76.0%
Fundamentalist/ism	Yes	476	40.0%	27	2.5%	503	22.2%
included	No	701	59.6%	1060	97.5%	1761	77.8%
Liberal/ism	Yes	203	17.2%	52	4.8%	255	11.3%
included?	No	974	82.8%	1035	95.2%	2009	88.7%
Terrorist/ism	yes	435	37.0%	91	8.4%	526	23.2%
included?	No	742	63.0%	996	91.6%	1738	76.8%
Ambassador/ial	Yes	194	16.5%	239	22.0%	433	19.1%
included?	No	983	83.5%	848	78.0%	1831	80.9%

Table 3.1 reveals that 'terrorism and/or acts of terrorism' were mentioned in 23.2 per cent of international (i.e. non-domestic) articles (n= 526), rising to a particularly disturbing 37.0 per cent of international articles in which 'Islam' was cited as being an influential factor in the report, or helpful in explaining the reported actions Muslim (n= 435). Similarly, 'violence and/or acts of violence' were present in 68.1 per cent of international articles (n= 1541), rising to a remarkable 79.0 per cent of articles in which Islam was cited as have an influential role in the reported action. By way of contrast, 'peace and/or acts of peace' were present in 24 per cent (n= 543) of these same articles, rising only slightly to 27.0 per cent (n= 318) of articles reporting 'Islamically influenced social action'. Further, many of these 318 articles were written on the subject of the Israeli/Palestinian 'peace process' — which is, after all, a state of *non*-peace given that the process is (ostensibly) intended to produce peace as an end result.[4]

Taking 'extremism', a report printed in the *Telegraph* (23 January 1998) foregrounded a representation of rural Pakistani Muslims which drew on both social and religious 'backwardness' in order to condemn their violent civil disobedience. This is clearly illustrated in the headline of the report: **Tribesmen threaten holy war over demand to pay power bills.** This rhetorical reference to "holy war" is repeated lower down the report, where the journalist states "tribal leaders shouted 'Death to WAPDA' [the Water and Power Development Authority] and promised to launch a *jihad* to protect their rights." It is unclear from this account whether the "tribal leaders" were actually calling for a "holy war", or whether "*jihad*" was being (more properly) used to refer to a 'struggle' to protect rights. Regardless, the headline's announcement of a "threaten[ed] holy war" presents the "promised [...] *jihad*" as a dangerous prospect.

The incivility, perhaps even barbarity, of the protagonists forms the major premise upon which their presumed 'danger' rests. This incivility is flagged in both the naming of the protagonists (as "Pathan tribesmen", "tribal leaders", "bearded tribesmen", and a tribal "Chief") and the contextualising description — they have "threatened to blow up the Warsak dam" and have already "burnt customs posts, government offices and official vehicles." The second paragraph for example, describes "Hundreds of bearded tribesmen, clad in black turbans and heavily armed". In choosing such a representation — arming and 'darkening' the men ["black turbans"], and the use of "clad", a more forceful and dramatic adjective than alternatives such as 'clothed' or 'dressed' — the journalist evokes the historic notion of 'the Muslim horde' in their negativisation.

A news article printed in the *Guardian* headlined **Ripples of fear through the Arab world** (17 November 1997) forwarded a more aggressive argument that the pan-Arab rhetoric of Jordanian Islamist politicians, inspired by the increasingly threatening American policy towards Iraq, posed a threat to the "stability" of the Middle East region. Julian Borger's choice of the Jordanian Islamic Action Front (IAF) to illustrate such an argument is significant since the Party's call for suicide attacks against American targets in Jordan, in the event of American attacks against Iraq, mark "a dramatic departure for the normally placid IAF — one of the most moderate Islamic opposition movements in the region." Borger provides additional material in order to argue that the IAF's previous 'moderatism' now appears to be slipping: the IAF

> boycotted this month's elections in protest at electoral and press laws which it claimed were anti-democratic, and Jordanian observers are worried that [this] extra-parliamentary Islamic opposition could be rapidly radicalised by the combination of a failed Israeli-Palestinian peace process, *perceived* US bias towards Israel and the *renewal of hostilities between* US-led forces and Iraq. [emphases added]

Taking the italicised words in the above excerpt: first, based solely upon the wide disparity between (for example) the military and economic aid given to Israel and that given to Palestine, the "perceived US bias towards Israel" is surely more reality that perception. Second, the structuring of expression in the nominalisation "renewal of hostilities" between the US and Iraq conceals both the overwhelmingly one-sided nature of this violence and the fact that this *US* hostility has continued unabated for much of the period since the 'end' of the 1991 Persian Gulf conflict — 'renewal' suggests otherwise. Aside from these italicised sections, Borger's argumentative reasoning is interesting since it is based on a single defining principle: the (violent; threatening) political actions of Islamist politicians are wholly explainable in reference to 'Muslim' struggles in the Middle East. This reasoning is then used by Borger, in conjunction with other authoritative sources to argue against the proposed US bombing of Iraq. The "Crown Prince Hassan", for example, is quoted saying "If there's going to be an attack against Iraq and if there's going to be an outcry, presumably an anti-Western outcry, it's going to be extremely destabilising". The possibility that the actions of the IAF are explainable in relation to internal Jordanian politics — particularly since the IAF is now excluded from a position in parliamentary debate and due political process — is passed up in favour of a homogenised and simplified 'Muslim threat' argument.

The lengths to which broadsheet newspapers occasionally go in order to press home an argument foregrounding the evil of 'Muslim terrorists' is quite remarkable. A frequently used rhetorical method is antithesis — the positioning of individuals, groups, ideologies, etc. in opposition to each other in an argument, in order to highlight their 'differences' for rhetorical effect. A model example of this was included in a three page article headlined **Terror by degree**, (*The Times* Saturday Magazine, 18 October 1997) which profiled "Ramsi Yousef", a suspect in the first unsuccessful bombing of the World Trade Center, and focused in particular on his time spent studying engineering at Swansea Institute of Higher Education. In order that the activities of this "Muslim fundamentalist", "murderer" and "international terrorist" are made still more malign, the article suggests that Yousef, along with Osama bin Laden, plotted against several "*moderate* governments" in the Middle East — which is quite a surprising description given that the list included "Algeria" and "Saudi Arabia".

Antithesis forms the very basis of the final article in this section: a review of a book on the Iranian revolution, entitled '*The Priest and the King*' by Desmond Harney, headlined **The Holy Terror** (*Sunday Times* Books supplement, 18 January 1998). The 'Priest' of the book title (and "The Holy Terror" referred to in the headline) "is, of course, the Ayatollah Khomeini, the dour, ruthless cleric whose followers overthrew the Shah of Iran, the hesitant, unhappy autocrat who was one of the most powerful allies of the West in the Middle East for almost four decades". This antithetical representation of the revolution (which, to a certain extent *is* invited by the title of the book) continues to be developed throughout the review: the "ruthless cleric" versus the reluctant, "unhappy autocrat". As part of this (re)presentation of the revolution, the Shah is transformed into a beneficent leader who had "tried to give his country *aspects* of 20th century life" (emphasis added). The details of *which* aspects of 20th century life the shah supported — capitalism, cronyism, torture, spiralling economic inequality but without popular or democratic involvement of the Iranian public in the political system — are not included in the review. Further, whilst the review suggests that it was the Shah's attempts at "liberalisation" which had "enabled the first of the demonstrations to start", there is very little about the atrocities and torture committed by the Shah which fermented this popular resentment. Even when the review refers to one 'massacre' of "scores of demonstrators", it is introduced as an exception to the rule and therefore in order to praise the Shah: "It is to the Shah's credit that he was not prepared to suppress the revolution by brute force, killing thousands, as he probably could have done." Khomeini on the other hand is described as "Grim and unbending", "the intransigent priest" and the bringer of "a most savage revolution".

> Controlled by Khomeini and his exiled helpers, the mullahs in Iran, whom the Shah had hitherto scorned [...] *crept out* and suddenly began to assume more and more power [...] turning the people towards the ayatollah and against everything western [emphases added]

Iranians, in both the excerpt above and elsewhere, are represented as "enraged, bitter and vicious", stupid, 'childlike' and swayed by "the professionalism of the propaganda". And here, suggests the review, lies "the awful problem posed by autocracy: the *alternative is almost always worse*, if only because of the repressed bitterness and frustration" of the revolutionaries (emphasis added). We do well to remember that similar arguments have been drawn upon to justify the continuation of repression throughout history — not least in reference to the black communities of apartheid-era South Africa. The upshot of the review reads:

> the revolution was complete. And deeply brutal and unpleasant it has been too. The abuses of human rights ordered by the mullahs at home or through terrorism abroad have been far, far worse than any that took place under the Shah.

Running through the review, and present most notably above, is an argument for 'the greater good': atrocities under the Shah (for the greater part deleted) were committed with a view to maintaining the western friendly status quo; those under Khomeini (in general cited and directly criticised) were committed in support of Islamic theocracy. The presupposition of the author therefore appears to be that Western-style, or capitalist friendly, societies are just and therefore qualify for the right to commit human rights abuses in their name (for the 'greater good'). On the other hand, the broadly 'Islamic' society brought in by Khomeini is inherently unjust, thus any revolution fought to introduce such a society — even one claiming the majority of public support — could never be for 'the greater good' and is therefore "far far worse".

Palestinian Authority controlled Bethlehem, at Christmas

Two articles, printed in separate broadsheets within three days of each other, appear intent on illustrating the negative effects which Muslims can have upon 'Western', or in this case Christian lives. The first of these news articles, **Tensions darken festive mood in Bethlehem**, (*The Times*, 22 December 1997) was stridently critical of what it labelled the "unceasing persecution [of Christians] under the Palestinian Authority", occurring at Christmas and in (of all places) "the town at the heart of the story of Christ's birth." The report states that such conclusions were the product of a "report published two months ago by the Israeli Prime Minister's Office" but the journalist, Christopher Walker, does not question the veracity of the report's claims despite the possibility that the Israeli government may be motivated by factors other than either the welfare of Christians or the 'pursuit of truth'.

Throughout, the article makes repeated mention of Bethlehem's demographic profile of Muslim-to-Christian residency. For example, the article quotes

> [...] Ranna Najjar, another Christian housewife in the West Bank town where the Muslim birth-rate far outstrips that of the Christians. "The city is not ours anymore. We gave up the city" she said.

Such a preoccupation with 'numbers' of racial/ethnically defined 'others' (what Hage (1998: 123) has called a "numbering pathology") is a benchmark of white racist talk and text (also see Daniels, 1997). The article also suggests that the majority Muslim population has brought a new sense of 'decay' to Bethlehem, stating that under Muslim rule, houses and streets have become "scarred with intifada slogans" (an assumedly 'Muslim' uprising), and that some Christians are now scared to openly celebrate Christmas: "I do not dare to go out on Christmas Eve any more. The Muslim boys call me and the other Christian girls whores [...] said Lina Attallah". The possibility that the low numbers of Christians living in Bethlehem may be attributable to their treatment under Jewish rule is backgrounded in order to facilitate the success of the article's principle argument of 'Muslim repression':

> Decimated by emigration and for the past two years living under the Muslim-dominated Palestinian Authority, Bethlehem's Christians now make up less that a third of the 39,000 population, compared with 80% during the period of the British Mandate which ended in 1948.

Here, the proportion of Christian emigration occurring under Israeli rule is notably absent. Indeed, it states lower down that Ms Lina Attallah "regrets *returning* from Texas to Bethlehem after the 1993 peace treaty which ended 27 years of Israeli military rule" (emphasis added), suggesting that it was, in fact, the Israeli rule which originally forced her to leave.

The article goes on to state that the majority Muslim population has resulted in the greater 'Islamicisation' of Bethlehem, to the disadvantage and even *exclusion* of Christianity. "Manger Square, the area in front of the Church of the Nativity", for example, is now "packed with Muslim worshippers every Friday because there is no longer enough room for all of them to pray inside the *imposing* Mosque of Omar" (emphasis added). Similarly, whereas "Greater Bethlehem, [...] only had 5 mosques in 1970, there are now 72." How this proliferation of Mosques affects Christian worship is unclear. What it suggests however, is that Walker believes that the 'rightful' status of Bethlehem's public space should be Christian. A similar attitude runs through a second article devoted to reporting Bethlehem at Christmas: **Tough and tawdry times in Manger Square** (*Guardian*, 24 December 1997). Here Bethlehem is described as: "a city where the wail of the muezzin [now] drowns out the peal of church bells"; where "more than half the citizens are unemployed [and] almost all are Muslims." However, the real focus of the article is on the sorry state of Christmas festivities under the rule of the Palestinian Authorities rather than the religious and cultural demography of the city:

> Two Christmases ago the birth of Jesus Christ was *hijacked* by the Palestinian leader Yasser Arafat, and turned into a political celebration of new found freedom [...] The nationalistic atmosphere prevailed again last year, with pilgrims *grimacing* in Manger Square when a dance band struck up as Midnight chimed. [emphasis added]

The excerpt above implicitly contrasts the unfavourable 'Palestinian Christmas present' with the more favourable 'Israeli Christmas past': the 'hijacking' (a highly significant verb for describing Palestinian action!) of Christmas under the auspices of Arafat's *PA* is represented as an unwarranted departure from normal practice. The implication that 'things were better' under Israeli rule is reiterated and contextualised lower down the report, where "Salim Lahhamm, a Christian Arab who organises pilgrim tours to the holy land", is quoted explaining why he believes that "this Christmas is the worst for business since the height of the intifada":

> "It's a double whammy effect", he explains. "Sixty percent of it has to do with what happened in Luxor (in Egypt, where Islamic fundamentalists massacred 60 tourists last month). The other 40 percent is about the peace process and the lack of confidence after the suicide bombs. The irony is that before the peace process we would not really have suffered from Luxor."

To be clear: although Lahhamm does not appear to be supporting a return to Israeli control, his remarks certainly appear to facilitate this argument, given that Christians, and perhaps (given the unemployment rates) even Muslims 'had it better' before the peace process. Further, it is interesting to note that the poor state of Bethlehem's tourism industry is apparently the worst it has been since "the *height* of the intifada" — another instance when 'Muslim activities' are assumed to have defined the public space.

The report concludes by stating that this year, following the deficiencies of the past two Christmases, "Bethlehem's *Roman Catholic* mayor, Hanna Nasser" (emphasis added) has decided that "Christmas will get its religion back": "We want only those who are willing to pray to be present in the square this year." The presence of this Palestinian-Authority-backed Christian public figure in the report is significant, since it goes some of the way to refuting the "unceasing persecution [of Christians] under the Palestinian Authority", alleged in *The Times'* report. The contrasting picture of Bethlehem which develops through the *Guardian* report is one of Palestinian incompetence rather than prejudice, and of poor motivation rather than Muslim extremism. Overwhelmingly however, the *Guardian* report still implies that Bethlehem's "tough and tawdry times" are attributable to Muslim activities — internal *PA* and external "Islamic fundamentalist" — rather than, for example, the hardships characteristic of all the Palestinian bantustans, provoked by Israeli economic blockades and 'border controls'. The silence of the journalist, David Sharrock, on these most elementary of contextualising factors is quite deafening.

Despotism: Threat to democracy

The following items of broadsheet reporting are all based, to varying degrees, on the assumption that Muslims and, in some cases 'Islam' in general, pose a threat to the internal stability of (Muslim) countries. This assumed threat usually takes the form of a 'threat to democracy', and corresponds closely with the enduring theme of 'Islamic despotism' (see Daniel, 1960).

The reporting of Turkey in broadsheet newspapers draws significantly upon the presupposed 'threat' which Islam poses to democracy. A report headlined **Turkey seeks Blair's backing over EU entry** for example, (*Telegraph* 10 December 1997) argues that Turkey is strategically very important, since it "stands on Nato's front-line, at a time when the threat comes no longer from the Soviet bloc but from militant Islam." In addition, the *Telegraph* suggests that since "Turkey offers the Middle East a unique example of a secular Islamic country that is a democracy" it should be granted EU membership. It is worth noting that the majority mandate given Necmettin Erbakan's Islamic Welfare Party in the Turkish general election, the military coup which ousted this government only months prior to this report being printed, and the ruthless suppression of Kurdish civil rights must *necessarily* be ignored in order to represent Turkey as a "democracy".

Similar information was deleted or (re)presented in reports printed in other broadsheets covering the possibility and desirability of granting Turkey membership to the EU. Robert Cornwell for example, in an *Independent* column headlined **Put diplomatic niceties aside and tell Turkey the truth** (11 December 1997), wrote:

> More serious still [than removing the chance of resolving 'the Cyprus issue'] if Europe spurns it anew, this strategically vital NATO country may turn its back on the West in favour of the Islamic world. This in turn, it is argued, would weaken its fragile democracy and offer a fresh opening for theocratic Islam: only six months ago, after all, the Islamic leaning Government of Necmettin Erbakan was eased out, under immense pressure from the Turkish military.

This passage is interesting for three principal reasons. First, the argument that without EU membership Turkey "may turn it's back on the West in favour of the Islamic world" assumes not only the standard ontological opposition between 'the West' and the 'Islamic world' but also that there is neither a third option nor any 'middle ground' for Turkey to opt for. The use of the noun phrase *"strategically vital NATO country"* underlines the argumentation of the piece, illustrating the importance of keeping Turkey 'on our side'.

Second, *"it is argued"* that Turkey's turn towards "the Islamic world", "would weaken its *fragile* democracy". This active subject deletion is a standard argumentative strategy, which tends to be adopted when a journalist's own position could not be concealed in the words of a quoted source. The potentially dubious status of the argument is exposed by simply asking: 'Who is this argued by?' It is also interesting to speculate on the use of the term "fragile democracy": what does this term suggest? It should be remembered that 'democracy' is a defining ontology for the majority of Western journalists (see van Ginneken, 1998). Thus a "*fragile* democracy" is one which should be protected — a kind of political china cup which should be shielded from the destructive influence of its own bovine nemesis. The use of such a term is especially ideologically significant when viewed in the light of the next point.

Third, the excerpt suggests that "the Islamic leaning Government of Necmettin Erbakan was *eased out*, under immense pressure from the Turkish military." This structuring of expression conjures a representation of an event akin to a bed-ridden grandparent helped to his feet by the philanthropic Turkish military rather than the *coup d'etat* which it arguably was. Under circumstances other than those of Turkey — a "*strategically vital* NATO country" remember — would the anti-democratic actions of the military have aroused more criticism in the broadsheet press? Lower down the column, Cornwell does state that "the *ousting* of Mr Erbakan [was] at basic odds with the civilian, democratic heritage of the EU", yet even this retelling of the event still avoids the term 'coup' and the implication that Turkey is, in fact, close to being a military dictatorship.

It is interesting to compare the representation of Turkish 'democracy' with the constitutional crisis which occurred in Pakistan at the end of 1997, made all the more interesting given the way the Bush administration courted the Pakistani military dictatorship post September 11 2001. The crisis itself developed from tensions between the three centres of political power in Pakistan — President Farooq Leghari; the judiciary, specifically the Chief Justice Sajjad Ali Shah; and the legislature, under the control of Prime Minister Nawaz Sharif. The story can be summarised at three levels: First and generally, as Nawaz Sharif's attempts to centralise power in the democratically elected Parliament. Second, more specifically, in Sharif's attempts to strengthen the position of the Prime Minster. Finally, and particularly, in response to two events: the repeal of Article 58(2) of the constitution which enabled the President to fire an elected Prime Minister at will,[5] and Prime Minister Sharif's criticisms of the Chief Justice for holding up legislation passed by Parliament, which resulted in him being charged for contempt of court.[6] The right-wing broadsheet press represented the political dispute in a different light:[7]

> That such chaos has come during a government with a record majority has merely hardened the impression that democracy and Pakistan do not mix. (**Pakistan on brink of army rule**, *Telegraph*, 1 December 1997)

> Pakistan has moved a notch closer to becoming a failed state and some argue it
> already is one. Islamic extremists sense their time may be coming as the nation
> staggers towards one of its greatest financial crises (**Sharif wins all as Pakistan state
> crumbles**, *The Times*, 3 December 1997)

As before, the use of the deleted subject in these articles is immediately apparent — who believes "democracy and Pakistan don't mix"? Who argues that
Pakistan is "a failed state"? Central to the conclusion that the crisis 'proved'
that Pakistan and democracy do not mix, was the representation of Prime
Minister Sharif as a dictatorial and authoritarian leader, motivated by self-
interested pursuit of power:

> Though the immediate crisis has passed, Pakistanis will be watchful that Mr Sharif
> does not try to erode further Presidential and judicial powers and so concentrate
> power in his own hands. (**Sharif victory as Pakistani president quits**, *Telegraph*, 3
> December 1997)
> Mr Sharif now looks unassailable, his authoritarian tendencies well established
> […] No elected leader has enjoyed so much power. With so few restraints, there
> will be overwhelming temptation to move towards a more dictatorial style of
> government. (**Sharif wins all as Pakistan state crumbles**, *The Times*, 3 December
> 1997)

By way of contrast, prior to the resolution of the stand-off on 3 December
1997, an editorial printed in *The Times* (2 December 1997) argued:

> **Islamabad on the brink: when the military may be the least worst option.** […The
> conflict] can only encourage opportunists and embittered tribal factions to violent
> action under the guise of defending democracy. Pakistan is a country in urgent
> need of reform, stability and clean government. […] an army take-over might be
> the least worst option.

How *The Times* can claim to be worried that Sharif is dragging the country
towards "a more dictatorial style of government" and yet simultaneously argue
(with a straight face) that "an army take-over might be the least worst option",
is at first glance truly baffling. The coherence and logic of these seemingly
contradictory arguments rests upon the 'Muslim-ness' which *The Times* rhetorically ascribes to Sharif. Thus, other reports drew specifically upon the
'Muslim' character of Sharif and his party in order to either criticise or derogate his (and their) political influence in Pakistan. One report argued that
Sharif was acting like a "Mughal Emperor" (**'Emperor' Sharif savours victory**,
Telegraph, 4 December 1997), whilst in an earlier report headlined **Sharif
supporters riot outside court** (*Telegraph*, 18 November 1997), the alleged
impudence or perhaps *illegitimacy* of Sharif's political power is clearly

illustrated: "In a *brazen* attempt to demonstrate its political clout, Mr Sharif's Pakistan Muslim League mobilised thousands of supporters outside the white marble Supreme Court building." The 'Muslim-ness' of Sharif's supporters is reiterated in the next sentence of this report, and related directly to notions of fanaticism, threat, and actual violence:

> As Mr Sharif entered the court, women party members read verses from the Koran and chanted *wildly*: "Sharif will win. God is with him". As the hearing dragged on for three hours, the crowd became restless and began to stone the police, who retaliated with baton charges. [emphasis added]

The journalist shows that a 'cult of personality' surrounds Sharif, inspiring a 'wild' fanaticism in his followers which, when unchannelled, can result in acts of violence and civil disobedience which need to be contained by security forces. It is also interesting to note that the 'wild', chanting Muslim party members inside the courtroom are identified as being women. Whether this facilitates the general argumentative line of an 'emotional' Muslim response is unclear.

In both of these brief case studies — Turkey and Pakistan — broadsheet newspapers appear wary or, particularly when reporting Turkey, *scared* of the prospect of Islamic-leaning democratically elected political parties. This aversion to democratically elected Muslim governments resulted in the backgrounding and, in some cases, the *deletion* of the Turkish *coup d'etat*, and the support for a similar course of action in the case of Pakistan. Whether this antipathy is in response to the expression of 'Muslim values' in the political sphere, the democratic empowerment of (broadly) Muslim populations, the democratic empowerment of 'third world' populations, or some other unidentified cause is unclear. What *is* clear is that broadsheet newspapers (particularly right-wing newspapers) believe 'Muslim government' and the free election of 'Muslim political parties' to be disadvantageous to the 'democracy' of Muslim countries.

Sexism: Social threat

Citing 'sexism' or, more specifically, the subjugation and repression of (often but not exclusively Muslim) women at the hands of either Muslim men or 'Muslim' value/social systems are argumentative strategies frequently used to disparage 'Islam'. 'Islam' and 'illiberal gendered social practice' are tied together by broadsheet newspapers via a two-part argumentative process: First, the social position of (Muslim) women is described in negative terminology, using either stylistic registers of repression and constraint, or else simply *labelled* as backward, 'un-Western', illiberal and hence undesirable. Second, through fallacious argument from part ('Muslim') to whole ('Islam'), the iniquitous social position of many (Muslim) women or the negative acts against women by 'Muslims' are uncontroversially ascribed to being carried out by *Islam* — either 'in the name of…' or 'sanctioned by…'. The representation of the 'veil' is a case in point, and the input and opinions of both Islamic and more broadly Muslim feminists are conspicuously absent from reporting because they would prove too problematic for the simplistic 'East vs. West', 'Muslim vs. Modernist' dichotomous representation of gender relations chosen in broadsheet reporting. Furthermore, although the more prejudicial (racist?) generalisations are observed more frequently in the reporting of the 'conservative' broadsheet press (in particular the *Daily Telegraph*) they are also recognisable in the reporting of the more 'liberal' broadsheets.

The passive, deferential demeanour which women — Muslim and otherwise — apparently have to adopt whilst in 'Muslim' countries formed a presupposition in many of the recorded items of reporting. A news-story printed in the *Independent* for example, reporting the celebrations in Tehran following Iran's successful entry to the 1998 World Cup finals (**Crowds hail hand of God in World Cup Triumph**, 4 December 1997), was based on the same presupposition of "women in deep purdah" present in the editorial discussed earlier in this chapter. The article reads: "As for the people, they went mad for joy. A few ladies, it was said, *even* joined their menfolk in the street" (emphasis added). The perceived discrepancy between how the journalist expects Iranian women to act and their reported celebrations, is illustrated in the use of "even" — a scalar implicature marking the highly deviate nature of the reported action and hence exposing the presupposition upon which such implicature is based: 'Iranian women don't do this kind of thing'.

On other occasions, to adopt and slightly adapt the cliché, journalists did not let the facts get in the way of a good opportunity to associate 'Islam' with 'sexism'. When Lucille McLaughlan, one of the British Nurses found guilty of murdering Australian Nurse Yvonne Gilford, got married whilst in a Saudi Arabian jail, the broadsheets' descriptions of her dress couldn't have been more different:

> The bride is reported to have worn a traditional Arabian dress and veil at the ceremony. (**Nurse weds in 'unforgettable' ceremony**, *Independent*, 1 December 1997)

> As two Saudi police officers looked on, McLaughlin, aged 32, exchanged rings with
> Mr Ferrie, aged 30, a tyre fitter. She wore traditional Arabian dress. (**Nurse weds in
> Saudi jail**, *Guardian* 1 December 1997)
>
> McLaughlan wore a smart Western-style dress, not the black abeya and veil that
> women in the *conservative Islamic* kingdom *have to* wear in public. (**Murder case
> nurse is given Saudi wedding with Western touches**, *Telegraph*, 1 December 1997;
> emphasis added)

In the *Telegraph* report, the (alleged) actions of McLaughlin — her decision to wear a "*smart* Western-style dress" — are represented as full virtued: an act of liberty in a land of conservative *Islamic* repression of women. In this way, the *Telegraph*'s representation of the marriage fits with the 'typology of *hijab* representation' suggested by Hage (1998): for the conservative press, the veil often represents "the subjugation of women to a non-national patriarchy. The desire to remove it is the desire to ensure that all women within the nation are subjugated to the dominant national patriarchal order" (p. 251). The *Telegraph*'s removal of the veil from McLaughlin's marriage illustrates the potentially disruptive influence which (the paper believes) non-national conservative patriarchy represents to the 'Western marriage', and the corresponding ideological importance that the image of the bride is (*re*)presented as one of the "Western touches" mentioned in the report's headline.

The Muslim veil, and the political significance of veiling on and for gender relations, formed the focus of the following two articles, both printed in the *Guardian*. In the first, headlined '**Coffee, tea or a headscarf?**' (5 December 1997) Kathy Evans describes the "austerity aboard the world's most Islamic airline" — IranAir. The first paragraph sets the tone for the remainder of the article:

> "You will please to put on your headscarf" [*sic*], said the matronly, heavily covered
> air hostess. This was not a request but an order to all women passengers, regard-
> less of nationality, to adopt Islamic dress.

In this excerpt, Evans skilfully combines several of the principal discourses within which the veil is located: the pressure to wear the veil comes solely from 'outside', rather than from the internalised (admittedly *social*) values of Muslim women; women are 'ordered' not 'requested' to wear the veil; and the (Iranian) veil is restrictive and burdensome, since it "heavily" not 'completely' covers the women. These discourses are also drawn upon lower down the article, where the Iranian actresses staring in the inflight films are similarly "heavily covered" and "*IranAir's* regulations are *enforced* even while its aircraft are parked in British airports" (emphases added).

Further, Evans' exact transcription of the "matronly" air hostess' inarticulate "order" is interesting. Here, by (allegedly) recalling *exactly* what the hostess said, Evans manages to obfuscate both the meaning and *function* of her statement; its illocutionary force could be interpreted as either a "request" or an "order". Once the speech act is made ambiguous in this way, Evans is able to explicitly *dis*ambiguate the meaning of the statement in favour of her own argument: it was "not a request, but an order". However, the air hostess *did* say "please", and the inclusion of this word appears to undermine the certainty in Evans' claim that the statement was an outright "order". In this way, the statement could have been presented and interpreted simply as the hostess' inarticulate attempt to politely request Evans to don her headscarf. This more generous interpretation of the statement would not, however, have produced a meaning so functional to, and supportive of, the broader argument of the article: Iranian *enforcement* of the veil.

The final article of this section (**Fashion statement lands 'fatwa'**, *Guardian*, 3 December 1997) combines the disparaging discourse of 'sexism and social threat' with that of 'extremism and Muslim violence' previously discussed. The first paragraph reads:

> A young Roman designer who put on a fashion show combining nudity with the Islamic *chador* was last night recovering under police guard from a beating at the hands of unidentified assailants.

The journalist, John Hooper, states that the attack followed "a string of threatening phone calls from callers with *foreign accents*" and "visits at his boutique from *Middle Eastern callers* showing particular interest in his nationality" (emphases added). These contextualising details are interesting, since, while they follow the "global homology" of the news-media — wherein violence will be "presented as ethnic or foreign in its origins" (Hartley & Montgomery, 1985: 244) — they are located in Italy, itself a 'foreign' country to the majority of the *Guardian*'s British readership. The 'angle' of 'foreign violence' is further highlighted in the excerpt above, through describing the designer, "Farhan Rahbarzadeh, the Italian born son of Iranian parents", as a "young *Roman* designer".

Rahbarzadeh's "fashion statement" referred to in the headline, designed to create as much publicity as possible at the "opening of his boutique", was certainly incendiary. The designer dressed three modelsw

> in black *chadors*, which [during the show] they let fall to the ground. One of the models turned out to be a man wearing nothing but a chastity belt. The other two

were women, one wearing nothing but a live python, the other a skimpy dress held together in such a way as to reveal a padlock at the crotch.

Continuing,

> Mr Rahbarzadeh said he had wanted to make a statement in favour of the liberation of Middle Eastern women. To symbolise their entrapment, he used a special fabric containing leaves and flowers encased in silicon.

Rahbarzadeh's "statement" therefore presupposes that "Middle Eastern women" (note the euphemism: these are not Israelis we're talking about) are both unliberated and trapped, and that the way out of such an entrapped state is to accede to the ('Western') commodification of the female body. In the upshot of the report, and echoing the reference in the headline, the journalist suggests that Rahbarzadeh's approach "seems to have made him the object of fashion's first *unofficial fatwa*." The use of "*fatwa*" to describe the attack against the designer, illustrates the journalists desire to present the story, and the issues which surround it, in as inflammatory a style as possible. An "unofficial fatwa" is an oxymoron, since a *fatwa* is a wholly official edict: a legal ruling given by a *mojtahed* — an individual qualified to interpret Islamic jurisprudence and if necessary draw new (at times different) understanding from it — something which the reporter is tacitly acknowledging in his use of the modifier "unofficial". The term only makes sense if we adopt the same prejudicial definition of a *fatwa* as that offered by Wynford Hicks in his (1998) book *English for Journalists*: "a death sentence".

The report therefore offers a series of negative argumentative propositions, which suggest that 'Islam', *in extremis*, poses a threat to the enlightenment project of 'the West': Presupposing that (Muslim) "Middle Eastern women" are unliberated — metonymically represented here as the *chador* — the journalist reports an the event in which a 'Western' man (significantly, an assimilated Iranian) attempted, albeit symbolically, to 'liberate' Muslim women. Faced with this challenge, "foreign" men with "Middle Eastern" accents attacked the designer — an attack which, despite being perpetrated by "unidentified assailants", is tied to 'Islam' through being described as a "fatwa". This in turn grants further support to the designer's original motivation for the 'fashion show': that 'Muslims' and perhaps 'Islam' as a whole, are in desperate need of the civilising influence of 'the West'. This argumentative conclusion is developed further in the analysis of articles included in the next chapter.

CHAPTER 4

The ideological square II

'The West' as civiliser

The civilising influence of 'the West' and 'Westernisation'

Following on from the previous chapter's discussion of how 'Muslim negativity' is constructed in reporting, the rhetorical conclusions of the articles analysed in this chapter represent the simultaneous contraposition of the ideological square's effect upon reporting: the positive representation of 'Our' social action. On the manner in which the ideological square shapes and curbs journalism, Van Ginneken (1998) suggests:

> Most citizens of major Western nations — and that includes most journalists — are deeply convinced that their society not only represents the very apex of civilisation, but is also willing to do all it can to help others reach this stage as soon as possible (p. 62)

These convictions are occasionally observable in the casual, rather extraneous editorialising which peppers even the most objective reporting. A model example of this, included in an otherwise rigorously objective report in the *Financial Times* (**Ataturk's legacy**, 20 January, 1998) reporting the banning of Turkey's Islamic Welfare Party, reads:

> Mr Erbakan has appealed to the European Court of Human Rights. Thus *even the most Islamically minded Turks* are discovering the value of European institutions. [emphasis added]

The scalar implicature present in "*even* the most Islamically minded Turks…" illustrates the presupposed cultural distance between European institutions and those who are "Islamically minded". By suggesting that it is the "value" rather than the 'presence' of these institutions which is being 'discovered', the report further implies that "Islamically minded Turks" are being enlightened by this contact with European politico-legal institutions.

Other reports suggest that the social values of Muslims are being improved by contact with 'the West'. An article headlined **Islamic dream wife proves**

elusive in today's Kuwait (*Guardian*, 17 December 1997) for example, Kathy Evans argues that due to "decades of exposure to Western culture, travel and television", Kuwaiti women are now convinced by the superiority of the 'western marriage'. The by-line reads: "Western ideals of equality held by Muslim women can make marriage difficult — if not out of the question", and Evans holds onto this conclusion despite including material in her article which could have resulted in a significantly different interpretation.

The evidence Evans presents to support her argument is certainly interesting. She states that there are an estimated "40,000 spinsters in Kuwait today, a figure unprecedented in the country's history." A manager of a mosque's marriage committee is quoted as saying "Kuwaiti men just do not trust the liberated girls", and the only quoted woman of the article, "Miriam, a 26 year old graduate working in a government ministry", says:

> No way am I going to obey my husband or allow him total control in my marriage. I want a western style marriage like you see on television where the responsibilities are shared.

On the basis of this evidence, Evans' conclusion — Western values are raising Kuwaiti women's aspirations for marriage, resulting in their becoming less attractive to Kuwaiti men with their Islamic values — appears quite plausible. Yet the article also includes two observations which cast doubts on the accuracy of this conclusion. First, the article cites "Mohammed, a young government clerk" and his "key requirements of his wife-to-be". Mohammed wants "someone, er, like Cindy Crawford — but of course she must have an Islamic ideology". The photograph which accompanies the article is a photomontage of Cindy Crawford wearing a *hijab*, and the caption argues Mohammed's "requirements" are representative: "Kuwaiti men want the face of Cindy Crawford but the ideology and veil of Islam". Evans' choice to focus on (and celebrate) the 'unrealisable' goal of a modern Kuwaiti wife with "an Islamic ideology" down-plays not only her accompanying observation that Kuwaiti men's aspirations for a Muslim Cindy Crawford are unrealistic, but also that they are similarly attributable to "decades of exposure to Western culture, travel and television".

Second, the article includes an observation which suggests that the high number of Kuwaiti spinsters may be attributable to a different set of forces altogether:

> With the majority of Kuwaiti women now working or choosing to study up to graduate level, many delay marriage until their mid-twenties or later.

So perhaps the "unprecedented" number of Kuwaiti spinsters may be attributable to changes in the personal ambitions of Kuwaiti women to work or
complete their education and therefore to marry at a later age. Kuwaiti women
are unquestionably changing their personal goals and aspirations, but to explain this purely by reference to the influence — and implied *superiority* — of
Western values, belies extreme ethnocentrism.

The improving influence which 'Western values' have on the 'Islamic
world' also forms a central argument in a news article headlined **Welcome to
the new Iran** (*Independent on Sunday*, 7 December 1997). In this article, the
by-line announces, "Robert Fisk found Tehran to be an efficient and tolerant
city. Until the veil slipped and the old order was revealed". This "old order" is
one in which: "Ayatollah Khomeini's massive portrait would glower down";
"Death to America" would ring "throughout the airport's black painted arrivals lounge"; "visitors to the grotty Laleh hotel […] would have to wipe their
shoes on a doormat depicting the American flag"; and Iranian official-dom was
characterised by "bearded civil servants, ladies in *chadors* […] dirty cups on the
desks, papers on the floor; no explanations. […] More bearded men, [and]
more dirty cups." Fisk's preoccupation with 'dirt' and particularly the 'ameni-
ties' in the "grotty" hotel are just one of the immediately recognizable approaches which this article takes in castigating Iran.

In contrast, when Fisk describes the (good) 'new Iran' he uses terms of
description which praises the country according to its acceptance of values he
identifies as being more 'Western'. It is clean, articulate (*in English*), deferential
(*to him*), increasingly high-tech and "efficient". Following an afternoon of
being passed 'from pillar to post' in search of his press pass, Fisk describes how
he "found an office of spotless hygiene where a young woman with immaculate
English apologised effusely for my problems. A brand new govt Mercedes was
purring at the door …[and] more polished young men promised me a press
pass in hours". In contrast to its previously austerity, "the arrivals lounge was
painted a gleaming white"; "The young man at immigration was clean-shaven
and wanted to talk about Iran's 2–2 draw with Australia"; and "gone is the
grubby doormat [of the Laleh hotel]; in its place lies a massive, finely stitched
Tabriz carpet of crimson and green gardens".

In summarising the report, Fisk asks: are these changes "a sign of the times?
Or just *a brief fling with reality* now that Mohamed Khatami […] is President".
The presupposed superiority of Western values is clearly illustrated here in
Fisk's 'question': under Khatami, the "new Iran" is coming to its senses and
recognising "reality". In this "new Iran", "there is a feeling that President

Khatami can present the human face of the revolution, where women's equality and youth are more important than punishment and suspicion". The 'Westernising' position of President Khatami in the reporting of Iran is developed further in the next section.

'Pluralism' in Iran

This section of the chapter analyses articles which reported the events and declarations of the Organisation of Islamic Countries (OIC) conference which took place in Tehran (9 December 1997). Broadsheet newspapers used this occasion to discuss civil and political pluralism in Iran and, in particular, the potential for 'positive change' — described as 'modernisation' by some, or 'Westernisation' by others — which they argued the election of President Khatami represented.

Using the OIC conference as a case study, the broadsheets presented Iranian political life as a rarefied power struggle taking place between actors representing two polarised political camps: the 'moderates' and the 'conservatives'. Although this 'two party split' does, to some extent, represent current Iranian ideological debate on issues such as civil society, citizen's rights and (in particular) political representation, it is, as Boroumand & Boroumand (2000) have illustrated, a gross simplification "epistemologically based on the 'good guy/bad guy dialectic'", which "precludes an understanding" of Iran (p.307). Within this simplified dialectic, President Khatami is the good "moderate", wishing "to liberalise the Islamic regime from within. He enjoys the support of the masses, but is challenged by the conservatives, who are violent, corrupt and unpopular" (Boroumand & Boroumand, 2000: 306–7). In other words, President Khatami is represented as the supporter of people's sovereignty (democratic; 'Western') and the Supreme Leader Khamenei, along with a homogenised corps of 'clerics', are the defenders of the Shari'a (autocratic; 'Islamic'). Accordingly, a perverse mutation occurs whereby the broadsheets report internal Iranian politics according to the recurrent manichean representation of 'Islam vs. the West'.

A *Telegraph* editorial headlined **Ayatollah greets Satan** (18 December 1997), argued that the political ground "is shifting in the hitherto rigidly antagonistic relationship between Iran and the United States", changes which

> stem from the election last May of Mr Khatami, a *moderate* who trounced the candidate favoured by the *conservative clerics*. His support came largely from women and young people, for whom 18 years of an Islamic republic had offered little encouragement. [emphasis added]

The editorial's primary argument is that, since Khatami is someone who the US find easier to deal with, he is closer to a 'Western' way of thinking than the "conservative clerics". This is supported by Khatami's syntactic opposition to the "clerics" who are presupposedly non-Western, by virtue of their 'Islamic-ness'.[1] This opposition is given greater weight by the second sentence of the excerpt which reveals that Khatami's electoral support came from "women and young people" dissatisfied with "an Islamic republic": a sexist, traditional and parochial country. This not only suggests that Khatami, being a "moderate", intends to move Iran away from being an Islamic Republic, but also implies that he played no part in governing the Islamic Republic — quite a startling suggestion given that President Khatami is a *hojatol-eslam* and served as the Minister of Culture and Islamic Guidance for more than 10 years.[2]

Similarly, an editorial printed in *The Times* (**Welcome to Tehran**, 9 December 1997) posits another value-laden figure of contrast: the occasion of the OIC conference, it suggests, "provides clues to the continuing struggle between *modernisers* and the *Islamic die-hards* for the soul of the country" (emphasis added). Although Khatami is only described as "the *relatively* reasonable new president" (emphasis added), the newspaper's antipathy towards his opposition — the "anti-Western revolutionary Iran" — is openly declared. The alternative to Khatami, *The Times* suggests, is an "ignorant and corrupt clergy attempting to sabotage cautious moves to liberalise the economy and the social climate". Whereas Khatami has "people power on his side" (democratic; 'good'):

> He will not attempt a volte-face over Middle East peace, anti-Americanism or Islamic zealotry [violence; fanaticism; 'bad'] so long as he and his allies are unable to confront the religious police [tyrannical; 'bad'] or question the obscurantist [dubious; unenlightened; 'bad'] legal code.

In a similar way to the *Telegraph*, *The Times* chooses to suggest that Khatami desires to bring about legal change in order to reposition both Iranian foreign policy and (seemingly) diminish the centrality of Islam to Iranian internal politics. This, presumably, is the result of the newspapers' inability to reconcile the notion that Khatami can be both 'moderate' *and* 'anti-American', can be someone who supports both the (allegedly "ignorant and corrupt") shi'a clergy *and* the liberalisation of the economy, or, most tellingly, that he can be both a 'Muslim' *and* a 'moderniser'.

The presupposed antithesis between Islam and reform is also present in the reporting of the 'liberal' broadsheets. So for example, when Robert Fisk suggests: "*If* President Khatami does *create* pluralism, his will be the only democratic nation in the Muslim Middle East" he presupposes that pluralism does not currently exist in Iran (**The Iranian political football is passed to the adults**, *Independent*, 9 December 1997; emphasis added). A contrasting, and slightly paradoxical *Guardian* news feature (**After the Shah, an endless dance of revolution**, 3 January 1998) appears to find difficulty in concluding that the landslide election victory of President Khatami suggests that Iran is democratic:

> Iran still falls short of any synthesis between its religious and its liberal traditions, while managing to maintain, it must be said, a system that has a genuine democratic dimension.

The journalist's recognition of Iran's "genuine democratic dimension" appears to be more a grudging admission than a ringing conclusion. Further, the journalist's structuring of the sentence reveals the distance he presupposes between, not only religion and liberalism, but also between religion and democracy — a system which Iran is "managing to maintain" despite its religious and liberal contrariety.

This 'difficulty' in reconciling Islam and liberalism/modernity is cast in a much more confrontational light in another *Guardian* article (**Top clerics enter the fray in the fight for the soul of Iran**, 10 December 1997). Here, Kathy Evans suggests that Iran is cut through by "a conflict" between

> the vocal and violent radicals and the silent majority of liberals and modernists struggling to produce a new vision of Islam seemingly at ease with, not threatened by, globalisation and modern technology.

In addition to the usual 'Islamists vs. the Modernists' schema, this passage also contains suggestions of the dictatorial and non-representative nature of Iran's leaders, at clear odds with the democratic nature of the Iranian system of government. Higher order themes of the *incommensurable* nature of Islam and modernity are also present, since the "liberals and modernists" are said to be "*struggling* to produce a *new* vision of Islam" reconciled with modernity, here represented as technology and the ideology of globalisation. The use of the adjective "new" implies that such an undertaking has not done before and as such this "vision" of Islam is, in fact, a '*revision*'. The use of the verb 'to struggle' in its present tense reiterates the ongoing nature of this task, suggesting that such a scheme is perhaps not that straightforward. There is something, this implies, in the nature of 'Islam' and/or 'modernity' that restricts their union.

Further to the suggestion that 'Islamism' and 'modernity' are exclusive, even incommensurable, this *Guardian* article suggests: Iranians can be placed exhaustively in either one of these ideological groupings; that despite the fact that "two thirds of the voters want the government to adopt more liberal social policies", those in the minority, (dogmatically) retaining loyalties to radical Islamism, dominate political debate; and thus whilst 'Liberalism' and 'Modernity' (antithetical to Islam) are the choices of the people, they are repressed by "the vocal and violent [Islamic] radicals". In this way, a global homology is suggested:

Modernity : popular support :: Islam : dictatorship

The actors included in this report are subsequently offered in personification of this homology — the Supreme Leader Khamenei as 'Islam'; President Khatami as 'modernity' — as indicated by the reported content of their respective speeches to the OIC. The *Guardian* argues that the speech given by Ayatollah Khamenei "contained echoes of the language of the early days of Iran's Islamic revolution. [...] and urged Muslims to be more united against Western cultural invasions." President Khatami,

> in contrast, spoke about human rights, the need for democracy in Muslim countries, and dialogue with the West. *Muslims*, he said, *had to use the West's scientific and social achievements to advance.* [emphasis added]

As suggested above, political and public debate in Iran is currently dominated by an ideological and social struggle, broadly the result of tensions between 'reformist' and 'conservative' religious coalitions. For British broadsheet newspapers, this contest for political power was variously interpreted as the efforts of the moderate President Khatami to 'reform' or 'liberalise' or 'modernise' or 'Westernise' Iran, in the face of an illiberal, intransigent Islamic dictatorship. This representation is first, inaccurate, since in contrast to the journalists' inability to conceive of a model of 'development' other than secular western democracy, President Khatami is not attempting to 'Westernise' Iranian democratic politics. In contrast, Khatami suggests Iran

> must wage a war on two fronts: against its own extremists and against the attraction of the humanistic West. To survive, according to Khatami, the Islamic regime needs modern religious thought, capable of attracting the youth and responding to the challenge of Western humanism, and a people ready to participate actively in the social and political life of their country. (Boroumand & Boroumand, 2000: 312).

Second, the dominant (schematic) representation of Iran is unhelpful since it suggests that the only criticisms of theocratic rule in general and of the *Velayet-e faqih* in particular, come from 'liberal' ('Westernised') politicians and scholars. Far reaching social and political critique employing complex and technical

Islamic argumentation is regularly printed in the Iranian press — particularly the women's press which has become "both a profession and a rallying point" (Keddie, 2000: 417) for Iranian women. Using gender inequality as a case example, Azadeh Kian-Thiébaut (1999) has argued that the reformist role of the women's press cannot be ignored in any analysis of contemporary political debate in Iran:

> Women's magazines [...] are playing a critical role in [Iran's] transformation. [...] The editors of these publications unanimously maintain that the inequality between men and women springs not from the Qur'an, but from religious authorities' misinterpretation of divine laws. [...] They also highlight contributions from reformist clerics, who are increasingly attentive to women's claims that Islamic laws must be adapted to the realities of contemporary Iranian society, in which women's social, economic, political and cultural activities have become integral. (Kian-Thiébaut, 1999: 15, cited in Keddie, 2000: 424)

It is lamentable that such important sites of social criticism and debate are ignored by the broadsheet press, seemingly because their ontological framework of 'Islam = backward; the West = progress' precludes the possibility that a 'progressive' argument could originate within and orientate itself towards an 'Islamic' value system.

Normalisation of Israeli aggression

Integral to the 'ideological square' is the complimentary representation of 'Our' social action in contrast with the negative representation of 'Their' social action. It is worth bearing in mind that deictic pronouns such as 'Us' and 'Them', 'Our' and 'Their', 'Self' and 'Other', etc. do not have any meaning other than their immediate application: their meaning is constantly negotiated and renegotiated in the context of specific reports, and actors included as 'We' and 'Our' in some reports (for example, the manner in which British newspapers positioned the French government during the NATO bombing of Serbia, 1999) are positioned as 'They' and 'Theirs' in others (for example, the manner in which French government are *re*positioned when debating/reporting the EU or the Euro). When analysing news reports in which it is not immediately clear who are being included in the position 'Us', it is possible to work backwards from this ideological double strategy, identifying whose opinions and social activities are represented positively and whose receive criticism. The negotiated status of the position 'Us' is clear in a number of articles, not least in the book review **The Holy Terror**, where the brutal dictator, the last Shah, is rhetorically welcomed into the fold (*Sunday Times* Books supplement, 18 January 1998; see previous chapter).

When reporting Israel and Palestine, the sampled broadsheet newspapers predominantly positioned Israel and Israeli Jews as 'We', thereby assuring their positive representation; and conversely, Palestine and Arabs — and not only *Muslim* Arabs — were positioned as 'They', prefacing a negative representation.[3] First, the acceptance of Israeli argumentation is clearly noticeable in the symbolic annexation of illegally occupied land. What this means is that 'Arab lands gained by violent invasion and illegally occupied by Israel' are very rarely so labelled, with the broadsheet press preferring to label such areas as the nominalisation 'the occupied territories' or increasingly as 'Israeli settlements'. For example, when Binyamin Netanyahu approved plans to build in Jabul Abu-Ghneim — a move illegal under both the UN convention and the Oslo Accord — the broadsheet press unerringly used the Hebrew name for this area of East Jerusalem: Har Homa. In one report the *Independent* went so far as to describe the annexation as "the Jewish neighbourhood planned for the outskirts of the city" (11 December 1997), providing the kind of euphemistic gloss that the Israeli government would no doubt consider to be very useful.

These strategies of symbolic annexation — facilitated by journalists' nominalising, backgrounding or deleting significant information — are also reflected in broadcast news coverage of Palestine, as illustrated in the recent work of Philo (2002). Through analysis of television news coverage of the 'intifadha' between 28th September and 16th October 2000 (89 bulletins), Philo (2002) argues that coverage is characterised by biases of both omission and commission — specifically the lack of historic contextualisation and stark "differences in the manner in which both 'sides' were presented" (p.4). Crucial information providing background and context to the violence and repression in Palestine, and the informed (sometimes critical) commentary of Israeli insiders — which are regularly included in the Hebrew press despite stringent and rigorously enforced military censorship (see Shahak, 1997) — rarely resurfaces in the British news media for example. Moving forward for the moment, another more recent example of British journalists failing to gain new angles from stories printed in the Israeli press, was the criminal invasion of the Jenin refugee camp under the banner of 'Operation Defensive Shield'. Reinhart (2003: 151), quoting a report from *Ha'aretz* written by Amir Oren, shows that prior to the military offensive into Jenin, the Israeli Army studied "relevant historical precedents" — including the Nazi takeover of the Warsaw ghetto:

> In order to prepare properly for the next campaign, one of the Israeli officers in the territories said […] it's justified — and in fact essential — to learn from every possible source. If the mission will be to seize a densely populated refugee camp, or take over the Casbah in Nablus, and if the commander's obligation is to try to execute the mission without casualties on either side, then he must first analyse and internalise the lessons of earlier battles — even, however shocking it may sound, even how the German army fought in the Warsaw ghetto. (originally in: Amir Oren, 'At the gates of Yassergrad', *Ha'aretz*, 25 January 2002)

Later, *Yediot Aharonot* repeatedly published articles criticising the Israeli Army's 'D-9 bulldozer units', which worked around the clock during the destruction of Jenin, 'erasing' the centre of the refugee camp by systematically demolishing hundreds of civilian homes. Tsadok Yehezkeli interviewed a bulldozer driver who proudly admitted demolishing homes for 75 hours without a break:

> […] Many people were inside houses we started to demolish. They would come out of the houses we were working on. I didn't see, with my own eyes, people dying under the blade of the D9. And I didn't see houses falling down on live people. But if there were any, I wouldn't care at all. I am sure people died inside these houses, but it was difficult to see, there was lots of dust everywhere and we worked a lot at night. I found joy with every house that came down, because I knew they [the Palestinians] didn't mind dying, but they care for their homes. If you knocked down a house, you buried 40 or 50 people for generations. If I am sorry for anything, it is for not tearing the whole camp down. (originally in: Tsadok Yehezkeli, Seven days Weekend magazine, *Yediot Aharanot*, 31 May 2002; cited in Reinhart, 2003: 164–5)

Information such as this surprisingly frank discussion of Army tactics, the policy of indiscriminate destruction of occupied civilian homes and the anti-Palestinian hatred which characterises the comments of the Army reservist in the second excerpt, were absent from British media coverage of the Jenin massacres. The ability of the Israeli Army, and later the Israeli government and Judiciary, to *deny* the massacre, to obstruct and eventually scuttle the planned UN investigation and to replace their early mortality figure with the staggeringly low estimate of 55 dead (see Reinhart, 2003), was in no small part attributable to the absence of commentary and contextualisation from 'inside' sources.

Further, using the results of focus groups representing a cross-section of ages and backgrounds, Philo (2002) shows that these and other distortions of news coverage of Israel/Palestine have resulted in a measurable impairment of public understanding. For example, despite there being around ten times more Palestinians killed and injured since the start of the al-Aqsa intifadha (1,306 Palestinians officially killed (of whom 239 were under the age of 18) and 100,047 injured between 29th September 2000 and 2nd June 2002–from www.jmcc.org), "only 30% of our sample of 300 young people believed this to be so. The same number believed either that the Israelis had the most casualties or that casualties were equal for both sides" (Philo, 2002: 3).

Second, explicit Israeli plans to consolidate lands taken through violent conquest were uncritically accepted. For example, a report headlined **Likud politician calls for Palestinian state** (*The Times*, 28 November 1997), shows a characteristic lack of critical insight into the reported claims of Likud chief whip Meir Sheerit, the Israeli politician central to the story. The opening paragraph of the story, written by Christopher Walker, reads:

> A leading member of Binyamin Netanyahu's ruling Likud party yesterday backed the creation of a limited Palestinian state in a new challenge to the policy of the embattled right-wing Israeli Prime Minister.

Through the use of the noun phrase "a new challenge", this excerpt clearly suggests that the "limited Palestinian state" proposed by Sheerit represents a change in direction, or perhaps a move *forward*, for the previously obstructive Likud party. This argumentative line is reiterated in the paragraphs which followed, suggesting, for example, that Netanyahu was stalling the 'peace process' in order to placate the demands of "extreme right-wing Jews furious that he plans to hand back more West Bank land to Palestinians". Against this party policy, Sheerit's "challenge" is described as a "surprise conversion" towards the objectives of the Oslo agreement.

On face value, Sheerit's comments do indeed appear to be quite radical. He is quoted as saying: "I think it is possible to achieve peace with the Palestinians"; and that "The most important thing is to initiate the establishment of a Palestinian state while we are still in power." However, lower down the article, details are given which should have cast serious doubts on the equity of Sheerit's planned "final settlement peace offer". Walker writes: "Under his proposal, Jerusalem would remain under Israeli sovereignty, the Jordan river would remain Israel's border and Israel would annex most of the 144 Jewish settlements." As anyone at all familiar with the region and its national borders should know, this plan would, of course, result in the legitimised *expansion* of Israel to include most of the land illegally occupied since 1967: East Jerusalem, the whole of the West Bank (in line with a border at the Jordan river) and 144 other 'settlements' which, although unspecified, must logically lie in territory *other* than the West Bank — presumably in Syria and Gaza. Not only does this plan go unexplained, uncontextualised and uncriticised, by presenting it in contrast to Netanyahu's "uncompromising" stance, Walker's report quite logically implies that it represents a compromise. This in turn supports Israel's claims to being the conciliatory party in the dispute and further undermines the Palestinian objections to the continued legalised theft of land which both this proposal and the Oslo Accords represent.

Third, violence proposed by Israel against sovereign (Muslim) states often goes similarly uncriticised by the broadsheet press — take the report **Israel steps up plans for air attacks on Iran** (*The Times*, 9 December 1997) for example. As the headline suggests, the article, again written by Christopher Walker, reports the "options" available to Israel in forming their "military contingency plans to neutralise Iran's Russian-backed missile and nuclear weapon programme". The 'need' for such a plan, already hinted at in its description above, was clearly articulated by the Israeli Defence Minister, Yitzhak Mordechai:

> "A country like Iran possessing such long range weaponry — a country that lacks stability, that is characterised by Islamic fundamentalism, by an extremist ideology that is striving to become a superpower in the Middle East — is very dangerous."

Such an accusation represents the classic approach of the propagandist, as illustrated by Ellul (1965: 58): "He who wants to provoke a war not only proclaims his own peaceful intentions but also accuses the other party of provocation. [...] He who wants to establish a dictatorship always insists his adversaries are bent on dictatorship." Israeli foreign policy, Shahak (1997) suggests, is not driven by "the 'wish for peace', so often assumed as the Israeli aim" (p.3); rather, like all states, Israel has "hegemonic aspirations. A state aspiring to hegemony in an area cannot tolerate other strong states in that area" (Ibid.). Should Iran have made similar argumentative claims about the hegemonic political ambitions, the religious fundamentalism (of, for example, the Gush Emunim) and the extremist ideology of Israel, they would no doubt be presented as either laughable or another example of Iranian belligerence. However, Shahak (1997) shows that such argumentative claims from Iran would in fact be well founded:

> Since the spring of 1992, public opinion in Israel is being prepared for the prospect of a war with Iran, to be fought to bring about Iran's total military and political defeat. In one version, Israel would attack Iran alone, in another it would 'persuade' the West to do the job. The indoctrination campaign to this effect is gaining in intensity. It is accompanied by what could be called semi-official horror scenarios purporting to detail what Iran could do to Israel, the West and the entire

world when it acquires nuclear weapons as it is expected to a few years hence. (Shahak, 1997: 54).

Shahak illustrates this point by quoting "respected and influential Israeli experts or commentators on strategic affairs" (1997: 58) whose opinions are regularly included in mainstream Israeli newspapers. Daniel Leshem for example, a member of the Centre for Strategic Research at Tel Aviv University, has been quoted proposing to "create the situation which would appear similar to that with Iraq before the Gulf crisis" (1997: 55; originally in *Al Hamishmar*, 19 February 1993). His proposed foreign policy is as sinister as it sounds:

> Iran claims sovereignty over three strategically located islands in the Gulf. Domination over those islands is capable of assuring domination not only over all the already active oil-fields of the area, but also over all the natural gas sources not yet exploited. We should hope that, emulating Iraq, Iran would contest the Gulf Emirates and Saudi Arabia over these islands and, repeating Saddam Hussein's mistake in Kuwait, start a war. […] This prospect is in my view quite likely, because patience plays no part in the Iranian mentality. But if they nevertheless refrain from starting a war, we should take advantage of their involvement in Islamic terrorism which already hurts the entire world. (Ibid.)

The report **Israel steps up plans for air attacks against Iran** should be viewed as part of this belligerent anti-Iranian heritage.

Returning to Walker's report, the greater part of the article is dedicated to describing "the two main options" that "Military planners are studying" as part of this anti-Iran plan. Either: "hitting Iranian missile plants in the cities of Shiraz, Kuramabad, Farhin and Semnan with the 'long arm' of its airforce, or targeting foreign scientists at the facilities rather than the buildings themselves." Walker then goes on to give further breathless descriptions of "advanced F15I fighter planes" and "surgical air strikes" identical to the well trodden rhetoric of militaristic techno-philia (discussed further in Chapter 6). Conspicuously absent from the discussion is any recognition of the *intrinsic illegality* of the plan, Israel's blind contempt for human life in proposing to bomb another nation without making any consideration for the welfare of Iranians, and the uncritical acceptance of Israel's seeming *right* to act accordingly on the part of Walker. Such a tacit support for the proposed Israeli offensive could only be achieved after: first, Iranian human life is degraded to a point where it is thought to be disposable; and second, Israel are licensed to engage in any and all illegal activities since (following their rhetorical repositioning into the in-group 'Us') they are perceived to be acting for 'the greater good'.

Attempted assassination of Khaled Meshal

A similarly nonchalant attitude towards state-sponsored terrorism (at least when it's perpetrated by 'Us' and directed towards Muslims) characterise the manner in which British broadsheet newspapers reported Mossad's attempted assassination of the leader of Hamas' politburo, Khaled Meshal. The exact details of the attack are still somewhat obscure, but this much is clear: on 26 September 1997, as Mr Meshal was entering his office building in the Jordanian capital Amman, two men approached him from behind and pressed a device to his ear. Meshal heard a loud noise, fell to the ground and immediately started shaking uncontrollably. The two men escaped in a waiting car containing a further two men, but were arrested later in the day by Jordanian police at which point they produced Canadian passports and were identified as Sean Kendall and Barry Beads. However, the two men refused to see the Canadian diplomat, their passports were discovered to be forgeries and when the remaining two assailants took refuge in the Israeli embassy suspicions gave way to an Israeli admission of guilt. Canada withdrew its ambassador to Israel; Israel brokered a deal to release Sheikh Ahmed Yassin, the spiritual leader of Hamas and, in what King Hussein called a "gesture of peace", deport him to Jordan. Finally, Israel was forced to send an 'antidote' to the Jordanian hospital where Meshal was recovering, fuelling speculation that the device was a chemical or biological weapon.

The leniency-verging-on-flippancy with which the broadsheets approached this story is characterised a *Guardian* article headlined **Mossad own goal rebounds on PM** (4 October 1997) — the sporting metaphor of the headline already diminishing the significance of the reported action. The attempt on Meshal's life resulted in hardly a word of criticism: the failed assassination is described as a "bungled attack" which has set "a bizarre new benchmark" in Mossad's "colourful history", the facts of which "are reminiscent of a paperback thriller." The reporter, Julian Borger, preferred to focus on the potentially negative effect which the *failure* of the mission will have on Netanyahu's credibility and political career. For example, a bold, closed captioned quote read "There is a growing feeling this government can't get it right — it just goes from screw-up to screw-up", drawing attention to the *failure* of the attack rather than its unquestioned illegality. Any mention of international law, of 'terrorism' or the implications of a sovereign state assassinating its political and/or criminal opponents was carefully avoided. Indeed Borger reframes the attempted assassination as another entry on the list of Mossad's "*daring* exploits" (emphasis added). Other examples on the list included "the raid on Entebbe and the abduction of Nazi war criminal Adolf Eichmann", thereby minimising the opportunities to object to the attempted assassination of the politician — these are, after all, the dashing boys of Mossad.

The report in the *Independent*, although arguing that "the attempted assassination" (also described as "zany") showed that Israel was "responding to political challenges in a very primitive way", also chose to frame the attack as a(nother) failure of Netanyahu's government rather than as a terrorist act (**Bibi flounders in sea of troubles after Hamas fiasco**, 4 October 1997). The *Telegraph* also avoided any suggestion that the "botched assassination attempt" amounted to state-sponsored terrorism, although they did make repeated and extended allegations of Meshal's involvement in Hamas' terrorist actions, despite his working for the party politburo rather than its armed wing (**Hamas leader tells how he survived murder attempt**, 4 October 1997). Similarly *The Times* labelled the attack as the "botched Mossad secret service operation in Jordan", and further suggested that "the Israeli public [had] expressed concern that the already fading image of Mossad's invincibility has suffered a severe blow" (**Calls for inquiry over Mossad plot**, 4 October 1997). Somewhere along the line, the fact that a state had attempted to assassinate a politician was lost.

The Sunday broadsheets were equally prone to normalising the attack on Meshal. In a report headlined **Netanyahu censored by Hamas truce offer** for example (*The Sunday Times*, 19 October 1997) the assassination attempt received the by now standard description of being a "bungled" operation. In addition, the report lower down stated:

> Netanyahu points to polls showing support for his decision, made after a suicide bombing in Jerusalem on July 30, to eliminate senior Hamas figures. But critics say the risk to the delicate relationship with Jordan should have ruled out carrying out any assassination attempt on Jordanian territory.

Note that it is not the plan to "eliminate senior Hamas figures" which "critics" balked at, but rather Netanyahu's decision to allow it to occur on Jordanian territory. The simple illegality of Netanyahu's plan, not to mention the scandalous possibility that the Israeli government may have developed an explicit 'shoot-to-kill' policy in 'dealing with' its political or even *criminal* opponents, are concerns which the journalist neither acknowledges nor criticises.

Finally, in an article summarising the consequences of the attack, the *Sunday Times* reported that an Israeli committee set up "to investigate a *bungled* attempt by Mossad agents to assassinate one of the leaders of Hamas, the *Islamic fundamentalist group*, is expected to recommend the dismissal of Danny Yatom, the head of the service" ('**Arab hunter' bids to control Mossad**, 9 November 1997; emphases added). The favourite to succeed Yatom was Meir Dagan — "a man who knows no fear" who during the first *intifadha* formed two "hit squads, codenamed 'Cherry' and 'Samson', to carry out assassinations in the West Bank and Gaza". Other than this obvious qualification to head Mossad, based as it is on a clear willingness to not let things as insignificant as the law or even basic humanity get in the way of operations, Dagan is also said to have:

- "established a covert death squad called 'Rimon' (grenade)" which "gunned down dozens of terrorists";
- "helped to establish a unit of about 30 soldiers acting as a hit squad in southern Lebanon";
- and is regarded as "one of the army's leading 'Arab hunters'."

The possibility that this man could head Mossad worried the reporter, Uzi Mahnaimi, who stated that his appointment "could seriously threaten Middle East stability" since he "is known to favour an increase in assassinations of those deemed subversive to Israel."[4] In contrast to the "gifted but uncontrollable" Dagan, the journalist, Mahnaimi, represents Danny Yatom as a reliable choice to continue leading Mossad, despite "the debacle in Amman". In the only evidence which the article provides in support of Yatom — taken from Yatom's own testimony "before the security services committee of the Knesset" — Mahnaimi suggests that Yatom "opposed the attack on Meshal, *preferring a plan to kill another target* on a different continent." That such scant regard for human life could be included in a broadsheet news report, not only without criticism but also in *support* of Yatom's suitability in leading Mossad, is particularly disturbing.

The whole approach of the British Broadsheet press to the reporting of Mossad's attempted assassination of Khaled Meshal was characterised by a low estimation of (Arab-Muslim) life, and their simultaneous acceptance of Israel acting with such murderous impunity — with some reports implying that Israel were justified in attempting to kill Meshal and other opponents. In this way, the reporting of the attempted assassination represents an archetypal example of the ideological square: whilst the terrorist acts of Hamas ('Meshal's fundamentalist group') are condemned, the equally terrorist act of Israel in attempting to assassinate him ('or perhaps they should have killed someone else') with a chemical/biological weapon, are implicitly accepted since they attracted no significant criticism.

As an epilogue to these events: Meir Dagan *was* eventually made Head of Mossad in September 2002, by his long time friend and wartime commander Prime Minister Ariel Sharon. The close association between Sharon and ex-General Dagan (also an active Likud member) developed and was cemented during the Yom Kippur war of 1973, when Dagan was the first officer to cross the Suez canal under Sharon's command. After replacing his more diplomatically orientated predecessor Ephraim Halevi, one of Mossad's first policy decisions under Dagan's leadership was, 'coincidentally', to authorise the assassination of individuals in 'friendly foreign countries' deemed to be a 'threat' to Israel. Although Israeli officials have refused to either confirm or deny that it has authorised such terrorist actions, the change in policy was revealed by former Mossad agents during interviews with the press agency UPI, and later confirmed by US intelligence officers.[5] The first recorded example of this 'new wave' of assassinations took place on or around 2 March 2003, when Abu Mohammed al-Masri, the alleged head of al-Qaeda in Lebanon, was killed by a car bomb as he arrived at mosque. Reacting to the murder, an Israeli security source said: "For us, there is now no difference between al-Qaeda, Islamic Jihad, Hamas, Hezbollah and others [...] We refer to them all as the Islamic terror syndicate" (in **Mossad hardman in first foreign kill**, Uzi Mahnaimi, *Sunday Times*, 9 March 2003). This is the first evidence that when it comes to "targeted killings", the "unconventional", "daring" and "controversial" Dagan [6]will not make the same mistakes as Danny Yatom: he will make sure his targets are dead.

CHAPTER 5

British Muslims

Difference, discord and threat in domestic reporting

Islam and 'the West'; Muslim and 'Westerner'[1]

In many domestic reports, a split between 'Islam' and 'the West', 'Muslim' and 'Westerner' is presented to the reader, contrasting actors, characteristics, philosophies and political and/or religious views thought to represent these two cultural 'camps'. This frequent tendency of the press to divide 'Islam' and 'the West', even in the domestic sample, has obvious implications for the social inclusion of British Muslims. It not only obviously serves to distance 'Us' British, 'Our' opinions, 'Our' public domain from 'Them' and 'Theirs', it also acts to symbolically divide British Muslims from the semantic domain 'British', excluding their opinions. This is achieved by one of two methods: the proxy split, where 'British' and 'Other' operate as the active referents, with Muslims being cited (along with others) as an example of the 'Other' category. Actors are divided into 'British' and 'non-British/immigrant', with (often *British*) Muslims being included within the second of these categories. Thus, 'Muslims' are identified as 'Other' by virtue of characteristics which they are presumed or perceived to lack: in other words, their lack of 'Britishness' divides 'Them' from 'Us'. The second method of division is an explicit split, where Islam and/or Muslims are identified as the 'Other' by virtue of values or characteristics which they are perceived to have: in short, their 'Islamic-ness' is used to divide 'Them' from 'Us'.

The 'proxy split' between British and Other

The schema adopted in the 'proxy split' is basic but global: it is based on a distinction between 'British' and 'non-British', the exact boundaries of which are never particularly well drawn — that would, of course, open them up to critique. The British Muslim communities are included within this 'non-British' grouping through either wilful manipulation of evidence, generalisation or ignorance: the impossibility of either 'white-Muslim' or 'non-white Englander' form central presuppositions of these texts. A strong example of British Muslims being associated with an ill-defined category of 'foreigner-other' is the article **'You've made us feel so welcome: In praise of Britain'**, written by Graham Turner (*Daily Telegraph* 17 January 1998). This news feature was based on a presupposed superiority of Britain, demarcating actors into 'Us' and 'Them' categories from the offset. The overheadline for example, states that:

> Pride, gratitude and sense of belonging typify the thousands of foreigners who have adopted Britain as their home. Their only complaint, amid all the compliments, is that the British themselves tend to run down their own country.

The prima facie division of 'Us' and 'Them' is clearly evident in this short statement, with the first sentence identifying the actors in the article as "foreigners". This distinction is extended in the second sentence through the co-location of the noun phrase 'the British' and the possessive-pronoun 'Their', which refers back to the "foreigners". This structuring of expression acts to exclude 'Them' from the in-group 'the British' since 'They' are reported as referring to 'Us' in the third person: 'Their complaint about us...' This presupposed division is continued throughout the text, as illustrated in this short list of examples:

> 'We often take Britain for granted. They do not.'
> "I am from India, and between England and India there is no comparison. If you said the whole world could come to Britain, half of India would immediately climb on a train and come. This is the best country in the world."
> "' You have to be born here to feel English, but I do feel British", [said] Saphie Ashtiany'
> "I still see myself as slightly foreign, but whereas Germans are totally unteasable [...] I do now enjoy both teasing and being teased, just like the English. So maybe I've made it?"

All of the actors referred to and/or quoted in the text were first generation immigrants. In order of appearance, the "foreigners" in the article are referred to as coming from India, Egypt, Germany, Iran, Germany (again), USA, Egypt (again), Jamaica, India (again), Ireland, and Kenya, the only 'English' voice being that of the journalist. It could therefore be said that the division between 'Britain' and 'Foreigner' only exists in the text by virtue of the fact that all the actors introduced are first generation immigrants, all of whom talk about themselves in such a way. But the text is not that benign. It was written, and hence its function lies, "in praise of Britain", and in order to achieve this Turner adopts a familiar strategic ritual of journalism, locating or concealing his truth claims in the words of the report's sources (see Tuchman, 1972). Although the newspaper is not directly 'responsible' for the divisions presupposed by the report's sources, their inclusion in the article to the absence of any contesting claims signals their assumed pertinence to the 'debate', and reveals the ideological commitment of the journalist. This ideological commitment is observable throughout the article in Turner's editorialising — take the last sentence of the article, for example:

> So, we have our faults, which are obvious, and we have made our mistakes, some of them terrible. We also, it seems, have our virtues, though our own dismal jimmies prefer not to recognise them. Is it very un-British to celebrate them occasionally?

Occurring after such extended self congratulation, the idea that it is somehow "un-British" to recognise "our virtues" and "celebrate them occasionally" appears rather ridiculous. Further, the claim that 'Our' British history is not celebrated does not stand up to even a cursory examination. In a final irony, this statement acts as the last (proxy) evidence of the 'un-Britishness' of the actors presented, since "recognising and occasionally celebrating the virtues of Britain" is all that Graham Turner has allowed 'Them' to do throughout the text.

The article also develops contrasts between Britain and 'Islamic countries', with the latter presented as inferior. This judgement of the lower status of 'Islamic countries' is subservient to the primary function of the text — "In praise of Britain" — as opposed to the explicit condemnation of 'Islamic countries'. Accordingly the evidence supporting this judgement presents positive elements of 'Our' national character which they are assumed to lack — in short, 'Our Britishness' — as opposed to foregrounding negative characteristics which 'They' are supposed to possess. The 'Iranian immigrant', Saphie Ashtiany, is included referring to the 'superior British character' as an even more primordial "nature":

> "I discovered that unspoken warmth and kindness is part of the British nature. There's also a strong anti-hysteric element in the national character. …Living here has actually changed my character. I'd have been far more excitable if I had stayed in Iran."

Zaki Badawi is also quoted 'in praise of Britain', but not before he is introduced in an uncharacteristically complementary way as "Dr Zaki Badawi, chairman of the Council of Imams and Mosques and perhaps Britain's most distinguished Muslim", adding credibility and authority to his words. His most prominent quote is cited below, numbered for ease of reference:

> "[1] As a young man in Egypt, [2] I never thought that I'd end my life in Britain. I wanted with all my heart to get the British out. I thought 'then we will have freedom'. [3] Well, of course the British are out, but freedom did not arrive. [4] Sadly, the Muslim world has not yet learnt the tolerance which you have in abundance here. [5] Islam advocates it, but our people do not live up to that standard."

In clause [1], Dr Badawi identifies himself as Egyptian, who, in clause [2] is shown to have had a dislike for Britain. This dislike is a result of the British 'being in' Egypt and the lack of freedom associated with their presence. The oppressive details of this 'presence' remain conspicuously absent from discussion. This dislike for the British is shown to have been misguided however, since as clause [3] suggests, the freedom thought to have been prevented by the British presence in Egypt was still found to be lacking after 'We' had left. This is explained by clause [4], where it is claimed that "the Muslim world" is a place lacking in 'British tolerance', a deficit which is identified, in clause [5], as being a fault of "our" (Egyptian) Muslim people, contrary to the tolerance advocated by Islam.

To reiterate: the inclusion of sources in this article is illustrative of the newspaper's commitment to a certain interpretation of 'Britain', 'Britishness' and the comparative position of 'Islam' and 'Muslims'. Quoting Zaki Badawi after being introduced as *authoritative* ("Dr"), *informed* ("chairman of the Council of Imams and Mosques") and of '*good character*' ("Britain's most distinguished Muslim") illustrates the 'communion' between Badawi's criticisms and the pragmatic goal of both the text and newspaper. The vagueness of his criticisms add to the general textual claim of British superiority. — What is meant by 'the Muslim world'? Is this geographically located, or does such a 'world' extend, *a la* Orientalist methodology, to include all Muslims? Is the whole of the 'Muslim world' meant to be intolerant, or just those who have the power to impose their will upon it? The ambiguity of Dr Badawi's statement and the criticism which it contains, adds breadth to whom it refers, expanding concentrically to include 'the Muslim world' and 'our [Muslim] people', all the while conforming with the text's pragmatic goal: "praising Britain".

Explicit Islam/West bifurcation

Although the vast majority of articles in the sample are based on an implicit assumption of difference — either as above, by contrasting 'English' and 'non-English' actors and/or characteristics, or through an implicit contrast between 'Islam' and 'the West' — occasionally such a bifurcation is suggested explicitly in the text.

If we first take an article entitled '**May your God go with you**' (*Independent Magazine* 20 December 1997), reporting a high level meeting between influential members and representatives of Judaism, Christianity and Islam. The journalist, Paul Vallely, states helpfully that "many of the views which *we in the West* hold about Islam are mythical, outdated or simply ignorant" (emphasis added), but seems to be unaware that such a statement contiguously propagates of one of the central 'myths' held about Islam: the assumption that the West is populated by "Us" non-Muslims and, by default, the East by "Them" Muslims. Building on this false start, Vallely then presents the by-now familiar stereotypical ideological conflict. On the one side, "we in the West" who are grounded in "[t]he offspring of the Enlightenment — science, capitalism, individualism and democracy". These constructs, he claims, are "a framework within which values can flourish, but [...] do not create those values." Opposing this framework, Vallely suggests, are

> contemporary Muslim fundamentalists, [who] react against the modernism of Western culture. [...] Muslims throughout the world feel humiliated by Western culture and, in particular, the economic, military power of the US, which is widely regarded throughout the Arab world as 'the Great Satan'.

The actors are thus identified, and the conflict itself presented as a battle for, or perhaps over, modernity: 'the West' supporting "science, capitalism, individualism and democracy"; and the "Muslims throughout the world feel[ing] humiliated" by this 'modernism'.

Such a statement is, of course, a gross generalisation, but rather than moderating the statement, Vallely extends the argument to "the UK, [where] the revival of Islam has similar roots." Here in the UK, Vallely suggests that this "revival of Islam" is characterised by "young British Asians [...] reading the Koran not just with fresh eyes but against a background of comparative depravation, exclusion, unemployment, low earnings and poor housing." Ignoring the fact that the *growth* of Islam is by no means isolated to young British Asians, this is as close as Vallely gets to a criticism of either 'the West' or of a modernity built on the apparently 'valueless' frameworks of capitalism and individualism.

Indeed, he describes the communities' reaction to such "alienation and racism" as a "widespread feeling of paranoia". This acts to background, or deny, the well-founded claims to disadvantage and ill-treatment referred to only three sentences before, with 'paranoia' conjuring associations of delusional mental illness.

Explicit divisions between 'Muslim' and 'Briton' are displayed not only in broadsheet representations of 'Islam' and 'Muslims', but also in the way symbols, artefacts and characteristics considered particularly or thoroughly 'Islamic' are represented. The broadsheet press' approach to the *hijab*, or veil, in the sampled coverage suggests that it is thought of in such a manner: as a metonym for Islam. As Hage (1998) suggests, members of both the political right and left see the *hijab* — as both cultural item and a symbol of certain aspects of Islamic culture and religion — as "a harmful presence that affects their own well-being" (Hage, 1998: 37). The exact manifestation of this 'harmful presence' differs according to the politics of the individual and in this case the newspaper. Therefore, the inclusion of the *hijab* in reporting highlights its rhetorical use in the text's argumentation, providing insights into newspapers' differential perceptions of 'Islam'. In order to clarify these differences, it is necessary to quote Hage (1998) at length:

> For example, scarves [can be] considered an unacceptable form of subjugating women or, as interviewee B put it: "It pains me to live in a society where such backward forms of subjugation are exhibited." In a more complex manner, to European women, scarves can represent an intolerable, because too visible, mode of subjugation that only serves to render their own subjugation more visible. Because nationalists follow a 'one nation one patriarchy' motto, the veil can also mean the subjugation of women to a non-national patriarchy. The desire to remove it is the desire to ensure that all women within the nation are subjugated to the dominant national patriarchal order. Finally, some non-Muslim migrant women, especially those who have a consciousness of themselves as Third World-looking, express a hatred of the scarf by fear of association. Here it is perceived as a migrant marker that some migrant women see as negatively affecting all migrant women by labeling them as backward. (Hage, 1998: 251)

With a dichotomy established between the veil and modernity, it becomes possible for any political ideologue to imbue the veil with whatever characteristics felt necessary to differentiate 'Them' from 'Us', and then — through the adoption of the Orientalist methodology of gross generalisation — to 'Islam' as a whole. The coverage of the *hijab* in the domestic sample falls well within these conceptions, each story in which the veil is mentioned adopting one or more of these schema. Sometimes differentiation is as far as the text goes — a simple

'Muslim' and 'British' split — leaving the possibility of rejection strategies based on this bifurcated allegiance, solely with the audience. On other occasions, the bifurcation is followed by either clearer implications, or else explicit identification, of the 'characteristics' which members of the two 'civilisations' are supposed to hold. Regardless, the female Muslims cited in broadsheet news articles become defined almost solely and inextricably in terms of their 'Muslim-ness', as is clear from the use of the *hijab* in the body of news-text:

> In the Turkish navy, female ratings do not wear a veil. Their uniforms are similar to those of Western servicewomen. (*Independent* 6 January, 1998)
> Robotics technician, Farida Khanum, 21, was bullied by other workers at a Luton car plant, one of whom mockingly put a cloth over his head and referred to her as "Yasser Arafat" […] her dismissal stemmed from her decision to wear the *hijab*, a head covering in line with Islamic modesty requirements. (*Independent* 15 January, 1998)
> The school, which has 180 pupils, operates a strict Islamic code […] Girls wear the Islamic headscarf, the *hijab*, and school stops for midday and afternoon prayers. (*Guardian* 10 January, 1998)

In the above *Guardian* article (**Muslim schools get grants**, 10 January 1998) for example, the "strict Islamic code" alleged to be in place in the school is distilled and represented by the newspaper in the form of two simple images: the *hijab* and prayer. The use of the adjective "strict", in connection with the *hijab* as manifestation of "Islamic code", ties its representation with enforcement and the subjugation of women. This approach also informs the representation of the *hijab* in the *Independent*, where three very young Muslim girls pictured wearing headscarves, are described as: "Girls in a British Islamic school, learning 'solid morals with discipline and respect'." (**Islamic vs. Secular**, *Independent* 25 October 1997).

Finally, a stylistic register of repression and constraint is also drawn upon by *The Daily Telegraph* in '**It's fashion, but who are the victims?**' The report, describing a catwalk show by fashion designer Hussein Chalayan, focuses upon the "bondage frocks" worn by the models, which were in fact stylised and in some cases surreal interpretations of female Muslim dress. The article adopts a more ridiculing or sneering tone to that of the two 'liberal' newspapers, describing the women as "stalking down the catwalk with bags on their heads", and dressed in "what looked like chadors, the black cloaks in which some of the Islamic faith protect the modesty of their women." Here, in a complex combination of image and inference, the journalist makes rhetorical use of the Muslim veil, comparing the fashion on display to the chador in order to criticise the designer's work: 'Bags, how ghastly!' This in effect transforms the alleged 'Islamic-ness' of the clothing into a term of derogation.

From this, I suggest that the *hijab*, in image and concept, is used by journalists as an indication of the Islamic-ness of either the theme or actors in an article. Wherever the *hijab* is mentioned in these texts, the author is specifically attempting to draw the readers attention to 'Islam', using the religion as a explanatory factor in the agency or motivation of the actors in the article, which is presented in contrast, or sometimes opposition, to the supposed normative base of 'Western/ised agency'. This does not equate to homogeneity in representing 'Islam' across the newspapers however, since as Hage (1998) suggests above, the *hijab* (and therefore the connoted 'Islam') are differentially perceived by the newspapers. Rather, the *hijab* is used by the newspaper to symbolise their particular 'Islam':

> For the right, Islam represents barbarism; for the left, medieval theocracy; for the centre, a kind of distasteful exoticism. In all camps, however, there is agreement that even though little enough is known about the Islamic world, there is not much to be approved of there. (Said, 1997: lv)

The ideological square in domestic reporting

The negative 'othering' of British Muslims is present in a range of sites across these domestic items of reporting. This, combined with broadsheet newspapers preference for backgrounding or excluding anti-Muslim discrimination and violence (see below) results in what Said (1997) has labelled journalism's "covering of Islam": "a one-sided activity that obscures what 'we' do, and highlights instead what Muslims and Arabs by their very nature are" (p. xxii). Such a pattern is premised on a double strategy contained in argumentative denials of racism, containing a "positive self-presentation, on the one hand, and a strategy of expressing a subtle, indirect [...] form of negative other-presentation, on the other hand" (van Dijk, 1992: 89).

'Fanatical' Muslim violence in the public sphere

'Muslim violence in the public sphere' represents a prominent approach to this negativisation. A remarkable 51.3 per cent (n= 79) of domestic articles which cited Islam as having an influence on the reported action, also reported or referred to 'violence or acts of violence'; only 12.3 per cent (n= 19) of these same articles reported or referred to 'peace and/or acts of peace'. A reporting frame emphasising 'Muslim violence' dominated the reporting of a campaign by Luton Muslims to have the name of a local bingo hall changed from 'Mecca' to something less insulting. Reports were printed on this topic in the *Guardian*, the *Independent* and *The Times*, with the newspapers picking up the story just as the (under-reported) campaign was beginning to be peppered with acts of frustrated violence. The ongoing nature of the campaign is acknowledged in a *Guardian* report (**Muslim ire over Mecca 'insult'**, 7 January, 1998), the first line of which states that "Muslims yesterday *stepped up* their campaign against Mecca, the chain of Bingo halls which they say takes the name of their holy city in vain" (emphasis added).

The articles report a meeting between the Rank Organisation, the owners of the bingo hall, and local Muslim representatives, with the majority of the information in all three of the news reports — identical for the most part — being taken from a press release of this meeting. Despite this public meeting forming the focus of the reported event, the news item in the *Independent* (**Mecca bingo hall outrages Muslims**, 7 January 1998) argued that the princi-pal approach of the Muslim community's campaign was:

> violent protest [...] They said it was an insult to Islam for the name of their holiest city to be associated with gambling, and on Christmas Day [no less!], bricks were thrown through the windows of the hall causing £3,000 of damage.

Instead of quoting any Muslims, the *Independent* journalist chooses to quote Councillor Hazel Simmons, the chairwomen of Equal Opportunities at Luton Council as saying "I personally believe this [the name] to be insensitive in what is now a truly multicultural society".

The press reports were universally critical of the Muslim campaign, they problematised the Luton Muslim community and 'Community relations' as a whole, and presented Muslim action as either reactionary and ideological, or else as fanatical violence. This may have been a result of the reports being derived from a press release summarising meeting which, judging by the material, was written by the Rank Organisation. Throughout, the actions of the Muslims were referred to as "demands", "violent protest" and "attacks", caused by their "anger and irritation", "ire" and "outrage". Only once were Muslims described as "asking" the Rank Organisation to "consider" the opin-ions of the community. Further, the actual "demands" of the community were systematically under-reported. Only in the *Independent* was it reported that the campaign was directed towards changing the name of a *single* bingo hall *back* to

'Top Rank', the name it had two months previously. *The Times* performs significant linguistic labour to conceal this fact from its report. The headline for example stated that '**Muslims want name change for Mecca bingo**', whilst the opening of the article is completely misleading:

> Muslim community leaders yesterday asked the owners of *a chain* of bingo halls to *change their name* because it was causing offence. The *arrival* of the Mecca bingo hall in Luton, Bedfordshire, has caused anger and irritation among Muslims [emphasis added]

The paragraph above not only suggests that it is the whole organisation which Luton Muslims wanted to change, but also conceals the recent renaming of the bingo hall by describing Mecca 'arriving' in Luton.

Similarly, the *Guardian* stated that the campaign was "against Mecca, the chain of bingo halls". Further, in the final paragraph of the article, the *Guardian* mentioned another, wholly unrelated campaign, organised by a completely different group of Muslims to convince Nike to alter a logo on one their running shoes. The function of this paragraph therefore appears to be: first, that the campaign "against Mecca" should be viewed within the context of a series of Muslim campaigns; and second, that these campaigns are the work of oversensitive Muslims who are objecting either just for the sake of it, or perhaps for political or ideological reasons.

In contrast to the way in which British Muslims were treated, the statements explaining the actions of the Rank Organisation were uncritically accepted, even when patently contradicted by the reported facts of the event. In the report by the *Independent* for example, the journalist paraphrased Rank as saying that "the name change was not insensitive, [but] was part of a policy of bringing their nation-wide chain of bingo halls under one name". What this therefore says, is that all Rank bingo halls across the nation were renamed without considering the areas in which they were located. Their own explanation therefore shows that, at the very least, Rank was inconsiderate, or ignorant of community sensitivities, but this glaring entailment was not pointed out by any of the newspapers. Something which all three newspapers *did* refer to was that the company had been trading since 1884, when "Two enterprising Victorian merchants chose the name Mecca for their new coffee house" (*The Times*). These "enterprising" men, *The Times* continues,

> could not have foreseen the trouble it would cause in the multicultural Britain of the 1990s. More than 100 years after the founding of the Mecca Smoking Café in London, it has fallen foul of Luton's 10,000 Muslims.

The process of division/rejection is apparent throughout *The Times'* article, as illustrated in both the quote above and also by the inclusion of "Mary, 55, who has worked in Bury Park [the area in question] for 20 years":

> "A couple of years ago *they* wanted to rename a street, where *they* had a mosque, Kashmir Street, but *everyone* objected and *we* put a stop to it. I just hope they don't burn it down while I'm in there" she said. [emphasis added]

Here, the source appears to mean 'everyone' in the sense of 'everyone who is allowed to have influence over the national space', since the name change would presumably not have been objected to by the Muslim community who proposed it. It should also be pointed out that "Mary" was the only person quoted throughout the whole of *The Times'* report. Not only does this help structure the readers' understanding of the event being reported, it also suggests that *The Times* felt that her version of the event was the most appropriate one to be reproduced.

Reporting discrimination

The manner in which 'discrimination' stories are reported is particularly interesting, since they could potentially conflict with the predominant approach in press reporting to background 'Our' negative traits. In the sample of newspapers studied, articles covering religious discrimination against British Muslim communities were *wholly* absent. Where examples of discrimination against Muslim minorities were reported, it was the specifically 'racial' element of such abuse which was marked for reference and not the possible 'religious' motivation. This is by no means a peculiarly 'British' phenomenon. A similar pattern was observed in Australia during the 1990–1 Persian Gulf Conflict, when 'widespread' attacks on Australian-Muslims and Arab-Australians, including the vandalisation of Muslim shop windows, the burning of mosques and tearing veils of Muslim women in the street, were consistently represented as racial attacks (see Hage, 1998: 27). The foregrounding of the 'racist' prejudice and discrimination is clearly noticeable in an article headlined **English cricket must bring Asians in from the cold** (*Daily Telegraph*, 4 October 1997). The author, Simon Hughes, clearly sets out his stall in the first paragraph of the article:

> Racial prejudice is still alive and kicking in English cricket. Thousands of man hours have been spent recently devising ways of improving our game, when one potential answer has been largely ignored for years: the proper integration of British-born Asians into the cricketing infrastructure.

The emphasis on "racial prejudice" continues throughout the article, back-grounding the possible explanation of religion in explaining prejudice and/or discrimination. The only references to religiously motivated discrimination come from either a quoted (Muslim) source — Ebad Mirza states "Faith plays a major part in their [Muslim boys'] life, so they have to go to mosque and fit in religious studies around school" — or else are couched in references to the 'religious needs' of these "British-born Asians":

> the culture of the senior game, orientated round the hop, wards off many players whose religion forbids them entering places serving alcohol. Rifts develop, exacer-bated by special Asian food requirements, and many [have] gone off to form their own sides.

Here Hughes suggests: it is the 'culture of the game' which excludes, not intolerance; it is the "special" religious rules and needs of Muslims which are the problem, not the unwillingness of 'Cricket' to accommodate or adapt existing practices; and the 'racial' explanation dominates *despite* citing religious practises as an explanation of the present exclusion of British Muslims.

The theme of 'racism' in sport is also central in an article entitled **Clubs urged to fight anti-Asian bias on the pitch** (*Independent*, 31 October 1997), written by Steve Boggan. The report focuses on a commendable scheme to remove racism from sport, specifically football, and this year was extended to include, as the headline suggests, an attempt to remove "anti-Asian bias". "Asian" is the noun of choice throughout, even though express reference is made to 'Islamophobic' remarks made towards an "Asian player" during a match: "What are you doing down there?" the bigot is reported as saying, "Praying to Allah for a goal?" This remark could, of course, have been moti-vated by 'racial' as opposed to 'religious' bigotry — the intention being to disparage someone of colour. But, for the reporter to have completely ignored the 'Islamophobic' content of the statement is disheartening, particularly since the article was printed only one week after the publication of the Runnymede Trust's research into British 'Islamophobia' (see below).

Racial abuse is not only directed towards 'Asians' in general, but also when attacking Muslims specifically. Referring to research completed with the Mo-roccan community in London, for example, Ghada Karmi stated that the women of the community told her:

> that if they put a scarf on and walked about, they might be set upon. One girl had been set upon by a gang of white youths who were shouting 'Paki, Paki' at this girl, 'Get out, go home Paki'. […]The girl made the point that she had been out in the

> same area without the headscarf on and nothing had ever happened to her, but the
> moment that she put the headscarf on this is what happened. (Karmi, 1999)

In this example, it was only when the girl in question looked like a Muslim that she was abused. When she went out dressed in 'western clothes', or even wore 'ethnic' dress such as her shalwar-kameez, no abuse was experienced. Without further complicating an already tangled maze of representations by the re-introduction of (public and journalistic attitudes to) the *hijab*, it seems apparent from these examples that despite its complex and inter-related nature, journalists present the prejudice and discrimination experienced by British Muslims in a surprisingly straightforward way: this discrimination is *racial* discrimination; those who are subject to such abuse are therefore so abused on the grounds of their *race*; and religion is not used as a category of exclusion or abuse. This contemporary 'anti-racist' attitude, that the religion of those who have suffered abuse has little or no direct relevance to the story, is highly significant. Not only does it impact on the reporting itself, it also contributes to the perception of an 'anti-Muslim bias', or what some have labelled 'Islamophobia', in the press. This problem has been skilfully discussed by Modood (1992) who states that

> The root problem is that contemporary anti-racism defines people in terms of their colour; Muslims — suffering all the problems that anti-racists identify — hardly ever think of themselves in terms of their colour. And so, in terms of their own being, Muslims feel most acutely those problems that the anti-racists are blind to; and respond weakly to those challenges that the antiracists want to meet with the most force. And there is no way out of this impasse if we remain wedded to a concept of racism that sees only colour discrimination as a cause and material deprivation as a result. (Modood, 1992: 272)

The reporting of 'Islamophobia'

The publication of Runnymede Trust's (1997) report, *Islamophobia: a challenge to us all* (22 October 1997) produced a flurry of news-reports, columns, and, in the wake of such press interest, reader's letters, commenting on both the findings and implications of the report. The manner in which the Runnymede Trust's study was actually reported is very interesting, due to the criticism which the survey levelled at both the press and wider 'British society'. Central to the majority of reporting was a rhetorical management of this criticism — an observation also made by Roger Hardy (BBC) whilst discussing the effect which the report has had on press reporting of Islam at a recent conference:

> I detect, not a tremendous mea culpa and breast-beating by editors and publishers
> and entrepreneurs in the media business, but a sense of defensiveness, which is
> something much less but maybe the beginnings of change. (Roger Hardy, 1999)

The reporting of the Runnymede Trust's study was characterised by four
argument management strategies, often occurring in combination in the
news-text:

– *deflecting* Runnymede criticism onto others
– subtle *countering* of criticism
– direct *refutation*
– or, on occasion, *ignoring* criticism altogether.

Two daily newspapers from the sample — the *Financial Times* and *The Times*
— did not report the publication of the survey *at all*, thereby adopting the
fourth of the criticism management strategies mentioned above: ignoring
criticism. Further, only 8 of the 26 articles reporting 'Islamophobia' printed in
the sampled newspapers were written by staff journalists, suggesting a lack of
interest in the Runnymede Trust's publication and the wider issue(s) of
'Islamophobia' on the part of the newspapers. The remaining 18 items were
readers' letters written in response to either the findings of the Runnymede
Trust or the manner in which its findings were reported, contextualised and
discussed — 14 of which were printed in the *Independent*. This response from
'the public' is significant, representing: 45 per cent of the total number of
sampled readers' letters written on domestic issues (n = 40); 20.2 per cent of
readers' letters across the whole sample (n = 89); 6.5 per cent of the whole
domestic stories sample (n = 276). or a massive 21.2 per cent of all domestic
articles printed in the *Independent* over the period in question (n= 66). This
interest was only matched by two other, similarly contentious subjects: 'Muslim schools and schooling' (n=17); and 'the advantages and disadvantages of
bombing Iraq' (n=13).

The findings of the Runnymede Trust were reported on 23 October 1997.
The news reports in the *Guardian* and *Independent* were accompanied on the
same page by other articles which acted to manage the Runnymede report's
criticisms, specifically the criticism of the press, through the way in which they
were contextualised and discussed. The *Guardian* article (**Muslim tykes 'happy
here'**, 23 October, 1998) for example, does not directly refute any of the
findings of the report (presumably the wholehearted denial of prejudice would
be dismissed by its liberal audience) but does display elements of the other
three criticism management strategies mentioned above: ignoring, deflecting

and countering criticism. First, the criticisms of the news media, and newspapers in particular, contained in the Runnymede survey are completely ignored. Second, the decision to describe discrimination as "racial slights" acknowledges the prejudice experienced by British Muslims, but deflects it away from the Runnymede's central concern with religious discrimination, and back towards 'race'. Third, the recommendation made by the Runnymede report for legislation combating religious discrimination, is subtlety countered through the presentation of contradictory evidence. This evidence is made all the more effective since it is drawn from Bradford, where parts of the survey were conducted: "In an area used by the trust as a testbed, pleasure about a wealth of kind words about Islam was tempered by doubts about further anti-discrimination laws. [...] 'It was a big problem in the 1960s and 70s, but is not a priority now'" one Muslim man is quoted as saying. A similar approach was also taken in the *Independent*.

The coverage of the story by the *Daily Telegraph* (**Survey calls for laws to combat 'Islamophobia'**, 23 October 1998) distorts the focus and findings of the survey even further. The first paragraph, for example, states: "Britain will be home to 2 million Muslims within about 20 years — almost double the number today and easily the largest non-Christian community in the country, according to a study published yesterday." The impression that the demographic growth of the British Muslim communities was one of the principal findings of the report continues for almost the whole of the first half of the article. Amongst other "significant findings", the report tells us that the Runnymede Trust has "... *disclosed* [not declared or affirmed] that there were now 613 mosques in Britain, compared to only a handful 30 years ago" (emphasis added), and also that:

> by 2001, there are likely to be 700,000 people of Pakistani background in Britain, two thirds of whom will have been born in the country, stabilising at around 900,000 in 2020.

What all this has to do with either 'Islamophobia' or the Runnymede report, is unclear until the journalist, Philip Johnston, helpfully informs readers that the building of new mosques, caused by the demands of a growth in the Muslim population, is an "area of cultural tension". Therefore, as the Muslim population increases over the next 20 years the "cultural tension" experienced will also increase. What this clearly represents is the journalistic equivalency of the linkage of 'race relations' with 'immigration': that an increase in the visible black and brown populations is likely "to impair the harmony, strength and cohesion of our public and social life and cause discord and unhappiness among all concerned."[2] The idea that the findings of the Runnymede Trust could be so wilfully misrepresented, drawing on standard xenophobic discourses of cultural and demographic 'swamping', is particularly offensive.

The remainder of this section is devoted to the *Independent*, the newspaper in which the majority of the coverage given to the Runnymede report was contained. After the *Independent*'s two initial news reports, Polly Toynbee wrote a column — headlined '**In defence of Islamophobia**' (23 October 1997) — attacking the assumptions and conclusions of the Runnymede report. The column began with Toynbee stating "I am an Islamophobe. [...] I judge Islam not by its words — the teachings of the Koran as interpreted by those Thought-for-a-day moderate Islamic theologians. I judge Islam by the religion's deeds in societies where it dominates. Does that make me a racist?" Toynbee went on to argue that it is not easy to treat Islam (and Muslims) with respect, since they describe "women as of inferior status, placing them one step behind in the divine order of things." The column adopted liberal argumentation — a rights-based discourse with a clear antipathy to religious expression in the public sphere — and applied the stock subjects used by 'liberals' when arguing against Islam: free speech, Rushdie and the *fatwa*; "Racism is the problem, not religion"; women & (in)equality; an alleged lack of Muslims denouncing atrocities in Islamic states; injustices of Saudi law; and a presupposed opposition of Islam and rationality.

Toynbee's column provoked a significant response: 14 letters and a further column were written in its wake, providing either congratulation, counter-argument or, eventually, counter-counter-argument in response to the column. This I have attempted to represent in Table 5.1 below.

In one sense the time and space devoted by the *Independent* to the discussion of the issues raised by the Runnymede Trust could be interpreted as a promising

Table 5.1. Responses to the Toynbee column, printed in *The Independent*

Date	Article	Stance
23 October	Polly Toynbee column: 'In defence of Islamophobia'	**anti**-Runnymede
25 October	Four letters criticising Toynbee	*pro*-Runnymede
	Two letters praising Straw's 'no new discrimination law'	**anti**-Runnymede
	One letter praising Toynbee	**anti**-Runnymede
25 October	Trevor Phillips' column: criticising Toynbee	*pro*-Runnymede
27 October	One letter praising Toynbee	**anti**-Runnymede
	Two letters criticising Toynbee	*pro*-Runnymede
28 October	Two letters criticising Toynbee	*pro*-Runnymede
	Two letters criticising Phillips	**anti**-Runnymede

advance, heralding the start of a new attitude of inclusion. And this could have been possible, were the discussion not based on the familiar, incendiary, reductive, distorted and unrepresentative issues and images around which Islam and Muslims are 'discussed'. In addition to the stereotypical themes mentioned above, Toynbee's more temperate position can be summarised as follows:

> No doubt some of the racism such [Bangladeshi] women suffer does spring from the fact that they are Muslims. But there is no hard evidence that poor, black, non-English speakers of other faiths are treated any better than Muslims. Racism is the problem, not religion.

There are similarities here with the earlier *Daily Telegraph* article reporting the exclusion of British Muslim cricketers: religious discrimination is denied to exist whilst simultaneously citing religious factors — the Bangladeshi women "are Muslims" — as motivating such prejudice and/or discrimination. Significantly Toynbee's argument is contradicted in an article printed only 16 pages earlier in the same newspaper. Here it states that "an individual Muslim is more likely to be the victim of racist violence when he or she is wearing Islamic dress or symbols. This applies to white Muslims [...] as well as to Asians" (**Straw rejects call for law to protect British Muslims**, *Independent*, 23 October 1997).

In addition to propagating inaccuracies and prejudicial representations masquerading as informed 'rationalist' criticism, Toynbee's column also limited the "disagreement space" (van Eemeren & Houtlosser, 1999) of the 'discussion'. This is illustrated in the foci of readers' letters responding to the column:

> Legislation in this and other countries allows educational pluralism which caters for all; it is popular with parents and academically successful. Denying Muslim parents the choice enjoyed by others [...] is unacceptable discrimination. (Ibrahim Hewitt, Development Officer, Association of Muslim Schools of UK and Eire, *Independent*, 25 October 1997)

> Polly Toynbee continues the persistent association of Islam with barbaric justice in referring to Saudi Arabian courts. Many Muslims, too, are horrified that justice in Saudi Arabia works as it does; they are equally horrified that this is described as Islamic. It may be Saudi justice, but it is not Islamic, any more than British justice is Christian. (Alex Hall, Centre for Research in Ethnic Relations, University of Warwick. 27 October 1997)

> Polly Toynbee has profoundly misunderstood the nature of education in her article. Values, religious or philosophical, cannot be separated from education. No school is value free [...] I would reject as strongly 'Rationalism on the rates' as I object to a system that excludes Muslim schools from state funding. (Ruth Chenoweth, Co-ordinator Third Sector Schools Alliance, *Independent*, 27 October)

In most of these responding articles, 'open' views of Islam predominate — an observation we would expect since they are argumentative responses prompted by the 'closed' views in Toynbee's article.[3] It could, therefore be argued that such letters are beneficial to the British Muslim communities, since they are intended as refinements, corrections or direct criticisms of what are considered as unacceptable, inappropriate or false representations of Islam. It is, however, equally easy to imagine that Muslims may "be made uncomfortable by the relentless insistence — even if it is put in the form of a debate — that her or his faith, culture and people are seen as a source of threat" (Said, 1997: xxi). Such a 'debate' informed both Toynbee's column and its argumentative responses, illustrating the extent to which derogatory, generalising and false representations of Islam and Muslims are still being discussed within the context of 'whether they are true or not'.

Muslim Terrorism: The atrocity at Luxor

The topic of terrorism is a perpetual feature of press representation and discussion about Islam and Muslims. Following the pattern of domestic reporting of Islam observed elsewhere (Poole, 1999, 2000), domestic stories about 'Muslim terrorism' "usually occur following an international event which provokes press speculation on the Islamic fundamentalist presence in the UK" (Poole, 2000: 5). The murder of 60 tourists at the Egyptian resort of Luxor (19 November 1997) provided a context for such reporting.

As Table 5.2 reveals, 'terrorist/ism and acts of terrorism' were mentioned in 15.9 per cent (n= 44) of the 276 articles in the domestic sample, rising to 23.4

Table 5.2. The 'Islamic-ness' of reported domestic negative actions

		Is Islam cited as a factor?				Total	
		Yes		No			
		Count	Col %	Count	Col %	Count	Col %
Fundamentalist/ism	Yes	43	27.9%	1	8%	44	15.9%
included?	No	111	72.1%	121	99.2%	232	84.1%
Liberal/ism	Yes	15	9.7%	3	2.5%	18	6.5%
included?	No	139	90.3%	119	97.5%	258	93.5%
Terroris/ism	Yes	36	23.4%	8	6.6%	44	15.9%
included?	No	118	76.6%	114	93.4%	232	84.1%
Ambassador/ial	Yes	4	2.6%	4	3.3%	8	2.9%
included?	No	150	97.4%	118	96.7%	268	97.1%

per cent of articles in which Islam was cited as an influential factor (n= 36). These findings point to a relationship between the reporting of 'Terrorism' and 'Islam' in the broadsheet press — a relationship which was found to be highly statistically significant (p< 0.000 across all chi-square tests) — but does not explain who the 'terrorists' were or the form which the 'terrorism' assumed. For this, a more detailed analysis is needed.

The massacre of tourists at the Egyptian resort of Luxor was a big story, producing 102 articles (4.0% of all articles); of these, 27 were located in a British (domestic) setting. Reporting developed from the initial reports of the event, through the effects of the event to both the UK and to a lesser extent Egypt, and onto the event consequences, including the post-Luxor accusations of President Mubarek regarding the 'haven' which the UK represents to anti-Egyptian/ Islamist terrorists. 15,670 centimetres of news reports were published on the subject of 'terrorism and Egypt' over the seven days which immediately followed the attack, representing 45.95 per cent of the total column centimetres reported about Egypt (34,105 cm). Thus, the way in which the events were tied to Britain and British people, and in particular the implications for British Islam and Muslims living in the UK was very interesting, providing insights into press conceptions of 'who and what *We* are', and 'who and what *They* are'.

Across the 27 articles, 99 actors were recorded as appearing as primary (n=27), secondary (n=27), tertiary (n=25) or quaternary (n=20) sources. Of these, 23 (23.2%) were referred to as being Muslims — less than the proportion for the domestic sample as a whole (n=269, 31.5%). Of these 23 Muslim actors, only 2 were not either terrorists, terrorist groups or members of illegal opposition groups. These two actors were a generic 'Islamic Pressure Group based in London' and generic 'Middle Eastern and South East Asian students', neither of whom were quoted. This shows the extent to which the millions of 'non-terrorist Muslims' were excluded from having their criticisms of the atrocity, and their disgust at its perpetrators, heard.

The representation of Islam in the articles was overwhelmingly negative: the 8 representations of Islam said by the Runnymede Trust to characterise an 'open' representation of Islam were *completely* absent from reporting. The reports predominantly argued that 'Islam vs. the West' is a 'natural' state of affairs (85.2%); Islam is 'separate' (70.4%); 'inferior' (88.9%); and an 'enemy' (88.9%). 'Fundamentalism' was mentioned in 77.8% of these domestic articles, illustrating very clearly the frame in which the story was reported. By contrast, 'liberal/moderate' were mentioned in 7.4% of articles, and seemed to appear in order to further hammer home the unjustified nature of the attacks, since the terms were used to describe "President Mubarek's moderate regime" (*The Times*, 18 November, 1997).

There were three themes around which the Luxor atrocity was reported: *tourism; security issues;* and *the human costs* of the atrocity, presented in a human interest format. These were the *only* themes used in the domestic reporting of the Luxor atrocity, with 'security' occurring over four times more regularly than either of the other two themes. This security agenda was essentially focused on the 'threat' which 'Islamic terrorists' represented to both Egyptian and British societies, and how this threat could be minimised. The lead editorial of *The Daily Telegraph* (**Islam's fifth column**, 19 November 1997) for example, contained remarkable arguments concerning the activities of Muslims in the UK — considered threatening by their very presence. The essential "problem" identified by the newspaper was "immigration", specifically the way in which "the United Kingdom has, in recent years, become a safe haven for a diverse array of extremist groups" whose "quarrels often spill over with lethal effect on to our soil, as exemplified by the assassinations of dissident elements here in London." The textual ambivalence of this passage acts to conceal the agency of the actions described, contributing to the generally threatening tone of 'the Muslims' identified in the editorial. These villains have found their way here, the paper claims, because of "our highly liberal asylum laws". "The truth is", the editorial continues rhetorically, "that there are too many people resident in this country today who use British liberty in order to take liberties." Among these villains are the aforementioned generic "Middle Eastern and Far East Asian students". These miscreants, the editorial argues, are here because of the "indiscriminate recruitment" of British Universities. This recruitment policy has brought "in its wake a small contingent of subversives" "from countries with terrorist regimes, who specialise in such disciplines as nuclear physics — no prizes for guessing what they're up to." Throughout terms such as "Islam", "the Muslim world", "terrorism", "terrorist regimes", "perilous activities", "threat" and others, are woven together into a prejudicial argument in which Muslims are homogenised and vilified (under both broad and specific negative accusations) in order to facilitate the success of the editorial's principal argument — 'We should keep Them out'.

The Security agenda gained in momentum with the introduction of the British government in the debate — as reported in articles such as '**Commons pledges to resist terrorism**' (*The Times* 19 November 1997), '**Anti-terror bill sparks fears of witch-hunt**' (*Guardian* 20 November 1997) and '**New law to combat foreign terrorists in Britain**' (*The Times* 20 November

1997). The involvement of the British government started with "Ministers and MPs speaking in the House of Commons, express[ing] their sympathies and condolences to the families bereaved by the Luxor massacre" (*The Times*, 19 November 1997), but by the next day had developed into proposed legislation directed at "Foreigners living in Britain who plot terrorist attacks abroad" (*The Times*, 20 November 1997). In the second paragraph of this article, the Home Secretary Jack Straw was paraphrased as saying "The new legislation will end Britain's reputation as a haven for Middle Eastern and other international terrorists", creating a new offence of conspiring "to commit violent outrages abroad" and possibly "making it illegal to raise funds in Britain for terrorist organisations abroad".[4]

The criticism that these proposals were met with received only intermittent and backgrounded coverage. *The Times*, for example, quoted the director of Liberty, Mr John Wadham, as saying we need "to take a careful look at how we can uphold Britain's place as a safe haven for the persecuted of the world [...] Locking up dissidents is not the solution" (*The Times*, 20 November 1997). The *Guardian* on the other hand stated that "Muslim charities and groups, in particular [...] fear the Government's proposal could lead to a witchhunt" (*Guardian*, 20 November 1997) and in doing so unfortunately implied that "Muslim charities and groups" fear the proposals because of what they *do* rather than because of what the Government *think* they do. A few days later, following another accusation from President Mubarek that Britain was harbouring terrorists, Jack Straw pushed the envelope further by saying:

> There is a very serious problem of people from abroad, *particularly from the Middle East*, seeking to use this country as a base, on the whole not for organising terrorism abroad, but for financing it or for seeking support for it. (*The Times*, 24 November 1997; emphasis added)

The headline of another report, '**London is not terror haven, say Ministers**', (*The Times*, 24 November 1997) paraphrased the Government as saying they "unreservedly condemned terrorism and took the threat from Muslim radicals very seriously". In a startling example of over-lexicalisation (Fowler *et al.*, 1979), these "Muslim radicals" are also described in the text as "Islamic extremists", "militant Islamists", "Islamic radical exiles", "Islamic exiles", "terrorists", groups involved in "Islamic terrorism" and even "Islamic asylum seekers". From this, it appears that the reporter, Michael Binyon, thinks the terms referred to above can be used interchangeably. Therefore, "Islamic terrorists" are "Islamic militants" are "Islamic radical exiles" are "Islamic asylum seekers", who "promote action against friendly governments" and "seek support from British Muslims". The promotion of such an interpretation is therefore particularly dangerous for the well-being of not only Muslims, but also non-Muslim asylum seekers living in the UK who are similarly tarred with the terrorist brush.

As before, *The Daily Telegraph* adopted a particularly vitriolic line towards the alleged 'terrorist threat' and the activities of radical Islamic groups in the UK. One headline, '**Leaders try to curb deadly threat from the world's Islamic fanatics**' — it's letters standing 2 centimetres high, printed across the top of two pages — presents *The Daily Telegraph* reading of events quite well. In the largest of four articles collected underneath, '**Law allows dissidents to plot from British bases**', Phillip Johnston places the presupposed "deadly threat" posed by Muslims firmly in a domestic context (*Daily Telegraph*, 20 November 1997). Muslims are presented not only as a threat to the countries which they are "campaigning to destabilise", but their activities also threaten to "spill onto the streets of London". His argument is achieved via a four part structure, illustrated in Table 5.3.

Table 5.3. Dichotomised representation of social actors and agendas

Sympathetic presentation	Unsympathetic presentation
Sources Jack Straw; Mr Straw (x4); Home Office (x3); Security authorities; MI5; Special Branch; British authorities; British citizens; Salman Rushdie; Algerian and French governments; French Security Chiefs; Israeli Security Chiefs.	*Sources* Kalim Siddiqui, 'who supported the fatwa'; Sheikh Omar Abdel-Rahman; 'the Blind Sheikh' (x2); Omar Bakri Mohammed (x5); Mohammed al-Massari (x3); terror organisations (x3); terror groups (x2); Islamic groups (x2); Islamic extremists; Islamic fundamentalists; overseas fundamentalists; militants; militant organisations; militant Islamic organisations; extreme British Muslim organisation; dissidents (x2); Hamas (x4); Hizbollah; Algerian GIA; Algeria's FIS; Gama'a al Islamia (Islamic Group); al-Muhajiroun (x3); Islamic Observation Centre; Hizb ut-Tahrir; Arab newspapers; Hamas' monthly magazine Filistine al-Muslima (Islamic Palestine)
Quoted sources Lord Lloyd of Berwick (42 words); Mr Straw (18 words); David Pryce-Jones, 'an authority on Muslim-Arab society' (64 words)	*Quoted sources* John Wadham, Liberty (33 words) Omar Bakri Mohammed (14 words)
Politics/Ideology democracy (x2); liberal democracy; free society	*Politics/Ideology* Muslim regime; Islamic militancy; khilafah — an Islamic state
'Place as subject' Britain (x4); London (x2); Western society (x2)	*'Place as subject'* the Islamic world; Muslim-Arab society; 'their homelands'; 'their own tyrannical country'

This four part structure fits with what Blommaert and Verschueren (1998) have called a 'management paradigm'. Accordingly, these Muslims

> do not only symbolise the intra-European enemy. They *are* the enemy. They seem to have penetrated in our midst, abusing our openness. They seem to form a threat to our society which risks destruction as a result of its own tolerance (Blommaert & Verschueren, 1998: 21)

First the 'threat' of Islam and Muslims is symbolically represented through the seemingly endless list of 'shadowy figures' and groups bent on "the overthrow of Western society". All cited Muslims are labelled with negative descriptive terms and, with the exception of Kalim Siddiqui, are labelled as being either foreign organisations or immigrants. Occasionally, it is only the perceived 'foreign-ness' — or more specifically, 'Middle Eastern-ness' — of these actors which marks them out as threatening. Johnston claims for example that "More Arab newspapers are published in London than anywhere else in the world", implying, through its very inclusion in an article about terrorism, that "Arab newspapers" — or perhaps Arabs in general — are involved in terrorist activities. These 'Muslim' actors are contrasted in the article with a set of almost universally 'official' actors, suggesting an authority and a legitimacy which the unsympathetic actors lack. The only two sympathetic non-official actors are, "British citizens" who "fall victim to terrorism abroad", and Salman Rushdie, himself the victim of a "death sentence" "supported" by some of those on the other side of the table. The extent to which negative action is dichotomised in this article, is therefore quite astonishing.

Second, the sources presented by Johnston in a sympathetic light are disproportionately quoted, weighting the article towards the individuals and groups offering critiques of these "Islamic groups". David Pryce-Jones for example, is first given complimentary introduction as "an authority of Muslim-Arab society", and is then quoted as saying:

> They [Muslims?..] show great sophistication in knowing how a Western society operates and *what its weaknesses* are. They can *exploit* the legal system, the human rights and asylum laws and other elements of a democracy *to which they don't themselves subscribe*. (emphasis added)

As usual, Mr Pryce-Jones' words betray his underlying anti-Muslim beliefs. 'Our' presupposed tolerance on the other hand is represented, as Blommaert and Vershueren (1998) suggested above, as a threat to our own society. In contrast to the sympathetic presentation of Pryce-Jones, John Wadham's opinion that "Locking up dissidents is not the solution", identical to the quote in the earlier article printed in *The Times* (20 November 1997), is held up as ridiculous. This again illustrates the functional way in which sources are often used by journalists in order to construct their own (prejudicial) arguments.

Third, through the negativisation of both actions and politics, the 'threat' of the "militant Islamic organisations" is foregrounded to the detriment of more positive work that some of them do in and for the communities in which they are based. The opinion of Johnston on this matter is made clear in Table 5.3 above, by the dichotomies he sets up between "democracy" and "Muslim regime", between "liberal democracy" and "Islamic militancy", and most tellingly between "free society" and "Islamic state". Here we see the constructive negativisation of Islam in action, whereby the previously fluid term of "Islamic state" is presented in opposition to "free society" without any further support.

Fourth, in case the reader has not received the message, the "tyrannical countries" of "the Islamic world" are referred to, seemingly as examples of places in which such "Islamic militancy" apparently has a more established hold than the sympathetically represented "British" and "Western society". The "free society" which 'We' enjoy is still represented as threatened however, since, as the concluding paragraph suggests, "there is concern that Britain could be increasingly vulnerable to international terrorism unless additional powers of the sort proposed by Mr Straw are forthcoming."

The extent to which the news agenda of the "deadly threat" of Muslims in Britain developed in the domestic sample, is illustrated in the presence of a 'benefit scrounger' story as a spin-off of the Luxor atrocity. The story was alluded to in *The Daily Telegraph* article analysed above, where the leader of al-Muhajiroun, Omar Bakri Mohammed, is referred to as having "five children and claims income support and disability benefit" despite being "dedicated to the overthrow of Western society". The schematic story received a full hearing in the *Sunday Times* (23 November 1997), in an article headlined '**Convicted Egyptian 'terrorists' living on benefits in Britain**'. This article reports "Three men sentenced to death for terrorist offences in Egypt [who] have been allowed to live in Britain where at least one of them has claimed thousands of pounds in social security benefits". The article goes on to develop tenuous links between the three men and "Muslim terror organisations" (both Egyptian and not) based on these convictions, despite protestations from one of the men that "The charges against me are based on testimony given under torture" and the journalists' own admission that the system of justice operating in Egyptian military courts has "been strongly criticised by international human rights organisations". At about two thirds of the way through article, the journalists seem to play a 'fanatical Muslim association' game, citing individuals and groups — Abu Hamza and the Finsbury Park Mosque, the Algerian *GIA*, the *al-Ansar* (Victory) newsletter — only tangentially related to the subject at hand. This builds a similar picture as *The Daily Telegraph* article above: an "underworld" of "Islamic extremists in Britain", whom Scotland Yard's terrorist branch are already having to arrest, seizing their "chemicals for making bombs". The message of the article is clear: 'Us against Them', 'They are terrorists', 'They are already here', and 'We are supporting Them through Social Security benefits'. It is hard to imagine a more negative representation of British Muslims.

Muslim schooling and Muslim pupils

The theme of Muslim pupils and schooling was an almost constant agenda running throughout the sample: 54 articles were recorded within the parent topic of 'Education' across the four month sample period. Within this parent topic, the topics of 'Religion in Education' and 'Funding religious schools' received the most coverage, being coded as either primary or secondary topics in 35 and 13 articles respectively. These articles reported the campaign for denominational Muslim schools, and the response to such a campaign from Government, journalists and members of the public. The story took a dramatic turn when voluntary aided status was granted to two Muslim schools on 9 January 1998, signally the end (or just the beginning?) of a long fought campaign for such recognition, and producing a flurry of articles on the subject in broadsheet newspapers. Education, and the schooling of younger children in particular, challenge the traditional separation of 'public' and 'private' spheres, since, in its role in the transmission of culture and social values, education necessarily spans the divide between the two. This creates a distinctive problem for British multiculturalism, traditionally founded on a philosophy of 'public assimilation/ private dissociation', especially when appeals to cultural freedom or even cultural relativism are made along religious lines. Argumentative distinctions exist between the themes of the reports printed before 9 January 1997, when voluntary aided status was granted, and those printed after. The analysis is therefore split into two sections in order to reflect and capture this editorial dimension.

'The Debate': For and against state funding for Muslim schools

The majority of items published on Muslim schooling before 9 January 1998 occurred as part of the 'Islamophobia' reporting agenda previously discussed. Accordingly, most of the articles printed were letters to the editor, and printed in the *Independent* in response to Polly Toynbee's column. The two principal recommendations of The Runnymede Trust's report — the funding of Muslim schools and new legislation outlawing religious discrimination — were often cited together in these articles, in order to argue that the broader theme of 'multiculturalism' was either a positive or negative philosophy in and for Britain. In these articles, 'multiculturalism' was used as a short-hand for the greater visibility, and perceived greater influence, of 'non-British' values and beliefs in and upon the British 'public sphere'. In addition, these articles presupposed: in its 'natural state', Britain and the British public sphere are 'white' and 'Christian'; the values and practices of 'ethnic minorities' should be studied and vetted, and only the 'acceptable' ones admitted into this public sphere. It was against this frame that the debate on Muslim schools and schooling occurred. Essentially, reporters and other correspondents asked: 'Do we (the white élite) consider Muslim schools to be an acceptable approach to education, here in Britain?'

The debate on denominational Muslim schooling is complex, with arguments for and against such schools drawing on a variety of discourses, for example: rights, both legal and moral; citizenship and inclusion; pedagogy; and the perceived 'effects' of Muslim schools on society (usually in the form of 'race relations'). The reporting of British Muslim schooling before the 9 January 1997 was almost wholly structured around such 'for' and 'against' argumentation, often locating arguments at the level of principle as opposed to policy. Looking first towards the readers' letters written on this subject, the main argument employed by those who disagree with denominational Muslim schools was that separate Muslim schools would be socially and racially divisive. Of course, simply citing 'divisions' only succeeds as an argument against Muslim schools when such 'divisions' are thought of as being negative *per se*. The exact nature of this negativity differs according to the (political) assumptions and commitments of the arguments' protagonists. For some, the 'divisions' approximated a religious or ethnic apartheid and hence ran counter to their multicultural principles:

> [...] the segregation of Muslim children would only reinforce the marginalisation which the Runnymede Trust rightly condemns. The provision of good secular

schools in which all children are educated together would surely be the best way to prevent so-called Islamophobia. (Nicholas Walter, Rationalist Press Association. *Guardian*, 24 October 1997)

[...] a largely integrated education system has been of immeasurable benefit to us all. If you don't believe this, witness [...] the hermetically-sealed Orthodox Jewish community in Stamford Hill (where I live) where there is no social interaction between children or adults of that community with anyone outside their own faith. The Government must do whatever it takes to avoid funding more religious schools. [...] Nothing less than the social fabric of our society is at stake. (Sabrina Aaronovitch, *Independent*, 28 October 1997)

In letters of this sort, the effects of separating Muslim pupils into denominational schools were extended beyond the education system, with protagonists arguing that they would be 'isolated', 'segregated' and 'marginalised' from society (read: 'white people') in general. This argumentative approach was based on two presuppositions: first, the (lack of) interaction between Muslim and non-Muslim in society, whereby schools were thought to provide the last (or for some protagonists the *only*) situation for social interaction between different social classes, faiths and communities. Second, these letters often presupposed that the standard of teaching in Muslim schools was lower than in secular schools, and therefore the attending Muslim children would be socially disadvantaged and marginalised through receiving a poor education.

For a select few, the divisions 'caused' by separate Muslim schools were said to create possible 'breeding grounds for Islamic fundamentalism', isolated from the usual 'checks and balances' of the mainstream culture. More usually, the divisions 'caused' by separate Muslim schools were thought to threaten (the related issues of) 'Muslim integration', Muslim acceptance of 'British values' and perhaps British values and identity themselves. These threatened 'effects' were additionally thought to encourage, or possibly *result*, in future violence between Muslim and non-Muslim communities:

Having seen the way that sectarian education has reinforced intercommunal violence in Northern Ireland, he [Jack Straw] should be looking at ways to reduce support for Christian schools rather than widening the scope of subsidised religious denominational indoctrination (Eric Thompson, *Independent* 25 October 1997)

[Criticising Muslim schools...] is not 'Islamophobia', but a reasonable and realistic opposition to the official encouragement of any kind of religious or non-religious divisions in an already dangerously divided society. (Nicolas Walter, Rationalist Press Association, *Independent* 28 October 1997)

Interestingly, the letters which took the firmest argumentative line against the supposedly 'divisive' nature of Muslim schools, also tended to congratulate

Jack Straw for "resisting demands to introduce legislation to protect Muslims from religious discrimination" (Eric Thompson, above). The strength of Eric Thompson's objection to Muslims schools is illustrated in the prejudicial language with which he describes religious schools: "subsidised religious denominational indoctrination" (Ibid.). Further, his linkage of the schooling issue with the demands for extending anti-discrimination laws is instructive, since both his positions are essentially based on denying British Muslims the advantages of civil society enjoyed by just about everybody else.

Similarly, Nicolas Walter elsewhere in his letter states that "liberals have the right to criticise objectionable aspects of religious or non-religious systems of belief and behaviour". The 'White fantasy' (Hage, 1998) of this "reasonable" man, regarding 'his' assumed "right" to manage the national space, is exposed by the presuppositions contained in his argument: He implicitly excludes Muslims from the position "liberal", and hence from having "the right" to be included and heard in debate, since criticising "objectionable aspects of non-religious systems of belief and behaviour" was exactly what Muslims were doing in the campaign for denominational schools. His point is, essentially, that such requests should be ignored.

News articles arguing against separate Muslim schooling employed very similar argumentation to the above readers' letters. '**Farrakhan opens UK blacks-only schools**' (*Independent on Sunday*, 19 October 1997) for example, drew upon the spectre of 'racial divisions', when it warned in its overheadline that "The separatist ideas of the controversial Nation of Islam are taking hold in Britain". The article made it clear that these schools not only separated children along religious and racial grounds, but are 'run by' Louis Farrakhan, who "has been accused of anti-Semitism and homophobia". The fact that supporters/members of the Nation of Islam form a extremely small minority, and are in no way representative, of Britain's Muslim communities, is a piece of background information which this article desperately needed to even approximate the appearance of unbiased reporting. A feature headlined '**How will they know who they are?**' (*Daily Telegraph*, 12 December 1997) presented a more complex argument against Muslim schools. The aim of multiculturalism — "to make children from other backgrounds feel at home because their culture is valued and celebrated" — is described as "praiseworthy" and yet also threatening and dangerous, since it is having negative effects upon "our own national identity and culture". Terms such as "multicultural swamp", "contested battleground", "disintegration", "the *decay* of our national culture", "the *advance* of multiculturalism" and Tebbit's own description of multiculturalism as "a divisive force" illustrate the arguments which the journalist, Graham Turner was presenting. Chris Woodhead, the then Chief Inspector of schools, is paraphrased as saying "there is a real *danger* that *bending over backwards* to pay attention to minority cultures is bound to have a negative effect on white children" (emphasis added). Finally, Turner explicitly argues that British schools should be Christian — "our national religion" — and that Muslim children should 'integrate'. This is evidenced by the praise he lays upon "John Cullis, head of Barclay Junior", who states (using a form of the racist semantic manoeuvre 'transfer') "I'm trying to Westernise them [Muslim and Hindu pupils] and unashamedly so […] because if we don't, they are not going to compete in the world".

The campaign *for* separate Muslim schools on the other hand, is based on the deceptively simple idea that the ideal environment for the development of Muslim youth is within a Muslim school system. This is in turn based on a critique of the present system, and specifically the monocultural and secular biases perceived to permeate modern schooling:

> […] to try to promote multiculturalism after disassociating all faiths from those cultures will not be accepted by Muslims […] Muslims do not expect the curriculum in state schools to be Islamic. What they do expect, however, is that the multicultural, multifaith character of Britain will be reflected in the curriculum and in the school ethos. (Mabud, (1992: 91), cited in Parker-Jenkins, 1995: 54).

With the present curriculum lacking such a focus on faith, schools are increasingly viewed by Muslims "as institutions intent on providing only a secular interpretation of reality …[and therefore] in conflict with the overall aim of raising children within a religious context" (Parker-Jenkins, 1995: 40). The themes of 'Muslim values', the cultural and/or religious needs of Muslim pupils and the wishes of Muslim parents, appeared frequently in readers' letters arguing 'for' Muslim schools, particularly the letters written in response to the negative argumentation of Polly Toynbee's column:

> […] divisions need not be damaging. They can celebrate the diversity of culture within multi-cultural societies. To force all children into secular schools against the wishes of their parents denies multi-culturalism and places Ms Toynbee alongside the Tebbits of the world. (Ibrahim Hewitt, Development Officer, Association of Muslim Schools of UK and Eire, *Independent*, 25 October 1997)
> [Re GCSE Islamic Studies] As part of their syllabus, the girls are taught to question the assumptions of their religion and to consider the rights and wrongs of other alternative points of view. […] They are not cut off from mainstream culture. (Samiya Mann, Zakaria Muslim Girls High School, *Independent*, 28 October 1997)

The fluidity of meaning connoted by societal divisions is clearly articulated in the letter written by Ibrahim Hewitt: "divisions need not be damaging", he argues. Hewitt follows this by making an argument which draws upon a rights-based discourse, previously used by Toynbee and no doubt immediately recognisable to the left-liberal audience of the *Independent*. By contrast, Samiya Mann argues *against* the idea that Muslim schools are culturally divisive, suggesting that the Muslim pupils in her own class are taught to assess critically "the rights and wrongs" of their own and others' religion and, besides which, are "not cut off from mainstream culture".

Following the Education Act (1944), the law does not pose any impediment to the granting of voluntary aided status to properly staffed and maintained Muslim private schools, since religious affiliation (of the school applying for funding) was not mentioned in the relevant section of the Act (ch.31). There is therefore an additional argument for equality before the law, whereby independent Muslim schools, of which there were 25 in 1993, should be accorded similar recognition as (for example) the 21 Jewish institutions which were receiving government funding at that time (Parker-Jenkins, 1995: 12).

> To deny parents in a pluralistic society an input into their children's religious and moral education, and to argue for the imposition by the state of one ideology over others, is the exact same approach which Polly Toynbee finds unacceptable in certain Islamic states. (Rev. Peter Trow, *Independent* 28 October 1997)
>
> Legislation in this and other countries allows educational pluralism which caters for all; it is popular with parents and academically successful. Denying Muslim parents the choice enjoyed by others […] is unacceptable discrimination (Ibrahim Hewitt, Development Officer, Association of Muslim Schools of UK and Eire, *Independent*, 25 October 1997)

Arguments for equality, such as those above, appear powerful, perhaps particularly to the readers of the *Independent*. By arguing that the 'right' to a "religious and moral education" (the two terms rhetorically tied together by Rev. Trow) is being denied to Muslim children, suggests double standards, which could in turn be interpreted as "discrimination" (as by Hewitt). Rev. Trow goes a stage further than arguing for 'equality' by drawing an analogy between Toynbee's scorn at "the same approach" in "certain Islamic states". In this way, he manages to accuse Toynbee of acting hypocritically at the same time as providing argumentative support for Muslim schools — an argumentative 'double-whammy'.

'The Reaction': For and against the state funding of Muslim schools

20 articles were written on Muslim schooling between 9 January 1998, when David Blunkett, the then Education and Employment Secretary approved grant-maintained status (later changed to 'voluntary aided' status, with a change of law) to two Muslim schools, and the end of the sample (31 January 1998). 10 of these articles were printed on 10 January, with all five daily broadsheet newspapers reporting the story, although with differing prominence and differing slightly in their use of information and argument. The *Financial Times* reported the story in a small article (72 centimetres) headlined '**Blunkett offers state funding**' (10 January, 1997), tucked away in their 'UK News Digest' column. Interestingly, the first line of the article stated that Blunkett's decision "reversed the government's traditional *policy* of *denying* them [Muslims] equal status with Anglican, Roman Catholic and Jewish schools" (emphasis added) — a claim which was absent or significantly mitigated in the remaining newspapers' reports. This news report was also the *only* article printed following the approval of funding, which did not refer to Yusuf Islam or his two previous incarnations, 'Cat Stevens' and 'Steven Georgiou'.

The *Independent* gave the story more prominence than the *Financial Times*, placing a large colour photograph flagging the story on the front page[5] and choosing to report it across a news item and a column. The news report (**Muslim schools win historic fight for state funding**, 10 January 1998) framed the funding of Muslim schools as an issue of religious and (seemingly) racial equality, made all the more pressing due to the low financial resources of many Muslim parents. The first paragraph read: "For years, Muslims have complained that white middle class parents could send their children to religious schools free while Muslim, often working class [and non-white?] parents had to pay". In addition, the equality of male and female Muslim pupils in these schools is earmarked as important enough to be mentioned three times — most significantly in Blunkett's reassurances "that these new schools will comply with the statutory provisions governing all maintained schools, such as delivering the national curriculum and offering *equal access* to the curriculum *for boys and girls*" (emphasis added). The foregrounding of equality in the *Independent* — both that Muslims should be treated equally and that, 'contrary to what you may think', these Muslim schools *will* treat female pupils equally — suggests a desire to convince its readership that the decision to fund Muslim schools was the correct one to make. This support was not received well by members of the newspaper's readership however, for example:

> It may sound reasonable for Muslims to want to maintain their culture and religious differences just as xenophobic whites do [...] It does not however help the integration of communities that is essential if we are to reduce future trouble. We should have no state funded schools based on religion. (M. Jones, *Independent*, 13 January 1998)

Here the issue of Muslim schooling is linked with under-defined "future trouble". By equating "Muslims" with "xenophobic whites" in the first line of the excerpt, the author is suggesting either: Muslims are *per se* "xenophobic" and as such nominal determiners ('xenophobic Muslims') can be dispensed with; or alternatively, the desire of Muslims to "maintain their culture and religious differences" is comparable, in degree or kind, to the corresponding desire of "xenophobic whites". To suggest that the desire of British Muslims to retain their 'Islamic-ness' is "reasonable" on the basis of this analogy suggests that the argument was chosen "not by selection of premises the [left-liberal] audience is likely to accept, but by selection of premises the audience is almost sure to reject" (van Eemeren et al., 1997: 226). This is shown in the second line of the excerpt where, in conclusion, the author associates British Muslims' abandonment of cultural and religious differences with "integration", whilst their sustaining or affirming of differences (cultural and religious pluralism by any other name) in Muslim schools is associated with "future trouble".

The manner in which *The Daily Telegraph* reported the story also appeared to depart from the paper's usually fierce position of 'integration'. The story was reported across three articles—a frontpage news report headlined '**Muslim schools gain state cash**' (the only newspaper to foreground the story in such a way) which provided the details and reactions to the decision, and two news-features which followed on page 8. In the first of these news-features ('**Jewish example helped solve dilemma**'), John Clare, *The Daily Telegraph*'s Education Editor, appears quite critical of the successive decisions to deny funding to Muslim schools, even asking "why denial should even have been considered." Underlying these rejections, Clare suggests, "was a prevalent view that immigrants should adjust to the British way of life rather than vice versa and that, in particular, the children of Asian immigrants should be educated alongside their white peers". In a newspaper as generally disdainful of multiculturalism as *The Daily Telegraph*, it is entirely possible that its readership would agree with such discrimination against Muslims and the reasons given in its justification (indeed an article written by Graham Turner, discussed above, makes such an argument). However, John Clare seems to have included such information in order to expose the injustice of the repeated rejections and the arrogance of demanding capitulative 'integration' rather than suggesting that the previous policy was valid.[6]

Yusuf Islam formed the centre of much of the reporting of Muslim schooling, with the manner in which he was treated almost directly analogous to the newspapers' coverage of the story: the *Financial Times* did not mention him; the *Guardian* appear confused, with commentary shifting between describing the school which he ran as operating "a strict Islamic code", explaining that Islam was "in Sarajevo accepting a peace prize" and humourous gibes regarding his former career[7]; and *The Daily Telegraph* centralised Islam, quoting him in the second paragraph of their (frontpage) news report. Interestingly, what appears to be the same quote from Yusuf Islam was used in a slightly different form in the report printed in *The Times* (**Muslims win right to their own state-funded schools**, 10 January 1998) — a form which reframed the content and implications of Islam's response in a subtle but threatening way. The quotes are compared in Table 5.4 below, and are analysed in accordance with the following rules of transcription:

- standard text: identical text in both articles
- *italic* text: lexical, syntactic or stylistic differences
- **bold** text: textual elements not present in the opposite text

Table 5.4. The comparative use of a quotation from Yusuf Islam

Daily Telegraph	The Times
We must realise that it only **affects** two Muslim schools in an ocean of thousands of Christian **and tens of thousands of secular** schools. So *the decision does not* change the world, **but it is certainly an historic one.**	It *is* only two Muslim schools in an ocean of thousands of Christian schools, so *it isn't going to* change the world, **but it will give a great hope to others.**

In both quotes it is the *symbolic* nature of the funding which is picked up on — 'two schools in an ocean of others doesn't change the world' — but the implications of the quotes are quite different. In *The Daily Telegraph*, despite the decision 'not changing the world', it is nonetheless "an historic one", and as such is important *in itself*. In *The Times* however, although the decision "isn't going to change the world", "it will give a *great hope to others*". Here, the journalist uses an elliptical sentence, eliding both who the "others" being referred to are and what these "others" hope *to do*. However, in the preceding paragraph of *The Times*' report, Zahar Ashraf (the parents' spokesman) is quoted as saying "Now that they know they will receive fair and equal treatment, *other Muslim schools should follow*" (emphasis added). This suggests that *The Times* thought the decision would "give a great hope [of funding] to others [other Muslim schools]", thereby shifting the meaning of the quote substantially. Further, *The Times* is not at all comfortable with the possibility that more Muslim schools will receive state-funding, as illustrated by the paragraph which immediately followed the quote from Yusuf Islam:

> The Rev. David Streater, secretary of the Church Society, said that the decision could have *serious consequences*. "Islam is not a quiescent faith — it is probably more evangelistic than Christianity itself — and this will be seen as *just a foot in the door*. We may be in an increasingly secular society, but this is still a generally Christian country and *we have to defend that*." [emphases added]

Here, state-funding for two Muslim schools, and the possibility that such schools will increase in the future, is represented as having possibly "serious consequences" to the 'Christian-ness' of 'Our' country — a 'Christian-ness' which "we have to defend". This threat, specifically to Christianity, is also flagged in *The Times'* removal of the reference to "tens of thousands of *secular* schools" (present in *The Daily Telegraph's* report) from the quote from Yusuf Islam. From this evidence, it appears that *The Times* manipulated and distorted the quote from Yusuf Islam in order to make him 'suggest' that these two schools were only the first of many which would be campaigning for state-funding (whether or not the quote from Zahar Ashraf was similarly altered is unclear due to the lack of a comparative quote). *The Times* then imbued the possibility that more Muslim schools will become state-funded with threat, specifically a threat to 'Our' Christian country posed by an "evangelistic" Islam with "a foot in the ['Our'] door". The source making such a claim — the Rev. David Streater — is not criticised or contested, illustrating the ascent given to his opinion by *The Times*. In contrast, *The Daily Telegraph* quote makes no such implication, with Yusuf Islam solely acknowledging the symbolic and historic nature of the decision.

'Positive' stories

There *were* domestic articles in which the bifurcation of 'Islam' and/vs. 'the West' is either not immediately apparent, or in which the dominant negative representation(s) of Islam and Muslims are backgrounded or wholly absent. Unfortunately, most of the items which included 'open' representations of Islam were readers' letters. The frequency with which such letters appeared in the domestic sample should not be a matter of wholehearted celebration, due to their function in contesting or correcting the inaccuracies of previous reporting and/or letters. In contrast, news reports and columns which foreground 'Open' representative characteristics are unquestionably a minority in the sample. But the fact that they exist draws attention to the dubious status of the truth claims of the dominant 'Closed' view. In addition, they show that it is still possible to kick against the financial, structural and organisational factors which collectively contribute to the overwhelmingly negative representation of Muslims in the broadsheet press, thereby illustrating a possible future for reporting the British Muslim communities in which a positive view predominates.

Islam vs. the West: A fallacy?

On occasion, articles dissented from the dominant representation of 'Islam vs. the West', arguing that such an opposition is erroneous at best. One approach to this dissent, clustered in the seven days either side of Christmas 1997, compared Islam and Christianity, drawing out the common tradition between the religions. The column '**Why the other lights of the world are not fakes**' (*Independent*, 2 January 1998) for example, inclusively referred to "We in the Abrahamic traditions", "the three great Abrahamic faiths" and the doctrines which Judaism, Islam and Christianity share. In one particularly 'open' passage, the author, Reverend Keith Ward, wrote:

> These three ways — the way of the people of the covenant, the community of divine law, the way of the 'body of Christ' — are all ways of mediating light in the darkness of building beauty from chaos, of incarnating justice and loving-kindness in the world.

The affirmation of the common heritage of the three Levant religions which this column includes hardly appeared anywhere else in the whole of the sample. Indeed, in some reports this common heritage was explicitly denied.[8]

A particularly interesting example of a positive representation of Islam (as opposed to Muslims) was an editorial, printed in the *Financial Times*, and headlined '**The faith of Abraham**'. This article was made all the more interesting for being printed on Christmas Eve, 1997. Here the *Financial Times* (which, as the editorial states is "as secular a newspaper as you could find") succumbs to the same seasonally affected reporting present across the rest of the sample at this time of year. But on this occasion, the editorial comes with a twist: the impending Christian celebrations are connected and discussed in relation to the Muslim Holy month of Ramadan which was due to start the following week. Perhaps this linkage was a result of the fact, again acknowledged by the editorial, that the newspaper has "readers around the world of all faiths and none" whose beliefs need accommodating. Regardless, the presentation of the common prophetic tradition of the faiths is refreshing:

> While abhorring the suggestion that Jesus or any other man could be God, their [Muslim's] own faith teaches them to respect both Jesus and Moses as divinely inspired precursors to their own Prophet. So Jews and Christians are "people of the book" sharing with Moslems [sic] the common root of the "religion of Abraham", and thus assured, in principle, of respect within Moslem society. (Financial Times, Editorial, 24 December, 1997)

There are however, two problematic features of this paragraph: First, some Muslims may take issue with the implication of the text that because Mohammed is presented as "their own Prophet", then Moses (Musa) and Jesus (Isa) are somehow 'not theirs'. This is clearly incorrect. Second, the use of the term 'Moslem' was a particularly inappropriate and unfortunate stylistic feature of the *Financial Times*, offensive in much the same way as the term 'Negro'. The *Financial Times* has now done away with this faulty phoneticism and throwback to colonialism, leaving only the mid-market, middle class, right-wing *Daily Mail* employing it as a matter of style.

In general however, the beneficial aspects of the editorial outweigh the negative. In addition to the inclusive comparison with Christianity, the editorial also acknowledges that Muslims are "often (as a recent inquiry discovered in Britain) the objects of ill-informed 'dread and dislike'." Faced with this racism the editorial argues that the "ready-made solution" offered by the West of a neutral public sphere "available to all for self-expression but to none for coercion", is far from successful in limiting either religiously inspired or religiously directed hatred. The Archbishop of Canterbury is quoted in support of this conclusion, stating that the "tolerance" of the neutral public sphere "too often 'equated merely with indifference'. Minorities that were only tolerated, he said, often 'end up feeling that they are being allowed to exist on sufferance, but that their existence is by no means secured'." The concluding paragraph of the editorial illustrates the generally good intentions of the newspaper:

> People of different faiths must go further [than toleration], showing respect for and interest in each other's traditions. [This means] …drawing on the values of peace and compassion that are shared by all the great world religions, and remembering, in the words of a British Moslem [sic] author the archbishop quoted, that

"both Islam and Christianity are ethical faiths, in which belief cannot be separated from behaviour".

Another approach which some articles took in dissenting from the dominantly 'closed' representation of Islam was to highlight the 'Britishness' of British Muslims. This argument most frequently occurred in readers' letters although was also included in some news reports.[9] An article headlined '**Britain's Muslims join forces to make one voice**' (*Independent*, 24 November 1997) for example, used the launch of the Muslim Council of Britain (MCB) as the event upon which a more inclusive representation of British Islam was placed. The article quotes Abdul-Wahid Hamed, spokesman for the MCB, as saying:

> The aim [of the MCB] is to highlight the fact that we are an asset to the nation and to celebrate the contribution we have made to society. We are also intent on sending the message that we are a mature community determined to play a full role in the future well-being of our country.

A reader's letter printed in *The Daily Telegraph*, written in response to a previous reader's letter written by Ray Honeyford,[10] employed historical supports for the argument that '**Islam is as British as Christianity**' (29 October 1997):

> If Mr Honeyford claims that Islamic civilisations have not contributed to the development of British institutions and culture, he betrays a breathtaking ignorance of the history of the British Isles and the extensive interaction between these islands and the Islamic world since Amr ibn al-As conquered Egypt in AD 642.

The majority of articles employing such argumentation were written on the issues and agenda of Muslim pupils and schooling, discussed in the previous section.

'Normalising' Muslim worship

The 'favourable comparison to Christianity' approach is also taken in an article printed in the *Guardian* called '**Fast food lessons of Ramadan**' (19 January 1998). The column, written by John Ryle, essentially aims to show the social and spiritual benefits of the abstinence associated with Ramadan, and goes on to draw attention to the very obvious precedent of Lent for fasting in Christianity. Although the article unfortunately starts with the familiar bemoaning of being deprived of sleep in Muslim countries (he calls the dawn call of the *muezzin* a "loud noise in the early hours", a "pre-dawn racket" and an "early morning din") the fasting itself is described with ringing endorsements. "Hunger affects the meaning of food," Ryle argues, "as well as the taste of it. Abstinence gives you back your appetite; it also gives you a glimpse of the sacred." As for the communal meal which breaks the fast at sunset, this "concentrates the mind, it forces you to see food as a blessing."

Where the article falters is in the journalists' *use* of Ramadan in the last two paragraphs. After the compliments above, Ryle goes on to say that fasting

> makes you wonder about restaurant critics, people who talk about food all the time. Do they have any idea of what it is like to go without? [...] Those who thank Marco Pierre White for their daily bread seem to be uninterested in the very appetite that food satisfies; they are guilty not so much of gluttony, as of superficiality.

The positive judgments loaded onto Muslim fasting in the first two thirds of the article therefore appears to have been designed as an argumentative re-source with which to attack food writers and restaurant critics. Of course, he is entitled to do this in an 'opinion column', but the argument does seem to be based on a presupposition that a Muslim wouldn't (or couldn't) be either a food writer, or someone who talks about food all the time. These presupposi-tions are based on generalisations (albeit intended to be complimentary) of 'who Muslims are' and 'what it is to be Muslim', and are probably a result of the fact that the evidence he draws from is taken from his own experiences of fasting in Afghanistan.

There is, contrary to the functionally ascetic picture painted by Ryle, a significant tradition of (over)indulgence in Ramadan, both in the nightly meal and especially the *Eid al-Fitr* (feast of breaking fast) at the end of the month. These 'celebratory' traditions are checked by, and frequently stand in opposi-tion to the very spiritual character of the month — a cultural-religious dy-namic which is placed in a much more central position in an equally positive, but ultimately more successful, second column about fasting and Ramadan printed in the *Guardian*. Written by Humera Khan of the women's group *an-Nisa* ('Women') and printed near to the *Eid* (*Guardian*, 24 January 1998), the article '**Celebrating with British Muslims**', as the name suggests, covers the British Muslim experience of Ramadan in a way not seen in other articles. This experience is related to the reader in four ways: First, from an internal, British Muslim perspective, Ramadan is described as

> a triumph of the spirit over the mundane, the communal over the individual. After a month of battling with the 'self' through control over mind, body and matter, Eid al-Fitr [...] is a day of joy and sharing marked by an Eid prayer performed by the community.

This is of course the standard account of Ramadan, as featured in the Ryle article above. Generally positive in style and content, it does have the tendency to both reify and homogenise the beliefs of Muslims, due to its lack of any social, cultural or historic contextualisation.

Second, Ms Khan builds upon this conventional, rather static introduction, developing the discussion to show the ways in which the "second or third generation British Muslims" like herself differ from their parents' generation in their approach to the celebrations. She states that although the communities

> have managed to maintain the values and ethos nurtured by our parents and grandparents, [...] where our Eid has changed is mainly to do with our attitude to the 30 days which precede it. Ramadan used to be a time of feasting and fasting with little spiritual reflection. It is now a time when we try to benefit from all the blessings that the holy month has to offer.

Such a representation of Muslim worship illustrates very clearly the inevitability of both continuity and change in the beliefs and practices of the British Muslim communities. The values which the largely immigrant Muslim communities brought with them to this country are still present (although undoubtedly to different degrees) in second and third generation Muslims, but changes in time and context brings changes in attitudes and practices.

Third, mainstream British society is introduced into the discussion in order to show the context in which such developments take place. This again, is an extremely positive step in the press' — and specifically the *Guardian's* — portrayal of the British Muslim communities, highlighting the interaction between the communities' internal attitudes to Ramadan, and the reaction(s) of the external communities:

> Bridging the divide between the traditional Eid to an Eid more reflective of our new lives in a new country has not [...] been straightforward. How do you perform your religious obligations, maintain the positive values and ethos handed down from generations, and also adjust to a society which is not only ignorant of your way of life, but sees you as some kind of alien?

Continuing, Ms Khan points out that "despite Islam being Britain's second largest religion the general public still do not understand much about us, or our way of life". This lack of understanding — or perhaps wilful ignorance — often translates to mere toleration, as opposed to acceptance and celebration of diversity in the public sphere.

Fourth and last, Ms Khan offers a hope for a better, more genuinely multicultural future. This is a future in which

> our children can see Eid lights along the high streets, when Blue Peter highlights more of the Muslim calendar, where schools become more imaginative in their presentation of Islam and where our children can talk about their religious celebrations and be fully accepted within the diversity of modern Britain.

Zokaei (n.d.) has argued that societal "inclusion is equivalent to the expression of solidarity and identification with wider groups" (p.3). Although the Muslim exclusion which Ms Khan's column refers to implies that mainstream 'white' society lacks this solidarity and identification with British Muslims, the column still 'feels' optimistic.

Covering British Islam and Muslims: A summary

There is, therefore, some distance still left to travel before the inclusion of Islam in British society is celebrated by broadsheet newspapers — a point also made at a recent conference by the ex-journalist, Edward Mortimer:

> I think that it is desirable that there should be something, some sort of superego implanted in the journalists, as there is effectively now with Jews and I think there has come to be, more or less, with Blacks. There are certain kinds of things that you just don't write because it is so evidently offensive, and unfortunately that superego is not yet sufficiently active where Muslims are concerned. (Edward Mortimer 1999)

The negativisation of British Muslims in broadsheet reporting is prefaced by two processes of division introduced earlier in the chapter — proxy and direct exclusion of 'Them' from 'Us'. In the first, British Muslims are excluded from the semantic position 'British' by virtue of the characteristics that they are perceived not to have: the characteristics of 'Britishness'; whilst in the second, British Muslims are excluded by virtue of the characteristics which they are perceived to have: their 'Islamicness'. Once this is acknowledged, it becomes particularly easy to brand these claims as racial, or more specifically racist, representations of British Muslims, and to dismiss them as essentialisation, simplification, false or ideological (Hage, 1998: 31). Following Hage, I argue that these acts and others like them, "are better conceived as nationalist practices: practices which assume, first, an image of a national space; secondly, an image of the nationalist himself or herself as master of this national space and, thirdly, an image of the 'ethnic/racial other' as a mere object within this space" (Hage, 1998: 28). In essence, they are based on a 'White fantasy' regarding the rights and abilities of mainstream 'White' society to regulate the parameters of

British society — to include or exclude — and they are as noticeable in conservative newspapers as they are in 'liberal' papers. Thus, although *The Daily Telegraph* and *The Times* were undoubtedly most responsible for the prejudicial tone of articles written on terrorism, the *Independent* and the *Guardian*, were not wholly blameless. Indeed there was a great deal of shared racism printed across these newspapers, amounting to an unacceptably negative representation of Islam and British Muslims

The features of a better multicultural future, mentioned in the article by Humera Khan discussed in the last section, are all issues of inclusive citizenship. They are a symbol, however small, of a commitment to the creation of a truly inclusive multicultural society: a society in which all Britons — regardless of tradition and identity — have a voice, a voice which is listened to, and moreover a voice which is respected. Despite the overwhelmingly negative representation of British Islam and Muslims, articles such as those discussed in the last section illustrate that (sections of) the British broadsheet press already realise that this 'multi-culture' *is* the future of Britain.

CHAPTER 6

The Iraq debacle

The reporting of Iraq during the UNSCOM stand-off

Arguing for 'intervention' in Iraq[1]

The history of war reporting is characterised by significant and often shocking levels of connivance between the military and the news media. As Knightly (2000) forcefully illustrates, with *very* few exceptions from the Crimean war, the so-called Indian mutiny, the Zulu wars of 1879 as well as the more familiar conflicts of the 20th century, the role which war correspondents played in reporting conflict has been the *promotion* of war, in which the war correspondents of the time disseminated propaganda sourced with those taking part in the killing. This dominant approach of war reporting has been given succour by, amongst other factors, the pressures of the market; the preferences of the audience during war not to be exposed to uncomfortable stories about failure, defeat and the death of 'Our Boys'; by the platitudinous fact that war fields are dangerous places which most journalists understandably want to avoid; and by journalism as a whole, especially the genre's need for authoritative, credible and available sources. During wartime — including periods immediately prior to conflict, characterised by media campaigning, preparation and promotion — almost every one of the authoritative sources that journalists rely upon, almost every PR officer or politician have, in one way or another, vested interests in relation to the conflict (Norstedt *et al.*, 2000: 384). In other words, journalists are flooded with propagandistic material which deliberately and systematically attempts "to shape perceptions, manipulate cognitions, and direct behaviour to achieve a response that furthers the desired intent of the propagandist" (Jowett & O'Donnell, 1992: 4), principally through manipulating the public's perception of the enemy, of the (potential) conflict and of their own government's conduct.

One approach during wartime is to reduce options and possibilities to an 'either/or' position. Typically, war propaganda "describes the actual conflict in a radically polarized way — as a struggle between the 'good guys and the bad guys' and in black and white" (Norstedt *et al.*, 2000: 384). Subsequently, a discourse dominated by propaganda will consequently only allow two positions: for and against. This creates a situation in which the only people referred to or quoted in the news are arguing either *for* or *against* war — a debate which presupposes 'We' have the right to be making such decisions. In particularly successful campaigns, sources are quoted offering competing *tactics* and *strategies* in a conflict or war which is already presumed will take place. And so it was during the build up to the US Desert Fox cruise missile attacks on Baghdad in 1998–attacks which were heralded by the period of coverage represented in this sample of broadsheet newspapers. During the build up to these cruise missile attacks, the reporting of Iraq was dominated by articles debating the desirability of the UK/US alliance invading Iraq and assassinating Saddam Hussein, ostensibly because the work of the United Nations Special Commission (UNSCOM) inspectors carrying out on-site inspections of Iraq's biological, chemical and missile capabilities was being restricted. Articles reporting Iraq during this period employed strikingly similar supporting arguments for intervention, to the extent that a schematic *discursive strategy* developed. This strategy is, in essence, an argument for intervention arising from the claims, themes, implications and a number of presuppositions present in the reports. This discursive strategy is illustrated in Figure 6.1 below.

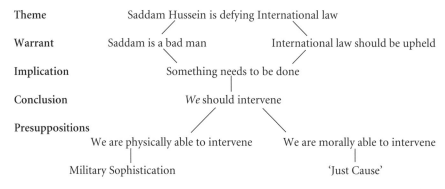

Figure 6.1. Discursive Strategy in the broadsheet reporting of Iraq

The universal theme of the reporting was 'Saddam Hussein's defiance of international law'. This theme ran through the top four coded topics — the 'UNSCOM stand-off' (n= 302), the 'threat of war' (n= 109), 'actions of international leaders' (n= 54), 'illegal weapons' (n= 134) — and others less frequently cited (e.g. 'sanctions', 'UN', 'terrorism'), totalling over 90 per cent of sampled Iraq articles. Additional to this theme were the claims that 'Saddam is a bad man', and 'international law should be upheld'. These claims often went unstated in the articles — hence their being labelled as argumentative 'warrants' in Figure 6.1 — illustrating the extent to which they are taken as 'givens'. Just as often however, evidence and argumentation were presented to back up these two claims. The combination of themes, claims and warrants of the reporting resulted in the implication that 'Something needs to be done' in Iraq.

However, the reporting of Iraq didn't stop there: it was under-cut by a further conclusion that '*We* should intervene'. The form that this intervention was proposed to take appeared to be directed by additional presuppositions. Necessarily, in order to suggest 'We *should* intervene', it must first be presupposed that 'We *can* intervene'. This presupposed ability takes the form of a *physical* ability and a *moral* ability, which are in turn based on presupposed military sophistication and a just cause. In other words, that we have the *military sophistication* to intervene — a sophistication which provides a *physical* ability to 'intervene' in Iraq; and secondly that military intervention is a just cause — thus, that we have the *moral* ability to act. Recently these two presuppositions have come to be practically inseparable, particularly since the development of the rhetoric of "military humanism" (see Chomsky, 1999, 2000; Hammond, 2000), or the idea, tested out in Kosova, that in order to save a country you have to bomb it. These presuppositions formed not only the backbone to much of the reporting, but were also argued explicitly in articles focusing on topics such as the 'UN', 'international law', 'diplomacy', 'actions of international leaders' and others.

This chapter should be viewed essentially as a study of political rhetoric. At a theoretical level, the chapter considers 'language in use', or put another way, the ability of discourse (particularly the powerful discourse genres like journalism) to *do* things. At a more empirical level (and keeping 'language in use' in mind), this chapter considers the reporting of Iraq during this period of coverage in relation to the efforts of powerful social agents to colonise the discursive/rhetorical power of élite journalism to serve their own interests. The argumentative discursive strategy introduced above informed the *vast* majority of reporting of Iraq and the 1997/8 UNSCOM 'stand-off'. Even when reports did *not* imply that 'We' — usually the US/UK cabal — should bomb Iraq, they were generally informed by the presuppositions in the lower section of Figure 6.1 above: that 'We' are *able* to direct morally and militarily defensible attacks on Iraq. These presuppositions were in turn confirmed, legitimated and reproduced in other more specialised reports presenting, amongst other subjects, the 'smart' military hardware of 'the Western powers', the precedence for intervention set by international law, the histories of atrocities by the Iraqi regime, etc. Each element of the above discursive strategy will now be presented and analysed, with a view to discussing how it confirmed or challenged the drive towards military aggression taken by the American and British governments.

Use of International law as an argumentative resource

International law was regularly referred to in this sample of Iraq articles, due primarily to the centrality of the UN, and specifically the UN Special Commission (UNSCOM), to the story. International law was selectively drawn upon to show that the actions of Saddam Hussein and/or his government were 'illegal', or an infringement of previous treaties or agreements. In an article printed in the *Daily Telegraph* (14 November 1997: 1) for example, Bill Richardson, the American Ambassador to the UN, was quoted as saying "Baghdad was pushing the crisis 'to the brink' and violating the UN Charter". The *Daily Telegraph* omitted to mention in this article that commentators such as Professor Francis Boyle (Professor of International Law and Arms Control at University of Illinois) thought that America was in violation of the same Charter by threatening to attack Iraq.

Despite the fact that the US and UK were practically alone in demanding Iraq's immediate and total capitulation of sovereignty, the élite press persistently and uncritically reproduced the US/UK argument that Saddam Hussein was 'defying international will'. The then British Foreign Secretary Robin Cook (who, on the eve of the 2003 US/UK invasion of Iraq, apparently relocated his long lost conscience) was quoted as stating "no option is ruled out by *the world community*" and, in the same article, the then Defence Secretary George Robertson stated that the actions of Saddam Hussein are "simply not acceptable to *the world community*" (*Daily Telegraph* **Invincible sent to the Gulf**, 17 January 1998, emphasis added). The then US Secretary of State, Madelaine Albright, was quoted in the *Guardian* (17 November 1997) arguing that the 'stand-off' was "not a dispute between Iraq and the US, but between Iraq and the law, Iraq and the world". Similarly, during her attempts to win support for military attacks from European and Gulf States, the *Financial Times* (29 January 1998) quotes her appeal for a "strong *international* response" (emphasis added) to Iraq.

Although the relevant Security Council Resolutions did not — and *do not* — authorise military attacks on Iraq, the Americans argued throughout the crisis that the decision for military aggression could be made without further recourse to the Security Council. In an article in the *Financial Times* headlined **'UN closer to tougher sanctions on Iraq'** (12 November 1997) for example, William Cohen, US Defence Secretary, "*reiterated* the US contention that there was '*inherent* authority' under existing UN resolutions for a military response" (emphasis added). Another article, headlined **'Defiant Saddam dares US to strike'** and printed in the *Sunday Times* (2 November 1997) reported that "Saddam" had "given Americans working in the UN arms inspection team in Iraq until Wednesday [three days] to leave". The report goes on to state that Richard Butler, the chairman of UNSCOM, considered this latest ultimatum to be "a breach of the 1991 cease-fire that ended the Gulf War". The implications of this are not spelt out by the newspaper, other than to imply that it was a little strong since it "drew a rebuke from the French, who said it was up to the Council to consider it a violation". In fact, a breach of the 1991 cease-fire could have led the way to full scale US military attacks on Iraq. Should the newspaper have included the implications of Butler's reaction in the report, it could have illustrated his threatening brinkmanship and the extent to which his views supported the American argument for military aggression.[2]

The UN Security Council, the major 'legal' player in the inspection crisis, was only represented by the sampled newspapers as performing a legitimate role when the decisions which it produced conformed to Anglo-American policy. Conversely, countries like France, Russia and China who opposed aggressive Anglo-American policy were criticised by the newspapers and even blamed for the 'stand-off'. The *Financial Times* for example, in an article headlined **'A win on points for Saddam Hussein'** (21 November 1997), suggests that "a damaging split" in the Security Council, produced "when France, Russia and China opposed a US and UK proposal for a small increase in sanctions to punish Baghdad's concealment of its weapons development", initiated the crisis. "It was that split", the newspaper continues, "which tempted the Iraqi dictator into his latest challenge to the sanctions regime". A similar point is made in a report printed the same day in the *Independent* (**'Baghdad claims victory in battle of nerves with US'**, 21 November 1997) where "divisions" in "the UN Security Council over what to do about Iraq" were identified as contributing to the crisis. On the same page as this *Independent* report, another article headlined **'Crisis over as Saddam lets inspectors back to work'** backgrounded a clear indication that *the US* were not adverse to

creating 'dis-unity' in the Security Council should the Council's decisions not
go their way. In response to a deal brokered in Geneva aimed at ending the
current stand-off, Mike McCurry, the White House spokesman is paraphrased
as saying: "the US would use its veto on the UN Security Council should there
be any alteration to the terms of former UN resolutions". This stated policy
illustrates the commitment of the USA to return the UNSCOM inspections to
a situation similar to the recently alleviated 'stand-off' should decisions be
made that they do not agree with. This stated intention was allowed to stand by
the journalists — Harriet Martin and Rupert Cornwell — without any comment, critique or contention.

Three days after the printing of this article, the *Independent* reported that
the US and UK had followed through with their commitment to veto any
alterations to the current inspections and sanctions regime which they disa-
greed with ('**Britain and US spike Saddam's guns over changes to arms inspections**', 24 November 1997). The report stated that "Russia had wanted the
commission to certify that Iraq had dismantled its nuclear programme and
long-range missiles" which would thereby close the chapter on UNSCOM
nuclear inspections. Considering that "the Vienna-based International Agency
for Atomic Energy has officially confirmed that Baghdad does not possess
atomic weapons, nor the means of manufacturing them" (Rouleau, 23 March
1998, Le Monde Diplomatique) Russia's request does appear acceptable. Not
only did the US and UK reject such a proposal, they went above and beyond the
requirements of S. C. Resolution 687 and demanded that Iraq "identify [the]
countries which sold it nuclear technology before the invasion of Kuwait".
Further, the article reported that the US and UK "were *jubilant* at the rebuff to
Iraq and Russia, which failed to win the full endorsement of France and China"
(emphasis added). Such celebration in continuing the sanctions regime again
elicited no critical response from the newspapers, either in their news reports
or their op./ed. columns, suggesting that the newspapers do not think 'dis-
unity' in the Security Council is problematic by when it is 'Our side' who are
being obstructive or imperious.

Finally for this section, a *Times* editorial ('**Seven Year Itch**', 31 October
1997), following the approach of the 'Western' governments at the time and
since, not only blames Saddam Hussein for the sanctions regime, but presents
the suffering of the Iraqi people as being actively *engineered* by Hussein:

> By seeing to it that some Iraqis go desperately hungry, Saddam has also succeeded
> in persuading the world that the people of Iraq, which is quite capable of growing
> enough food to supply its populace, are starving because of UN sanctions.

This passage not only counters the correct view that it is the UN sanctions which are to blame for the suffering endured by the Iraqi people, but also provides a *humanitarian* pretext for military intervention, in addition to the legal and geopolitical arguments already used. By combining these arguments the newspaper is enabled to state, in a forceful and emotive conclusion, that "[t]he West [...] must ensure that retaliation severely damages the military and security apparatus that underpins his [Hussein's] regime".

The 'ideological square' in reporting Iraq

The 'ideological square' is a particularly important aspect of the dominant discursive strategy in these sampled articles on Iraq, since it provides the basis of presumed 'moral' justification for military intervention. The analysed texts concur with and support a reading of the reported events functional to the military aims of the 'Western' governments. Since semantic and argumentative moves are discussed throughout this chapter, this section will focus on key examples of lexical and syntactic structuring of expression. Numerous alternative examples of lexical and syntactic structuring of expression exist, which could have been analysed.

A report headlined '**Iraq faces countdown to attack**' and printed in the *Daily Telegraph* (19 January 1998), contains several interesting textual features illustrating the ideological commitments of the journalist and newspaper. First, the article's use of noun phrases is interesting: "Saddam Hussein" is only called by his full name in the first line of the text; is labelled as "dictator" on two occasions (one in the 'overheadline'); as "the Iraqi dictator" on one occasion in the second paragraph; as "the tyrant" in the third paragraph; as "the Iraqi leader" in the second to last paragraph; and as "Saddam" on ten other occasions. "Iraq" is mentioned as an actor on two occasions. In contrast, the actors positioned in conflict with Iraq and Saddam Hussein are presented more collectively and more positively. The collective nouns cited were: "America", (3 times); "Britain"; "Washington and its allies"; "senior government offcials"; "UN"; and "United Nations inspectors". Individuals cited were: "Madeleine Albright, Secretary of State"; "Bill Richardson, America's ambassador to the UN"; "Britain's Defence Secretary, George Robertson"; "Sir Edward Heath" (twice); "Richard Butler, head of the UN's compliance team"; and the shorter "Mr Butler" (twice). The contrast between Iraqi and non-Iraqi actors is striking. Although each 'side' were cited a comparable number of times (n= 19; n=

16 respectively), Iraqi actors were dominated by President Saddam Hussein, or more specifically by "Saddam", whilst the non-Iraqis were either collectivised or else were individuals given their full honorific titles. The consequence of these lexical choices is that the conflict appears to be both personalised and justified: the collective efforts of the US, the UK and the UN against "Saddam", "the tyrant" and "Iraqi dictator".

Second, the way in which aggressive transitive actions attributed to the 'non-Iraqi side' are presented is interesting. Throughout the article, the "attack" referred to in the headline is mitigated, passivised or nominalised (as in the headline), which effectively backgrounds or occasionally removes the agency of the attackers. The closest the report gets to a foregrounding of agency is in the first paragraph, numbered here for ease of reference:

> [1] America warned Saddam Hussein yesterday that [2] it is closer to using *a military attack to end Iraq's efforts to block United Nations inspectors.*

In clause two, the whole of the italicised section represents one single noun phrase — the 'object' which 'it' [America] intends 'to use'. Even here, where the presence of aggressive American agency is strongest, the expression is structured in such a way as to provide the readership with the justification for the "military attack", qualifying the very noun phrase which proposes it: "to end Iraq's efforts to block United Nations inspectors". Elsewhere, the proposed American military aggression is expressed as "military force", "the military option", "military action", "military strikes" and "the military-based response", displaying the kind of over-wording indicative of an "intense ideological preoccupation" (Fowler *et al.*, 1979). On two other occasions, the newspaper uses the terms "punitive missile strike" and "punitive cruise missile attacks" which again provide a justification for the military attack in a similar way to the numbered quotation above. The addition of the adjective in this case is therefore highly ideological, providing the reader with an objective for the 'military strike' (i.e. a punishment for "Saddam", "the tyrant"), and moreover, through the *choice* of the adjective, that this objective is a 'just' and 'justifiable' one.

Third, the article employs non-obligatory rhetorical devices such as metaphor in order that certain meanings of the reported action be emphasised in the minds-eye of the reader. The visit to Baghdad by Richard Butler, the head of UNSCOM for example is described in the article as "the final test of whether to unleash American cruise missiles against the tyrant". The choice of the lexical metaphor "unleash" to describe the launching of cruise missiles is attractive since it imbues the bombs with life and taps into the more literary metaphor '[unleashing] the dogs of war'. The attack is further justified through the use of the noun phrase "the tyrant" to describe Saddam Hussein, since the missiles are being 'unleashed against the tyrant' and not Iraq. This very simple structuring of expression acts to limit the possibilities of dissent in much the same way that the classical rhetorical argument 'fighting for peace' does.

Throughout the majority of the articles reporting the UNSCOM 'stand-off', the sampled newspapers metaphorically employ an authoritarian discourse of discipline (Fairclough, 1995a: 95) to describe the reported action, switching between 'parent-to-child' and 'master-to-pet' relations of discipline. Saddam Hussein and Iraq were cast in the relationship's subordinate role and 'Western' (US and UK) actors are represented as dominant. The *Financial Times* (15 November 1997), for example clearly employ this disciplinary metaphor in an article headlined '**The US has a big stick, but it can talk softly**'. This metaphor is continued through the article in terms such as "punitive strikes" and in the evaluation that previous US air attacks on Iraq (e.g. January 1993, September 1996) were "too lenient". The article uses an 'insolent animal' metaphor most clearly in the claim that the Clinton Administration were wondering "how to bring Iraqi President Saddam Hussein *to heel*", suggesting that Hussein was somehow comparable to a wayward puppy. The same day the *Independent* stated that Iraq had "*defied* the United States" ('**Last superpower defied by friends and enemies alike**', my emphasis). Lower down in the article, where a Pentagon spokesman criticises Iraq's request to limit the number of US weapons inspectors, the disciplinary discourse shifts to a *legal-punitive* metaphor: the Pentagon official is quoted as saying "It is as though an ex-convict were trying to pick its own parole officer". The disciplinary image of the 'big stick' was also used in an article printed in the *Daily Telegraph* (18 November 1997): first in the headline — '**Western ability to wield the big stick at Saddam is slipping away**', and also as "the military stick" later in the article.

Such formulations were built up across the sample, wherein Saddam Hussein was persistently described as a subordinate who has not 'learnt his lesson' and should therefore be 'punished' and 'brought back in line' with the (US/UK) 'international community'. Representing the UNSCOM inspections 'stand-off' in such a way tends to implicitly invoke "an imperialist and indeed racist ideology of relations between nations, which contributes to the continuity of imperialist and neo-colonialist relations in practice" (Fairclough, 1995a: 102). With this in mind, these formulations appear highly functional to the call of the United States and Britain to attack Iraq.

If we next look at lexical style across other sampled articles it becomes apparent that, through the journalists' choices of verb phrase, Iraqi actions are foregrounded, described fully and presented as 'negative'; in contrast, the proposed Western 'military action' is backgrounded and euphemised in order to de-emphasise its negative effects. In one edition of *The Times* (14 November 1997) for example, the military attacks proposed by the American and British governments are labelled: "Gulf Action" (in the headline), "grave consequences", and "a military confrontation" in a front page article; and as a "strike", a "strike against Iraq", the "military option" (in a headline, p.19), "military action", "further measures" and the proposal to "punish Iraq militarily" across seven other articles (p.18–19). This not only illustrates the same intense over-wording suggested earlier, but is also highly ideological, since all but two of the above descriptions of 'Western' military violence conceal the 'agents' and 'objects' (the 'affected') of such violence.

A classic example of the dichotomous 'ideological square' developed in the sampled Iraq articles between the verbs 'to warn' and 'to threaten': the actions of Iraq and Iraqi actors being represented as 'threats', whilst the actions of 'the West' and 'Western' actors were represented as 'warnings'. Below are a few select examples of this dichotomous representation, included in chronological order. Iraqi and 'Western' speech acts are italicised throughout:

> A senior Pentagon official last night gave a *warning* that any Iraqi attempt to shoot down US reconnaissance aircraft would be considered an act of war and be met with a military response. As Iraq renewed its *threats*, America *urged* the United Nations to implement tougher sanctions against Iraq. (*The Times*, 8 November 1997)
>
> **Clinton *refuses* to rule out attack after Iraq *threat*.** [...] Iraq *threatened* to shoot down U-2 spy planes on UN missions. [...] James Rubin, State Department Spokesman, *said*: 'We have made it clear that any attempt to shoot them down would be a serious mistake'." (*Daily Telegraph*, 8 November 1997)
>
> [...] a senior Iraq official *threatened* to shoot down US spy planes if they resumed flights over his country. A senior Pentagon official *said* yesterday that any Iraqi attempt to shoot down a UN surveillance plane would be considered an act of war (*Guardian*, 8 November 1997)
>
> William Cohen *said* that if Iraq acted on its week-old *threat* to shoot down a U2 plane, this would be tantamount to "an act of war". (*Independent*, 10 November 1997)
>
> The United States is *proposing* an intensive bombing campaign against Iraq next month... How will Saddam respond to a renewed air war? [...] He could *threaten* Kuwait again, as he did in 1994 (*Independent* , 27 January 1998)

In each of the five examples above, American and United Nations (Kofi Annan) actions which could be construed as 'threats' or at the very least 'threaten*ing*' are de-emphasised through the lexical choices of the journalists. In contrast, the actions of Iraq and Iraqi actors *are* labelled as 'threats'.

Moving on to the *syntactic* structuring of expression, the choices of sentence construction made in the sampled Iraq articles further highlight the 'ideological square' discussed above. Mirroring the findings of Kress (1983), the use of the verb/adjective pairing "is/are likely" in the sampled newspapers illustrates the (ideological) presuppositions and commitments of those using it. The first line of an article headlined '**Israel 'threatens nuclear reply' to Iraq germ attack**' and printed in *The Times* (29 January 1998) for example, states:

> With tension mounting in the Gulf, the CIA has given a warning that Iraq *is likely* to fire scud missiles armed with non-conventional warheads at Israel if attacked by the Americans, according to a report in *Yediot Aharonot.* (emphasis added)

The excerpt is a complex, multi-layered sentence, containing a number of interesting linguistic dimensions. First, the 'factuality' of the sentence (and therefore of the threat) is emphasised through the journalists' use of two features: the action of the CIA is labelled "a warning" as opposed to 'a claim'; and the constructive role of the Israeli newspaper *Yediot Aharonot* in the story is backgrounded to the final clause of the sentence. Shahak (1997) describes this newspaper as a "quality paper" but which "tends to include all views in the framework of Zionism" (p.8). The stake of the paper in the story should therefore be viewed from within this ideological commitment. Second, it is interesting to speculate on what the motivations of the CIA were in press releasing such information to Israeli newspapers. What did they expect, or intend *Yediot Aharonot* and their readership would *do* with such information? Moreover, what were the CIA actually *doing* with such information if UNSCOM was as uncorrupted by espionage and covert operations as the Americans claimed throughout the stand-off? These questions were, of course, not broached by *The Times*.

Returning to the verb/adjective pairing "is likely", the usage in this case is a little more complex than the example discussed by Kress (1983). It is unclear whether the syntactic choice "is likely" was made by the CIA, *Yediot Aharonot* or the journalists who wrote the article, and for this reason, I'll sideline the issue of authorial agency and focus on the claim: Through using "is likely", the factual 'existence' of the proposed missile attack is stressed, regardless of onlooker perceptions, in a way which would not be possible with the alternative 'seems certain'. This syntactic choice therefore increases the 'threat' posed to Israel by Iraq. In addition, the use of the culturally consonant phrases "Scud missiles" and "non-conventional warheads" (both 'bad bombs', in contrast to 'good bombs' like the US 'Patriot'), combined with the "warning" speech act, result in the newspaper presenting an especially threatening sequence of events.

By way of comparison, the alternative verb/adjective pairing 'seems certain' was adopted in other Iraq articles. In the *Daily Telegraph* article headlined **'Clinton refuses to rule out attack after Iraq threat'** (8 November 1997) for example, the journalist Hugh Davies wrote:

> Experience has proven that in disputes with UN inspectors, the Iraqis have backed off only when military action *seems certain.* (emphasis added)

Here, through the use of the verb/adjective pairing "seems certain", Hugh Davies suggests that the Iraqis only 'back off' from a dispute when military action seems certain *to them.* This chosen syntactic construction acts to de-emphasise the existential, i.e. very real US/UK military action. Unilateral US/UK military attacks were, after all, not only carried out on occasions before and since this article was printed, they were in fact an almost daily ritual within the 'no-fly zone' of northern and southern Iraq. In this way, by using this particular verb/adjective pairing Davies encourages the audience to 'read' the reported event as a symbolic conflict being 'fought' by diplomats in the rooms of, amongst other places, the UN. Thus, to say that "the Iraqis have backed off only when military action seems certain [to them]" simultaneously suggests that Iraqi perception is the most important aspect of the crisis, whilst presuming that the decision to react militarily has not been already made. As such, the presentation of the reported event contained with the chosen verb/adjective pairing, contributes to the 'ideological square' mentioned above. The military threats of American and British forces are reframed as simple posturing, devoid of any real intent to attack Iraq.

'Good bombs': The sophistication and/or superiority of 'Our' weaponry

Articles show-casing the military vehicles, weaponry, equipment and personnel being sent to the Persian Gulf were common in these élite newspapers. These articles almost universally focused on American and British military equipment being sent to the Gulf region, with few references to the armed forces of other 'allied' countries. When other armed forces were mentioned, they tended to be in the lower sections of articles. An article headlined '**Invincible is prepared for Gulf action**' (*The Times*, 14 November) for example, mentions "six Chilean helicopter technicians [who] will be left behind to form a skeleton staff at a UN monitoring centre" in the final paragraph of an article covering 325 column centimetres. The remainder of this article makes no mistake of informing the readership of exactly who and what will be involved in the majority of the (proposed) attacks: a British "strike force", sent "to the Gulf to support the Americans in any military action against Iraq". The report includes breathless descriptions of "the RAF Harriers", which are "more powerful and have a longer range than the Sea Harriers", and which may be allocated to *HMS Invincible*. These military vehicles and personnel were being sent to the Gulf, with the full backing of the newspaper, to join the "US forces in the Gulf — 2,000 personnel, 17 warships and 200 aircraft", all of whom "were on full alert".

The same day (14 November 1997), in an article headlined '**US fine-tunes its military machine**', the *Guardian* provided a list of the American and British "hardware" stationed in and sent to the Gulf (reproduced *exactly* as it appeared, 'bullet points' and all):

> United States forces have a wide choice of equipment available to do the job, including:
> – Tomahawk cruise missiles, both ship- and submarine-launched, which they say are twice as accurate as the ones used during the Gulf War
> – Anti-radiation missiles designed to home in on air defence missile radars
> – F-117 Stealth fighters and carrier-borne aircraft equipped with various 'smart' weapons, such as laser-guided bombs.
> To these can also be added a dozen RAF Tornadoes [...] also fitted with the Tiald laser-bombing system.

The list continues for much of the report's remaining 300 column centimetres, although not in the 'bullet points' seen above. The report mentions the "US Naval battle group" including "the [*nuclear*] aircraft carrier Nimitz", "British warships", "US combat aircraft" and the "US ground forces" in Kuwait, "where, *coincidentally*, a British infantry battalion, The King's Regiment, is on manoeuvres [...] this weekend" (emphasis added). This article's central function is to communicate the strength and, above all, the high technological sophistication of the weaponry available to American and (to a lesser extent) British forces to attack Iraq. The excerpt above states that this military hardware is "available to *do the job*", a "job" which the newspaper does not mount serious opposition to, despite it routinely acknowledging the inevitable "risk of 'collateral damage' — jargon for killing civilians". Absent from this promotion of Our military sophistication are the numbers of civilians which these weapons have butchered.

The technophilia of weaponry formed a significant angle in these Iraq articles, as it did during the build-up to the bombing of Iraq in 1991. Where the 'star weapon' bombing Iraq in 1991 was undoubtedly the 'smart bomb', during the period of this study the bomb of choice was the B-61 'bunker bomb' — ordnance which America has since used to kill Afghans and Iraqis, both civilian and military. Several articles mentioned the power and sophistication of the 'bunker bomb', one of which was headlined '**Pentagon tests 'bunker buster' for Iraq raids**' (*The Times*, 30 January 1998). The leader of this article states: "NEW BOMBS CAN DESTROY SADDAM'S HIDDEN BIOLOGICAL WEAPONS, WRITES IAN BRODIE", which of course assumes that such biological weapons do in fact exist. The real interest in analysing this article lies in its rhetoric — directed towards convincing the readership that these bombs *should* be used to "destroy" the "hidden biological weapons" referred to in the leader. The first paragraph, apparently written without a trace of irony, reads:

> The Pentagon, which unveiled precision-guided 'smart bombs' during the Gulf War, yesterday promised *even smarter bombs* if and when America and Britain launch new raids against President Saddam Hussein's weapons programme in Iraq. (emphasis added)

This first paragraph introduces the premise which the remainder of the article attempts to support: that these new bombs are "smarter" than the largely discredited "smart bombs" used against Iraq in 1991. It is interesting that the Pentagon still felt that the label 'smart' was the best way of mitigating the bomb's destructive capabilities, despite the acknowledged failures of 'smart' technology during the bombing of Iraq in 1991. The new name for the bomb — the "bunker buster" — also supports the conclusion that the bomb will destroy buildings, as opposed to Iraqis. No doubt this name was chosen from a list of options employing the kind of catchy alliteration guaranteed to secure good copy in the press yet retaining reference to its ostensible function. Perhaps the plans to name the bomb the 'Saddam Smasher', the 'Dictator Dismemberer', the 'Iraqi Incinerator', or the more inclusive 'Arab Annihilator' were passed over at an earlier stage for fears that they would foreground its actual effects to an unacceptable degree.

The reasoning for the bomb's proposed usage is supplied by Brodie, suggesting that "Pentagon officials are *acutely* aware of the moral and political problems that could be created if bombing raids release anthrax and botulism spores or poison gas into the atmosphere where they could kill thousands of civilians" (emphasis added). The US military claim that, motivated by a desire to prevent Iraqi civilian exposure to chemical/biological weapons, they have "developed a weapon *it is believed* can vaporise the germ and chemical warfare agents Saddam *is* hiding" (emphasis added). — Note the doubt in the 'bunker buster's' ability to actually do 'the job' of destroying 'Saddam's bio/chem weapons' and the accompanying declaration that such weapons do in fact exist. Brodie's statement that the Pentagon is "acutely aware of the moral and political problems" in adopting military tactics which 'inadvertently' kill Iraqi civilians, therefore implies that the US are keen to avoid killing civilians. This claim is entirely inconsistent with not only the attitude of the American State Department towards Iraq during the inspections crisis,[3] but also the US military use of nuclear weaponry — which is what munitions containing depleted uranium *are* — during the 1991 and 2003 Iraq conflicts. The radioactive dust created by the millions of tonnes of uranium dropped around Basra and in the southern deserts of Iraq continues to encourage cancers (particularly in children) in excess of that seen across the rest of the country, which are themselves *far* above the cancer rates prior to 1991. Ian Brodie does not treat this specious 'military humanism' with such disdain however, suggesting that the avoidance of civilian deaths was the primary objective of the development of this weapon.

The article goes on to state that research and development for the bomb has occurred in two, seemingly unconnected ways: "*a* bomb filled with rocket fuel has set off a 30 second inferno that rose to several thousand degrees during testing" (emphasis added); and new "5,000lb laser guided penetration bombs or missiles, pencil shaped and with hardened nose cones" have been developed in order to "penetrate reinforced concrete bunkers as many as four floors underground". The article goes on to describe in breathless, pseudo-sexual language, the "*penetration*" of such "bunker busters", which "can scythe through layers of metal and reinforced concrete" and not explode "until it has fully *penetrated* the bunker*" (emphasis added). This is apparently done through the use of "a *new* delayed fuse" (emphasis added) — the use of the modifier 'new' suggesting an improvement or development in existing delayed fuses. This 'new fuse' is central to the functioning of the bomb since it allows it to "count the number of floors it goes through as the bomb *penetrates* the *bunkers*".

The testing of the bomb has not, however, been particularly successful, and the fallible nature of this new "smarter" weapon can be exposed with a closer, more critical reading of the claims in Brodie's report itself. The article states:

>As an example, the fuse can be programmed to detonate on the fourth floor. American television viewers saw Pentagon videotape of a 'bunker buster' smashing its way through four walls of concrete before exploding.

First, the obvious conclusion that we are meant to come to in reading these two sentences, is that they are connected: that the bomb *can* be programmed to explode after 'smashing' through four floors/walls, and that this *is* what happened in the example broadcast to the American people. But the two sentences, and the events they describe, are not necessarily connected by any causal relationship. The excerpt is an example of an enthymeme, which, through omitting a premise, pushes the audience to create "coherence in the incomplete argument by consciously or unconsciously supplying the 'missing link' from the premises in their own belief system" (Gill & Whedbee, 1997: 175). The suggested relationship between the two sentences does not therefore exist, but is left for us to infer based on the expectations for narrative coherence that we impose upon texts.

Second, and related to the first point above, we must wonder why it is that the "bunker buster" is so fond of the fourth floor of 'the bunker'. If it can indeed be programmed to explode on whatever floor it wishes, why do all the references and examples in the article only refer to the bomb exploding after passing through four levels of concrete? As "Frank Robbins, research director at the Elgin base" is quoted as saying: "the fuse that counts the floors is still being tested". The image that this therefore paints is of a weapon which *can* penetrate four floors or concrete walls and, due to the incomplete nature of its research and development always *does* penetrate four floors or concrete walls. What is therefore being described is a weapon of such blinding technology that it is able — with the help of a reinforced nose-cone and rocket propulsion — to smash through four concrete walls before coming to a stop. These "smarter" bombs therefore appear remarkably similar to the previous, more cerebrally challenged bombs, merely with a hard-hat welded to the front. Despite this, "Mr Robbins said it [the development of the fuse] is far enough along to be fitted on 'bunker busters' already sent to the Gulf". This rather frank admission from the "research director" should have added fuel to the suggestion that this latest American incursion into Iraq is being used as a testing ground for military equipment — an arms fair of a more practical nature. This implication is missed by Ian Brodie.

As mentioned at the start of this section, articles reporting the military vehicles, weaponry, equipment and personnel were common during the sampled newspapers. Through these articles' almost universal focus on American and British military equipment, the presumption that 'we are physically able to intervene due to military superiority' is supported. In addition to this physical ability, the way in which 'Our' weaponry is presented in these articles — "precision-guided", "smarter weapons" which "vaporise [Saddam's] germ and chemical warfare agents" without harming civilians — also supports the presumed 'moral ability to intervene'.

'Bad bombs': The threat of 'Their' weaponry

Accompanying articles celebrating 'Our' military prowess, referred to above, were the seemingly contradictory articles in which the threat of 'Their' weapons was emphasised. The capability or otherwise of Iraq to produce and launch chemical, biological and nuclear weaponry was, of course, a frequently cited topic of the sampled Iraq articles (n= 134; 25.2% of Iraq articles), since it formed the crux issue of the UNSCOM inspections and resulting 'stand-off'. The existence of these weapons could clearly be thought of as threatening *per se*, since they are designed to kill in horrific and often indiscriminate ways. Further, it could be argued the presence of these weapons in the Middle East, an area with a particular reputation for 'unrest', could be construed as 'threatening' to the peace or 'stability' (*hegemony*) of the region. But the fact that Israel's nuclear and (possibly) chemical/biological weapons programmes were not treated as '*per se* threatening', casts doubt on both of the arguments given above and exposes the implicit racism in the US/UK preoccupation with Iraq.

Within the 134 articles which mentioned 'Iraqi illegal weaponry', a variety of linguistic and discursive features were employed to specifically highlight the threat of these weapons to '*Us*'. Israel was also included in the position 'We', and the possibility that Iraq would launch chemical or biological warheads at Tel Aviv was frequently cited — particularly in the periods of peak preoccupation in the weeks before 17 November 1997 and 31 January 1998. The article, headlined '**Israelis prepare for attack**' and printed in *The Times* (17 November 1997) for example reports that, in light of the threat posed by "non-conventional Scuds attacks", "as many as 6,000 [Israeli] people a day are visiting gas mask distribution points". An article on the same page headlined '**Saddam given warning over Scud offensive**', claimed that it was only "Israel's implied threat to use nuclear weapons [...] that stopped Saddam from launching Scuds armed with chemical and biological warheads against Tel Aviv" during the 1991 conflict with Iraq. With a characteristic lack of diplomacy, Richard

Butler, the head of UNSCOM, made alarmist references to the threat Saddam Hussein and Iraqi weapons may pose to Israel — allegations which were reported by all of the sampled newspapers. The *Independent* for example, in an article headlined '**US seeks support for Iraqi airstrikes**' (28 January 1998) suggests that Butler said "Iraq had enough biological weapons to 'blow away Tel Aviv.'" Earlier, Butler had claimed that "Saddam is hiding about 200 tonnes of VX gas" ('**Children hunger for peace in Iraq crisis**', *Independent*, 27 November 1997), a claim which was later used by America as 'proof' that 'the UN' thought Saddam both held and was concealing chemical weapons.

Elsewhere, articles included rhetorical figures of speech in order to make the argument that 'Saddam poses a threat' even clearer to the audience. The *Sunday Times*, in an article headlined '**Saddam hides secret arsenal behind women and children**' (16 November 1997), claimed that "a warhead containing enough anthrax virus to kill tens of thousand of people, for example, need be *no bigger than a suitcase*" (my emphasis). In a similar move, William Cohen was reported by most of the sampled newspapers holding up a 5lb bag of sugar and claiming that "such a bag filled with anthrax bacteria could kill half Washington's population if it were spread over the city" (*The Times*, 17 November 1997).[4] The *Financial Times*, based the whole of an article to William Cohen's allegations ('**Iraq 'may have huge nerve gas stockpile**'', 26 November 1997). The first paragraph of the article stated Cohen's claim that "Iraq may possess enough of a nerve gas known as VX to kill the world's entire population". This claim is also rephrased lower down the article and loaded with even more hyperbole: Cohen is cited "stressing the danger posed by Iraqi weapons of mass destruction to *humanity as a whole*". This claimed 'threat to humanity' is supported by two additional claims (all italics, my emphasis): "One *drop* [of VX] on your finger will produce death in a matter of mere moments"; and "the UN believes that Saddam may have produced as much as *200 tonnes* of VX [...] theoretically enough to kill *every* man, woman and child *on the face of the earth*". The threat of the nerve gas in Saddam's hands in driven home even further to the American public by Cohen stating: "The front lines are no longer overseas — it can be in any American city".[5]

Despite British and American claims to the contrary, the actual existence of Iraq's chemical and biological weapons was unproven during the sample period and remains unproven at the time of writing. This inevitably led to a variety of western warmongers using 'rhetorical vagueness' in order to produce an ambiguous sense of uneasiness and threat, which journalists dutifully reproduced in their reports. Despite the accusatory declaration of the headline '**Saddam**

hides secret arsenal behind women and children' (discussed above), the article itself could only make reference to "a frightening amount of anthrax" which Iraq "could" produce using pharmaceutical fermenters. On other occasions, the claims being made regarding the 'threat' or Iraq were so couched, hedged and mitigated to be almost devoid of any real content. An article printed in the *Independent* headlined '**Britain warns of Saddam's timebomb'** (19 November 1997) for example, quoted a British "intelligence assessment" which stated:

> Provided it still has key components — and that is unclear — Iraq could within a few months build, with little risk of detection, missiles capable of hitting Israel and key targets in Saudi Arabia. (emphasis added)

What this assessment therefore states is that Iraq *may* be able to produce missiles *providing* it has certain key (i.e. essential) components, the likelihood of which is unclear.

Finally, an article printed in *The Times*, headlined '**Clinton cites Tokyo attack as a warning'** (17 November 1997), combines several of the linguistic features mentioned above in the form of an especially strong rhetorical argument for intervention. As the headline suggests, President Clinton used the deaths of Japanese civilians in the March 1995 sarin gas attack on the Tokyo underground in an analogous argument of 'what can happen when these weapons fall into the wrong hands'. The first paragraph sets the scene of the UNSCOM stand-off with typical hyperbole: "The crisis with Iraq is not a replay of the Gulf War but *a battle against organised forces of destruction*, President Clinton said yesterday" (emphasis added). The pseudo-apocalyptic language drawn upon in the opening paragraph, lends a histrionic feel to the article. Casting Iraq as an example of, or perhaps possessed by the "organised forces of destruction" clearly negativises Iraqi action and justification. The deaths of the Japanese civilians in Tokyo is referred to "as an omen" of the "battle" suggested in the first paragraph. Clinton continues:

> Think about it in terms of the innocent Japanese who died in the subway and how important it is for every responsible government in the world to do everything possible not to let big stores of chemical or biological weapons fall into the wrong hands.

The reference to "every responsible government in the world" is a barely concealed swipe at the governments of France, China and the Russian Federation who were, for whatever reason, less than enthusiastic about the policy being advocated by America. What Clinton actually demands in the above excerpt is also interesting to discuss. First, he calls to "responsible governments" to remove "*big* stores of chemical or biological weapons [from] …the wrong hands". Does this mean that if Saddam Hussein had a *small* store of chemical or biological weapons that would be okay? Second, Clinton is not calling for the total eradication of chemical or biological weapons, merely that large numbers of them should be kept from falling "into the wrong hands". This of course accords exactly with America's long-term policy on *their* production of chemical and biological weapons, as illustrated by their persistent and dogmatic refusal to ratify the (1986) Declaration on the Prohibition of the Development, Production and Stockpiling of Bacteriological (Biological) and Toxin Weapons and Their Destruction.[6] Third, arguing that chemical and biological weapons should not be allowed to "fall into the wrong [i.e. Saddam Hussein's] hands" suggests that this is how Saddam Hussein previously acquired them: they 'fell into his hands'. This of course completely removes the very active role which, amongst others, Britain and the United States played in selling 'weapons of mass destruction' and technology necessary for manufacturing such weapons to Iraq and Saddam Hussein.

The first two paragraphs of this article therefore structure the "crisis with Iraq" as a battle between the "organised forces of destruction" and "responsible government". The United States is firmly cast in the second of these positions, despite their hypocritical approach to bacteriological weapons proliferation and very active role in the creation of the 'force of destruction' that is Saddam Hussein.[7]

President Saddam Hussein's 'removal' from power

The presuppositions and implications of the dominant discursive strategy supported an argument advocating the removal of President Saddam Hussein from power in Iraq. In some articles reporting Iraq and the UNSCOM 'stand-off' this argument was placed in a much more central position, wherein journalists either explicitly supported the argument, wrote about 'Saddam's removal' in the form of a 'for-and-against debate', or else elliptically and euphemistically advocated military intervention to 'solve the problem of Saddam'. These articles form the focus of this next section.

The arguments for military intervention and the assassination of Saddam Hussein were presented and discussed as 'options' open to 'Us' in resolving the 'stand-off'. In an editorial headlined '**Iraq: diminishing options**' (12 November 1997), the *Guardian* presents such an argument:

> Sooner or later, the Council will almost certainly have to consider military action, a choice which is far from satisfactory and yet may be necessary, because not to take it would lead to an even worse situation.

Perhaps most interestingly, here this editorial attempts to allay the presumed reticence of the *Guardian*-reader to military aggression by suggesting is prevents "*an even worse situation*" (emphasis added). The newspaper therefore adopts a 'consequentialist' view to the "military action", based on a utilitarian principle whereby punishment (in this case the proposed "military action") is "an intrinsic mischief" whose use can only be justified by its countering "some greater mischief or evil" (Atkin, 2000: 2). In achieving this criterion of justification, the *Guardian* suggests that not punishing Iraq simply would lead to an (intentionally ambiguous) "even worse situation". Coincidently, the editorial's argument for military intervention closely mirrors the view of Downing Street at that time. Quoted in the *Financial Times* (**Blair joins US in warning Iraq over hidden weapons**, 29 January 1998), Prime Minister Tony Blair presented an almost identical argument: "if he [Saddam Hussein] isn't stopped — and stopped soon — the effects will be worse for the whole of the region in the long term".

The *Financial Times* also summarised the 'options' which may end the 'UNSCOM crisis' in an feature article headlined '**Saddam stand-off**' (20 January 1998) — the overheadline to the article stated 'DAVID GARDNER LOOKS AT THE LIMITED OPTIONS FOR DEALING WITH A DEFIANT IRAQI REGIME'. To the journalist's credit, the article argues that all "the limited options" will be limited in success: the American demand for "full compliance" is described as almost unenforceable; previous cruise missile attacks only served to "strengthen Mr Saddam"; and the much discussed "targeted attacks against […] weapons installations" are also dismissed since "there is little guarantee such strikes would hit easily concealable germ and nerve gas agents". The options discussed were, of course, 'the limited options of *the US and UK*', presupposing that they were in the position — morally and physically — to take such options. Further, the article suggests another option: "an alternative government-in-exile to Mr Saddam, with a generous programme to reconstruct Iraq built around it." This "option" open to 'the West' is not objected to as strongly as with the others — the journalist merely suggests that it "is unlikely to yield *short-term* results" (emphasis added). The failures of the alternative 'options' suggested appear even more marked in light of this partial criticism. This, along with Gardner describing the deposition of Saddam Hussein as signalling 'the West's' "good intentions" suggests that the long-term removal of the "defiant Iraqi regime" is the "option" which he is endorsing.

The 'consequentialist argument' used in a *Guardian* editorial discussed above, is also drawn upon in a column printed by the *Guardian*, headlined **'Still armed and dangerous'** (31 January 1998). The column, written by Martin Woolacott, 'debates' the possible ways in which 'We' are to 'deal with Saddam', with the overheadline of the article illustrating its primary argument: 'DROP-PING BOMBS ON IRAQ MAY BE THE LEAST WORST OPTION'. He rightly suggests that "bombing Iraq with the intention of destroying part of the regime's mass-destruction capacity is a risky business that will not bring an easy solution to the problem posed by Saddam". However, his evaluation that bombing "will not bring an *easy* solution" suggests that it will bring 'a solution' nonetheless. He then goes on to identify further "problems" with destroying "the regime's mass-destruction capacity":

> After four or six or 10 days of bombing, what if Saddam is still defiant? What if the bombing should inadvertently spread chemical or biological stocks? What if the bombing left intact some biological or chemical capacity?

These problems and others are swept aside in the final paragraph however, where Woolacott concludes:

> There is no answer to these questions, except to say that alternative, if it is to let Saddam prevail, is worse. This is a deep game, and it should be played with the intention of denying him the advantage and not with any predisposition to either force or diplomacy, even if it seems likely that force, for all its manifest disadvantages, will in the end be needed.

This, I feel, is one of the most depressing passages of the sampled Iraq articles for three reasons. First, Woolacott is essentially arguing for war: a war on Iraq's WoMD; a war on Saddam Hussein. This war is justified, he feels, despite the appalling possibility of large numbers of Iraqi civilians being killed by the inadvertent "spread [of] chemical and biological stocks", the Iraqis who would inevitably be killed by 'allied' bombs and the Iraqis who may be killed by Saddam Hussein in predictable massacres of 'treacherous' or rebellious civilians in the north and south of Iraq. Woolacott skips over these possibilities — there is, he states "no answer to these questions" — in favour of implying that letting "Saddam prevail" would be 'worse for the world'.

Second, Woolacott suggests that the strategy towards Iraq "is a deep game" which should be played without "any predisposition to either force or diplomacy". Aside from the fact that he appears to show a very clear predisposition towards using "force" to solve the "problem" of Saddam, the very idea that "force" and "diplomacy" should be regarded as equally acceptable courses of action is appalling, showing an incredibly lax regard for Iraqi life. That this disregard can then be labelled a "game", albeit a "deep" one (whatever *that* is meant to mean) I find particularly disturbing. Third, the proposed violence is backed despite Woolacott acknowledging that Saddam Hussein may remain in power and "defiant" at the end of it all. It is undoubtedly the case that Saddam Hussein and his regime were both guilty and capable of despicable and unimaginable acts of cruelty. But it is sad that a columnist in a 'quality' British newspaper found himself able to argue for a course of action which could conceivably result in comparably pernicious effects, yet which also seems to offer little or no possibility of changing the circumstances which precipitated such action.

The assassination of Saddam Hussein was an 'option' which, the sampled newspapers argued, was being backed with some vigour in the United States too. Several of the sampled Iraq articles focused centrally upon the arguments being put 'for' and 'against' this course of action by the American 'public', American politicians and American newspapers. The *Guardian* for example printed an article reporting American support for the assassination of Saddam Hussein, in an article headlined '**Public opinion wants Clinton to 'sock it to Saddam**" (15 November 1997). The *Daily Telegraph* also printed an article, headlined '**Tired of words, Americans want to end the 'Beast of Baghdad**" (13 November 1997), which argued strongly for the assassination of Saddam Hussein. The article opens by employing the openly rhetorical figure "The Average American" (capitals in original), representing an 'appeal to group feeling' in support for the argument in the headline. The article also quotes Thomas Friedman of the *New York Times*, a notorious hawk, who wrote:

> Saddam Hussein is the reason God invented cruise missiles [...] Cruise missiles are simply the only way to deal with him. [...] So if and when Saddam pushes beyond the brink, and we get that one good shot, let's make sure it's a head shot.

A third article on this subject, headlined '**America considers how to bring about the death of a President**', was printed in *The Times* (18 November 1997). Where this article differs considerably is in the fact that it more accurately locates the 'ASSASSINATION DEBATE', referred to in the leader, with élite political commentators, such as Friedman cited above, and the American government. The journalist — Ian Brodie *again* — quotes American notables who back the plan to assassinate Hussein: "George Stephanopoulos, formerly a close aide to President Clinton, said: 'We should kill him.'" To his credit however, Brodie quotes an "Executive Order" of the United States which shows that such a course of action would not only break International laws, but would also contravene American domestic law:

> Execution of foreign leaders by government agents was outlawed by Executive Order 12333 signed by President Reagan, It says: 'No person employed by or acting on behalf of the United States Government shall engage in, or conspire to engage in, assassination.'

Unfortunately the importance of this paragraph to the options being 'debated' was de-emphasised through it being placed as the penultimate paragraph of the article. This is, of course, a significant observation. Should it have been placed as the second paragraph — after where the article states "A debate is growing in the United States over the moral and practical issues of assassinating President Saddam Hussein" — then the article would have given a very strong implication that the assassination of Saddam Hussein should not even be discussed, never mind considered as a 'moral' or 'practical' option. Needless to say the highly relevant "Executive Order" which makes it illegal for the United States to "engage in, or conspire to engage in" the assassination of Saddam Hussein, was conspicuously absent from all other sampled Iraq articles, in *The Times* and the other titles, both previous to and following its inclusion in this single article.

Articles contesting the dominant discursive strategy

There were articles which dissented from the discursive strategy analysed and presented. Such articles were very much in the minority, and tended to be concentrated in columns and readers' letters. They contested the dominant discursive strategy at all levels, but tended to focus on three points: first, dissenting articles argued that Britain and the US do not propose to attack *all* countries which break international law. This entails an inconsistency on the part of Britain and the US, which in turn implies that their actions towards Iraq are unjust. A reader's letter, written by Cathy Aitchison and printed in the *Guardian* (15 November 1997) makes this point quite forcefully. The *whole* of the letter reads:

> How dare the US strut around the world, insisting on complete compliance with UN resolutions which suit it and ignoring those which don't?

Arguments from this strategy were clearly intended to undermine the presupposed 'moral basis' for the attacks. Israel was the country most frequently referred to as 'escaping' the criticism of the UN and the military wrath of 'the West'. A *Guardian* column, written by Paul Foot and headlined '**State terrorism unpunished by the UN**' (17 November 1997), makes such an argument. The first paragraph sets the scene, purposefully not mentioning the country whose "terrorism" has gone unpunished in order to highlight the hypocrisy of the US/UK position toward Iraq:

> Senior UN officials have looked on helplessly as angry UN resolutions have been repeatedly ignored. Murderous invasions of a neighbouring country, all of them banned by the UN Charter and overwhelmingly condemned by the General Assembly, have been carried out with impunity. At the same time there has been mounting oppression, torture and house-bombing against opposition forces, and secret stockpiling of a nuclear arsenal. The regime concerned is in Tel Aviv. No state on earth has shown such cynical disregard for the UN as has Israel.

Much of what is written in the above paragraph is unquestionably correct. It was however referred to only very rarely in these Iraq articles, and nowhere in language as emotive as in Paul Foot's article. The rhetoric is particularly powerful: UN officials are 'helpless'; UN resolutions are not only "angry" but are "*repeatedly* ignored"; Israel does not just 'invade' but does so 'murderously' and "with impunity" and has used "oppression, torture and house-bombing against opposition forces". In fact, so emotive is the language that the reader may be persuaded into thinking that Foot is 'biased', 'unobjective' or else has an agenda in criticising Israel. Further down the article he quotes Geoff Simons from his "recent book on the United Nations" where he states: "Israel is currently in violation, to a greater or lesser extent, of UN resolutions 338, 465, 476, 672, 673 and 681." In addition he argues: "In 1996 Israel bombed south Lebanon again, targeting a UN base and killing hundreds of refugees who were sheltering there". This section provides particularly compelling evidence of the extent to which Israel 'defies' international law, and perhaps goes some way to supporting the rhetorical accusation of "State terrorism" in the headline. But in answer to the question "Will the UN go in?", Foot concludes:

> No it won't. [...] Ignoring UN resolutions and building up nuclear arsenals only become matters for armed intervention when the regime concerned is (temporarily) hostile to the United States and cheap oil supplies are in peril.

Here not only is the hypocrisy of the proposed anti-Iraqi attacks exposed, but a reason for these attacks is also given: the geo-political and economic interests of America. This accusation of base American self-interest goes a long way to undermining the presupposed 'moral' basis to the military intervention. As stated above, such arguments were rarely made and never with such ferocity.

Second, some articles questioned the alleged 'precision accuracy' of 'Western' military hardware. These articles based their criticisms on the low success rate of weaponry used in the 1991 attacks on Iraq, and occasionally attempted to derail the claim that such weapons could be used as part of an 'ethical' bombing strategy. One article, headlined '**Can America match its mouth with its muscle?**' and printed in the *Independent* (15 November 1997), presented a wealth of evidence taken from "a highly critical report by the [US] General Accounting Office (GAO)", to support the argument that "American air power was nothing like as accurate or effective in the Gulf War as was claimed by the Pentagon." The report from the GAO, reproduced in part by the *Independent*, "systematically deflates the claims, made by manufacturers and the US Department of Defence alike, for the effectiveness of most weapons systems." For example, the ability of the "air-to-ground Maverick missile, costing $100,000 (£61,000) each, to hit anything was impaired or sometimes made impossible by clouds, haze, smoke and dust." Further, the US-led coalition was only able to hit:

> multi-story buildings and other large immobile targets with accuracy. Thus, US planes hit telecommunications towers, the oil refinery and power station at Doura on the capital's southern outskirts as well as bridges spanning the Tigris. But it could not destroy smaller mobile targets such as tanks and artillery pieces.

What this therefore means is that the civilian infrastructure is easy to hit, but not the security and military apparatus. This argument therefore enables the reader to infer that should Iraqi civilians actually be able to avoid being hurt or killed by the proposed 'Western' attacks, their quality of life would be severely reduced (as it was following the targeting of civilian areas during the 1991 Persian Gulf Conflict) due to the destruction of the infrastructure and public utilities.

The third dissenting argumentative strategy argued against the whole basis for military intervention. By this strategy, the claims and presuppositions of the dominant strategy were generally accepted (Saddam Hussein *was* defying the international will; He *was* a bad man; and international law *should* be upheld) but the implied conclusion, that we should therefore bomb Iraq or attempt to kill him specifically, were rejected in favour of non-violent action. A series of five readers' letters, printed in the *Guardian* (17 November 1997) made such an argument, although the headline that they were placed under — '**Let America fight its own battles**' — appeared to suggest that they were actually objecting to *British* involvement in bombing Iraq rather than opposing the bombing of Iraq *per se*. One of these letters even criticised the decision of the *Guardian* to include

> a big picture of an American warplane on the front page [...] Printing the picture can only arouse the atavistic conviction that war is exciting, which is the last thing the world needs in a time of international tension. This week, please give us a picture of diplomats working hard to keep war at bay. (Leonard Pepper, Oxford)

By far the most significant of these five letters, in terms of size (it was the largest), placement (it was positioned first) and political importance, was written by four Members of Parliament — Tony Benn, Tam Dalyell, Ken Livingstone and John McDonnell — accompanied by Ron Huzzard and Rae Street. The approach taken in this letter is to shift the role of the 'aggressor' towards the American and British governments, which in turn helps to negativise the 'Western' approach to Iraq. This is illustrated in the letter's opening paragraph:

> We note with concern the growing threat by the United States of yet another military attack on Iraq, backed by the British government. [...] There is no justification for bombing Iraq yet again, almost seven years since the end of the Gulf War.

Lower down, the letter attacks the stated reason for America's continuing support for military attacks on Iraq, and suggests an alternative theory for this proposed aggression:

> We suspect that Washington's continued belligerence towards Iraq has little to do with saving the world from destruction and much to do with protecting US domination of the world's oil supplies.

Here the mitigation of the claim — "We *suspect*" — is counteracted by the rhetorical strength of the claim itself — "*continued belligerence*" and "protecting US *domination*". Their dismissal of the US stated war aim is enabled by the letter's use of hyperbole — "saving *the world* from *destruction*" ridicules the US in its self-appointed role of protector.

The derisory tone of the letter is heightened by its claim that perhaps "the safety of the world would be better served if weapons of mass destruction were removed from [...] countries like the US and Britain". What this sentence does is quite cleverly redefine the American 'war aim' of "saving the world from destruction" into the more specific intention of 'removing weapons of mass destruction'. This definition enables the authors to allege an inconsistency on the part of the US:

> Israel is known to be a nuclear weapons state and has been defying UN resolutions
> for years. Yet the US does not threaten to bomb it, nor should it. Likewise,
> Turkey's recent military incursions into the north of Iraq in pursuit of the Kurds
> have gone unchallenged.

Therefore, the authors are using an example of the first dissenting strategy
discussed above — alleged inconsistencies — in order to contest the US
argument for military aggression. This constitutes a strategic rhetorical use of
the topic potential on offer to the authors of the letter, since to argue inconsistent adherence to a principle does not refute the applicability of the principle in
the case discussed. However, the letter aims to show how the arguments
offered by the US and Britain — weapons of mass destruction, international
law — do not justify bombing Iraq since these same arguments apply in the
case of Israel and Turkey. There must therefore be an alternative reason why
the US wants to bomb Iraq — which the letter suggests is the US desire to
maintain its "domination of the world's oil supplies", an argument which is
immoral and therefore unacceptable.

The lack of dissent in the sampled Iraq news reports may be partly the
result of the space required to support a claim which contests the dominant
discursive strategy. On the other hand, should the news reports have been
more critical regarding the claims made by US and British officials, not providing column space for them to '*warn* Iraq not to make their *threats*', and
approached the proposed military aggression as an intrinsic evil which must be
used defensively, with restraint and *only* where no other option could bring
possible success, then dissent would have been possible in the most abbreviated
of reports. The decisions of journalists and newspapers to accept, and in most
cases *support*, the argument to direct military aggression at Iraq for the crimes
of its government, must be viewed in light of this.

The importance of UNSCOM to 'unconnected' Iraq articles

The story of the UNSCOM weapons inspections and 'stand-off' dominated the
articles reporting Iraq. There were however a few articles which, on the surface
at least, appeared to report Iraq and Iraqi actors from a different frame of
reference that that provided by the UNSCOM crisis. One story, reported by the
sampled newspapers on 6 November 1997, involving the sentencing of six Iraqi
men for the hijack of a civil aircraft appeared to provide an opportunity for
archetypal 'crime' reports. In a report headlined '**Lenient sentence for Iraqi**

hijackers' printed by the *Guardian*, it was the hijackers themselves who appeared to be given more sympathy than the victims of the ordeal:

> Acknowledging the *horrors* the men had *suffered* in their homeland, and a *plea* by the jurors for lenience, the judge said the men had carried out an offence of the greatest possible gravity and that he *had* to jail them in order to deter others. (emphasis added)

The journalist, Allison Daniels, appears to feel so strongly that these Iraqi men represent "worthy victims" of an enemy regime (see Herman & Chomsky, 1994: 37–87) that the victims of the crime itself are almost forgotten. The Iraqi men's actions are described as "an offence of the greatest possible gravity"; the third paragraph states that the passengers and crew "had all been *terrified*"; and three paragraphs later it states in an almost cursory way that "an air hostess was taken hostage and a passenger was stabbed". No other mention of the distress or injuries to passengers or crew is made for the remaining 103 centimetres of column space. This, compared with the repeated references made to the "horrors", the "unimaginable torture" and the "20th century hell" experienced by the men in *Saddam Hussein's* Iraq.

One would perhaps expect the *Daily Telegraph*, as a traditionally conservative newspaper, to take a different line on the (lenient) sentencing of these hijackers than that taken by the *Guardian*. And indeed they did, but the sympathies of the newspaper were still firmly placed with the hijackers, to a degree which they were not in, for example, the more recent case of the Afghani jet hijacking at Stansted airport. These sympathies are suggested in the headline to the article: '**Asylum-seekers jailed for jet hijack**' (6 November 1997). This headline foregrounds the 'victimhood' of the Iraqi men in a way which alternative headlines focusing on their criminality (such as 'Muslim hijackers seek asylum') wouldn't. In the fourth paragraph, the report states that the hijackers,

> gave evidence of the *brutality* of Saddam Hussein's regime, the *deaths, disappearance, torture* and *sexual abuse* of members of their families and friends. Several had been *sentenced to death* for refusing to join the Iraqi army to fight against fellow Shi'ites. (emphasis added)

By contrast, the victims of the hijacking are mentioned in the seventh paragraph, where the judge states that they "must have been 'reduced to *abject terror*' by the threats and were not to know that the men brandishing knives and fake grenades were not fanatical terrorists" (emphasis added). This very effectively acknowledges the distress which the passengers and crew were no doubt in, but at the same time reduces it, by stating that they were never in any 'real' danger since the grenades were "fake" and these men "were not fanatical terrorists".

This report, and the previous report from the *Guardian*, is therefore functional to the dominant discursive strategy present across much of the Iraq articles reporting the UNSCOM 'stand-off'. The claims and explanations of the Iraqi hijackers' actions are all related directly to the "horror", the "terror", the "death" and "torture" which are seemingly routine in *Saddam Hussein's* Iraq. The claims of these articles therefore support the argument for military aggression on the grounds of 'humanitarian need' — the Iraqis *want* us to bomb their country and rid them of their dictator — and are perhaps all the more persuasive precisely because they appear, at first reading, to 'be about' a completely different event.

'Fancy a trip to Iraq?'

The sampled newspapers displayed a particularly low level of interest in Iraqi civil society. Moreover, most of these articles are written from a position in which the 'threat of Iraq' — militarily, civilly and socially — was emphasised. This can be illustrated quite clearly if we examine, for example, two articles which coded 'travel' as their primary topic. Both of these articles are on the same subject — a British national, Phil Haines, visiting Iraq as a tourist in order to complete his personal ambition to visit every sovereign country on Earth — but interestingly, they are published over two months apart and by different newspapers. The first story was headlined '**Last stop for the man who has been everywhere**' and printed in the *Independent on Sunday* (23 November 1997). The primary aim of the text was to argue that 'the travels of Phil Haines form a great achievement'. The journalist provides two supports for this claim:

1. 'Mr Haines has been to all 192 sovereign countries'
2. 'The latest countries read like a list of war zones'

How this story is connected to Iraq is in the textual realisation of the second supporting reason, wherein Iraq is cited as the latest in this "list of war zones: Afghanistan, Angola, Liberia, Sierra Leone, Somalia and now Iraq". The threat of these war zones to Mr Haines' personal safety must necessarily be emphasised in order for the text to remain coherent. The threat posed by Iraq was achieved via alluding to the familiar, high-profile UNSCOM story. In fact, the audience's familiarity with the ongoing saga of weapons inspections is *relied* upon, since, without either direct reference or explanation, the journalist derives claims of the unaccommodating nature of Iraq *directly* from this recent history. This is noticeable in the first paragraph (numbered here for ease of reference), where both the action and the actors are identified without any further contextualisation of the nature and relevance of the surrounding events:

> [1] Not even the threat of war, nor nuclear attack, [2] could have stopped Phil Haines from going on holiday to Iraq last week. [3] While US and British forces menaced the Gulf, [4] he and a few friends were cheerfully speeding towards the almost deserted Karameh border post [5] — and a remarkable record.

Here, the journalist is simply presenting Iraq as a dangerous place to be. The mention in clause 4 of the "US and British forces menac[ing] the Gulf" must also be read in connection to instrumental aim of the text to represent Iraq as a war zone. Thus, although it is novel to see 'the Allies' represented as "menac[ing] the Gulf", the sentence supports the argument that the Gulf is 'a generally threatening place to be', and as such remains functional within the text. Indeed, describing the "forces" (interesting that they are not Armies) in such a way, without the luxury of being informed of their motivation, perhaps *increases* the perceived threat, since such threats seem undirected, open-ended and unexplained.

In summary then, in order for the second supporting reason ('The latest countries read like a list of war zones') to be accepted, the journalist needs to provide a concise example of a war zone. The easiest way to do this is to provide an archetypal 'war zone' which Mr Haines has visited. Thus, Iraq is offered in such a way: as a rhetorical 'place as subject' — a 'war zone' — drawing upon perceptions of the country which it can be assumed were fairly well inscribed in the imagination of the public at that time.

The second article, headlined '**Fancy a trip to Iraq?**' and printed in the *Daily Telegraph* (31 January 1998), prefers to adopt the more familiar travel writing genre. The use of this headline and the adoption of some of the formal features of travel writing (the recommended company, centred around a 'package deal', suggestions of excursions and sites of interest) during the period in which 'the UNSCOM stand-off' received the most copious and extensive coverage, are clearly intended to be read as ironic. The weapons inspections in Iraq would be well known to anyone with a passing interest in current affairs, and this knowledge is alluded to in the first paragraph of the article:

> [1] With a task force gathering in the Gulf, [2] diplomats shuttling furiously, [3] and Saddam Hussein growling defiance, [4] one man is still determined to take his Easter holiday in Iraq. [5] And for £1,350 you can go, too.

Once again, we see the assumptions of the journalist coming to the fore. The above passage is written on the assumption that the audience will know who the actors referred to are, and the relations between them: who constitutes the "task force", what the diplomats are attempting to achieve with their "shuttling", and most importantly who Saddam Hussein is and to whom he is "growling defiance". But just in case the reader did not know the exactitudes of the crisis, the sentence is structured in such a way to imply an unattractive situation regardless of details. The whole of the first three clauses, with the addition of the adverb 'still' in [4], function as an adverbial phrase contingent to the central fourth clause. Other adverbs signalling contingency include 'although', and 'despite', thus an alternative way of writing the sentence could have been:

> [1–3] [Despite all this], [4] one man is still determined to take his Easter holiday in Iraq.

This alternative version would have functioned adequately, communicating that the man in question is determined to holiday in Iraq, regardless of the obstacles placed in front of him — an invitation which is extended to the reader in exchange for the rather princely sum of £1,350.

Thus, evidence is provided to show that Iraq is, depending on your point of view, somewhere between a rather dubious choice for a holiday and a potential death-trap. The journalist seems to sense that not enough evidence has been provided to *prove* the undesirable nature of Iraq, and the second paragraph acknowledges this, stating:

> [6] It may not be everybody's idea of the perfect package, [7] but Phil Haines, [8] the director of Live Ltd, [9] a travel company he runs from his home in Twickenham, Middlesex, [10] is determined to go ahead with it.

At this point in the article, the only information provided for the reader on which to base a decision of whether or not this *is* their "perfect [holiday] package", is that which is alluded to regarding the general nature of Iraq: the gathering task force, shuttle diplomacy and the 'canine' (cf. "growling") Saddam Hussein. It is highly doubtful that this would appeal to very many people at all and hence the use of 'not everybody' (line 6) is clearly intended to be ironic, transgressing, as it does, the Gricean maxim of 'Quality' (1967: 53). But there are some people to whom this holiday — with its apparent fair share of adrenaline — may appeal, so it become necessary, in the third paragraph, to further pervert the travel writing genre through citing some of what the journalist calls the 'highlights' of the holiday:

[11] A gruelling journey overland from Jordan, [12] an Aids test at the border, [13] and a room at a hotel where you are invited to wipe your feet on a mosaic of George Bush [14] are among the highlights.

The choice of the three elements given as "the highlights" (clauses 11–13) is interesting, and deserves further examination. First, the choice of the adjective "gruelling" provides Iraq with a very obviously negative frame of reference from the onset. Second, each of the three cited "highlights" are signifiers of stereotypical representations of the Middle East and, by association, Iraq. Taking each one in turn:

1. "A gruelling journey overland from Jordan": peripheral nation; substandard transportation [cf. gruelling];
2. "an Aids test at the border": unclean/unhealthy; intrusive; suspicious;
3. "wipe your feet on a mosaic of George Bush": grudge-bearing; anti-western

As such, these elements — considered by the journalist to *characterise* the holiday — must be viewed as part of the greater stylistic register from which they are drawn: the Middle East as socially and culturally un(der)developed.

Lastly, the three elements are mentioned as being *among* the highlights, implying that there are others. What this means is that the journalist has played a visibly active role in the choice of what to single out as worthy of particular reference, as opposed to alternate options. Three of these 'other', presumably less illustrious, highlights, are backgrounded in the text, relegated to the latter half of a sentence, two thirds of the way down the article:

Visas are arranged through an agency in Baghdad, and stops will include the souks in that city, the Hanging Gardens of Babylon and the ziggurat at Ur.

This structuring of information is highly significant, since foregrounding information in this way encourages a reading in which the three stereotypical elements (in clauses 11–14) are granted a higher significance than that accorded to one of the Wonders of the Ancient World. The mention of these tourist sites appears almost as a *concession* to the main argument of the article, that 'Iraq is an undesirable place to visit'. But the added information cannot be regarded as a concession in the truest sense of the word since despite the introduction of this new contestive material, the article continues along much the same lines as it did previously. In this sense, the information operates as a "show concession", ostensibly providing "evidence that the speaker appreciates the other side's point of view, displaying to listeners that the speaker is not wholly blind to other's positions" (Antaki & Wetherell, 1999: 24). The article gains a sense of 'objectivity' through the inclusion of the concession, and the argument being presented about Iraq being an undesirable place to visit becomes all the more convincing because of it.

Coda

When approaching the reporting of Iraq we should ask ourselves: what function do these texts play? Gill and Whedbee (1997) try to encourage critics to "view texts as pragmatic: a rhetorical text responds to or interacts with societal issues or problems, and it produces some action upon or change in the world" (p.161). Adopting their approach, it is instructive to bear in mind that the two 'tourist texts' were originally printed during or immediately following large peaks in the number of articles reporting Iraq — 23 November 1997 and 31 January 1998. It therefore seems highly suspect that the only two 'travel' articles covering Iraq in the sample, focusing on the exploits of the same man, occur in close proximity to these large peaks in reporting. The UNSCOM stand-off is present in the two articles in the form of a background, assumed threat: it is cited as a reason for not visiting, and hence *learning* about the nation and its peoples. This lack of understanding is highly functional to the interventionist aims of the sampled newspapers' dominant discursive strategy, a point also made by Traber and Davis (1991):

> Ignorance of the affairs of a nation's ordinary people is useful in the construction of the image of an enemy. The less we know of the enemy the easier it is to create the image that we wish. The mass media have built up or, at least, reinforced a social cosmology which divides the world into angels and devils, the good and the bad (Traber & Davis (1991: 9) cited in Keeble (1997: 59)).

The two articles analysed here can hardly be regarded as conventional examples of the 'travel writing' genre. Rather they seem to be developing a 'stay at home' genre when it comes to travelling to 'threatening Iraq', an agenda which seems highly functional to the broader concerns of reporting the UNSCOM stand-off.

The discursive strategy featured in Figure 6.1 formed the principal thematic feature of the sampled Iraq articles. The presuppositions and implications of this strategy supported an argument which firstly advocated military intervention in Iraq and secondly, but less frequently, advocated the assassination (or the more euphemistic 'removal') of President Saddam Hussein from power. Clearly, 'We' can only (metaphorically) 'unleash' this (euphemistic) 'military action', if 'We' are actually able to *do* so. 'Our' physical and moral ability to bomb Iraq is therefore presupposed in most articles and forms a central argumentative claim in others. The reporting of the UNSCOM 'stand-off' therefore constitutes a 'Discourse of Military Intervention', in which the lexical, syntactic, semantic and structural choices in the texts are functional to their pragmatic role: justifying bombing Iraq and 'removing' Saddam Hussein.

Chapter 7

Conviction, truth, blame and a shifting agenda

The reporting of Algeria

Introduction[1]

Is the reporting of Africa racist? Does, as Baffour Ankomah (2001) has argued, a 'heart of darkness' rhetoric dominate and constantly recur in the reporting of Africa (also see Badawi, 1988), and in what ways is this reporting frame, with its emphasis on barbarity and underdevelopment, further complicated, affected or shaped when reporting majority Muslim North African countries? As Harrison and Palmer (1986) argue, not only has coverage of Africa declined and continues to decline since the 1950s, only certain stories about Africa — principally war, coups, famine and the actions and interests of white Africans (previously in South Africa, currently in Zimbabwe) — are reported. "The point worth emphasising", they suggest, "is that only the spectacular, the bizarre or the truly horrific tend to reach our screens, thus reinforcing our stereotypes of Africa and Africans" (p. 82).

In contrast with many studies of critical discourse analysis, in which analysts merely play lip-service to the integration of linguistic and socio-political critique, this chapter of the book is focused at the level of *social practices*. In the case of Algeria, like with many dictatorial regimes, it is essential that analysis focuses on *sources* (the Algerian Junta, Western European Governments) and *forces* (capitalism, anti-Muslimism) outside the newsroom, and the effects which they can have upon reporting, since it is to the benefit of the Algerian Junta, of Western European Governments as well as in the interests of capitalism that Algeria is represented as 'a heart of darkness'. This approach accords closely to what Reisigl and Wodak (2002: 33) call "a sociodiagnostic critique". With such a critique, "the analyst exceeds the purely textual or discourse internal sphere. She or he makes use of her or his background and contextual knowledge and embeds the communicative or interactional structures of a discursive event in a wider frame of social and political relations, processes and circumstances" (Ibid.). The more standard approach to CDA (the "text or discourse immanent critique", Reisigl & Wodak, 2002: 32) involves an analytic 'move' from texts to social practices, primarily employing conventional discourse-linguistic tools to illuminate (presupposed, manifest, implied) textual meaning in order to offer deductive observations on how prejudicial (or misrepresentative) reporting of the civilian massacres is dialectically related to anti-Muslim racism. In contrast, the analytical approach of this chapter moves 'the other way' — *from* social practices *to* texts, via discursive (news gathering) practices — with the data used to illuminate the restrictive/constructive effect(s) which social practices have on newspaper discursive practices (and hence on the contents and implications of the texts).

'An internal conflict': Quantitative patterns in the reporting of Algeria

The broadsheet reporting of Algeria was marked by a strikingly consistent topical focus — death, 'terrorism' and 'Islam' — and equally striking shifts in the apportioning of blame for these deaths. The supremacy of these topics inevitably 'framed' Algeria as a country simply *of* conflict, death and politics — a stereotypical representation which was then explained with reference to Islam and the activities of Algerian Muslims. 139 articles (57.5%) specifically reported the deaths caused by the conflict as a primary topic: 78 focused on 'civilian deaths' (32.2%), 12 emphasised 'terrorism' (5.0%) and 49 focused on 'civil war' in general (20.2%). Almost every article reported Algeria from within a 'conflict frame'. The EU diplomatic mission to 'investigate terrorism' was a regular theme of later reports (n= 34; 14.0%); and was additionally reported as 'diplomacy' (n= 2; 0.8) or the 'actions of international leaders' (n= 10; 4.1%). The Algerian municipal 'elections' received minimal coverage (n= 5; 2.1%) as did the 'demonstrations' organised by Algerian citizens following the announcement of the (fraudulent?) election results (n= 7; 2.9%). In stark contrast to the scale of coverage granted to death, war and (high) politics: the 'cultural' lives of Algerians received scant coverage in a total of only *four* articles — 'travel', 'literature', 'music' and 'faith' (all n= 1; 0.4%); and the oil industry was reported as a primary topic in only two articles (0.8%), despite the clear and significant influence of the several international oil companies currently active in 'prospecting' for Algerian oil and gas.

Indeed international contextualisation was, until the short-lived intervention of an EU investigative 'troika' of nations (see below), almost entirely absent from the reporting of Algeria. Only 27 articles (11.2%) were located in a country other than Algeria, which is perhaps remarkable considering the difficulties of British journalists in gaining any access to the country. In addition, only 85 articles (35.1%) cited more the one country, meaning that in 64.9% (n= 157) of articles reporting Algeria during this sample period, 'Algeria' was the only country considered to have had an influence on the reported action. What this framing of the story inevitably meant was that the Algerian conflict was presented as an 'internal' dispute, thereby backgrounding the influence and interests of both other countries — specifically France — and the oil companies with a financial stake in Algeria.

So, if individuals, organisations, Governments and companies outside of Algeria were assumedly unconnected with its civil war, then who did journalists present as agents or perpetrators of the violence? Time and time again, Muslims and 'Muslim groups' had this role thrust upon them: in 83.5% (n= 202) of the reports on and from Algeria, 'Islam' was cited as an influential factor in explaining or accounting for the reported violence. Further, the role in which broadsheet newspapers placed 'Muslims' in the conflict — as aggressor or victim — can be inferred if this same variable (which coded whether Islam was thought to be connected with, or the cause of the reported actions) is cross tabulated with the Runnymede Trust's eight suggested binary argumentative positions, characterising 'open' or 'closed' views of Islam and Muslims. Selected results of this cross tabulation are provided in Table 7.1 below.

Table 7.1. Representation of Islam and Muslims, by 'Islamic agency'

| | | Is Islam cited as a factor? | | | | Total | |
| | | Yes | | No | | | |
		Count	Col %	Count	Col %	Count	Col %
Represented as: separate/interacting	Separate	152	75.2%	4	10.0%	156	64.5%
	Interacting	6	3.0%			6	2.5%
	No response	44	21.8%	36	90.0%	80	33.1%
Total		202	100.0%	40	100.0%	242	100.0%
Represented as: enemy/partner	Enemy	145	71.8%	2	5.0%	147	60.7%
	Partner	12	5.9%			12	5.0%
	No response	45	22.3%	38	95.0%	83	34.3%
Total		202	100.0%	40	100.0%	242	100.0%
Islam vs the west: natural/problematic	Natural	128	63.4%	1	2.5%	129	53.3%
	Problematic	9	4.5%	1	2.5%	10	4.1%
	No response	65	32.2%	38	95.0%	103	42.6%
Total		202	100.0%	40	100.0%	242	100.0%

Table 7.1 shows that the majority of Algerian articles represented Muslims as being 'separate' (64.5%; n= 156), 'inferior' (64.5%; n= 156), an 'enemy' (60.7%; n= 147) and the erroneous enmity between 'Islam' and 'the West' as 'natural' (53.3%; n= 129). These percentages increase markedly when articles citing 'Islamic agency' are analysed separately. When chi-square tests were performed on the four binary variables in Table 7.2 and the 'Islamic agency' variable, the results for all four tests were highly significant: in each case, p= 0.000 for all measures, suggesting a high dependency between 'Islamic agency' and negative argumentative representation. These findings show that 'Islam' and 'Muslims' were represented in overwhelmingly negative terms when broadsheet newspapers reported Algeria, and also suggest that 'Islam' was used, *in itself*, as an argumentative resource in the derogation of Algerian Muslims.

The next set of questions which need to be broached involve locating journalistic *agency* for these argumentative claims about Islam and Algerian Muslims. Broadly: who is responsible for this negative argumentative representation? The picture painted by Table 7.1 above, is of an undifferentiated negative coverage of Algerian Muslims, but in fact the coverage of Algeria differed greatly between the seven broadsheet newspapers sampled. Table 7.2 below illustrates this, by revealing the total position each broadsheet newspaper took with regard to the binaried argumentative positions suggested by the Runnymede Trust (1997).

Table 7.2. The argumentative representation of Islam, by newspaper

	Closed Representations		Open Representation		Ratio: Open to Closed Representation
	Mean	Sum	Mean	Sum	
Financial Times	1.88	81	.67	29	2.81
Guardian	2.57	139	.11	6	23.36
Independent	2.64	119	.27	12	9.78
Telegraph	2.75	88	.22	7	12.50
The Times	2.69	145	.46	25	5.85
IoS	3.71	26	.14	1	26.50
Sunday Times	3.86	27	.43	3	8.98
Total	2.58	625	.34	83	7.59

Table 7.2 shows the total number (Sum) of 'open' and 'closed' binary representations of Islam and Muslims, the mean number per article and the ratio between 'open' and 'closed' representations for each newspaper. The table

shows that all newspapers' 'closed' means were substantially greater than 'open' means: items printed in *The Sunday Times* contained the highest mean number of 'closed' representations of Islam, at an average of 3.86 'closed' representations per article. However it the ratios between 'open' and 'closed' representations which are the most striking feature of the above table. Take the *Guardian*: by only including 6 'open' representations of Islam (i.e. criticising 'Islamophobia'; that 'Muslims are diverse'; 'Muslims are our equal'; 'Muslims are our partners, not our enemies'; etc.) across 54 articles, the *Guardian* ensured that it achieved a ratio of 23.36 'closed' representations of Algerian Muslims for every 'open' representation. By this ratio, the *Independent on Sunday* produced the most 'Islamophobic' representation of Algeria: its readership was over 26 times more likely to be subjected to a 'closed' representation of Algerian Muslims than to an 'open' one. The dominance of this prejudicial reporting, and the wide divergence between 'open' and 'closed' representations, are represented graphically in Graph 7.1.

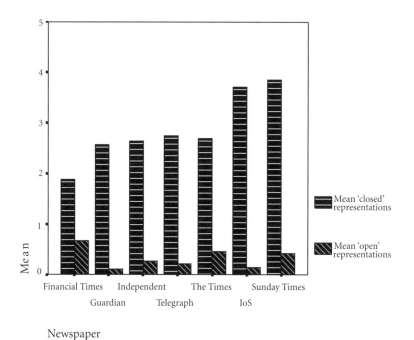

Graph 7.1. Representing Algerian Muslims

It is interesting to note the differences between Sunday and Daily newspapers, with Sunday newspapers including a higher proportion of 'closed' representations (3.79 per article) than the dailies (2.51 per article). The greater length of articles in Sunday newspapers (the mean length of items in Sunday newspapers was 340cm compared to 173.8cm in daily newspapers) provides little explanation for an increase in this ratio, since the increased size of newspaper reports didn't produce an equal increase in the number of 'open' representations. This suggests that the greater degree of anti-Muslim prejudice in Sunday newspapers may be directly attributable to the inability of these journalists to write, at length, about Islam and Muslims without recourse to 'closed' stereotypical representations. Whilst this is a rather disheartening finding, it does appear to suggest that the more objective, 'hard' news formats prevalent in daily broadsheets — and especially the *Financial Times* — provide the most 'open' forum for the representation of Islam.

The by-lined source of these articles is also an important variable to take into consideration, particularly in the case of Algeria, where visas and access were only granted to certain media organisations.

Table 7.3. Summarised by-line for Algerian and 'Other' articles

| | Country | | | | Total | |
| | Algeria | | All other countries | | | |
	Count	Col %	Count	Col %	Count	Col %
Staff Journalist	160	66.1%	1771	77.1%	1931	76.0%
Press Agency	64	26.4%	320	13.9%	384	15.1%
No source given	7	2.9%	109	4.7%	116	4.6%
All other sources	11	4.5%	98	4.3%	109	4.3%
Total	242	100.0%	2298	100.0%	2540	100.0%

Table 7.3 shows that the percentage of Algerian articles sourced to press agencies (26.4%) is almost twice that of the remainder of the sample (13.9%). This high figure is no doubt the result of the difficulties newspapers and journalists had in obtaining access to Algeria. In situations such as Algeria — a 'newsworthy' story which British journalists were unable (or unwilling) to gain physical access to — broadsheets rely upon copy wired from press agencies based where the story is breaking. This was found to be significant when the themes and argumentation of press agency reports were compared to those written by staff journalists — particularly staff journalists writing from Algeria.

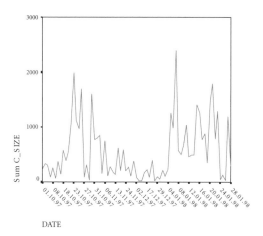

Graph 7.2. Algerian articles' daily column centimetres

Finally, Graph 7.2, shows that the reporting of Algeria fitted broadly into three sections: the period up to and including the reporting of Algerian municipal elections, which caused a peak in coverage on 23 October 1997; second, a mid-period characterised by steadily decreasing press interest, reporting the ongoing conflict and the deaths of civilians; and third, a rejuvenated interest in the Algerian conflict in January 1998, corresponding roughly with the start of the Muslim Holy month of Ramadan.

Thus, until Ramadan, the reporting of Algeria was 'tailing off' into occasional and short articles. However, once Ramadan had started, broadsheet newspapers showed a renewed interest in a conflict which was now provided with an explicitly Muslim 'peg', or angle, on which to 'hang' the story. As stated above, 'violence' and 'terrorism' formed integral parts of the broadsheet reporting of Algeria. This relationship is clearly illustrated in two further graphs (see below) representing the occurrences of the words 'violence (and acts of violence)' and 'terrorism (and acts of terrorism)' across the four month sample.

Graphs 7.3 and 7.4 closely mirror the distribution of articles in Graph 7.2, illustrating the importance of 'violence' and 'terrorism' to broadsheet newspaper reporting of Algeria. Simple put: as the number of reports or column centimetres increased, so did the occurrence of 'violence' and 'terrorism', in very closely related quantities. Reports referring to 'violence' and 'terrorism' peak during Ramadan — giving an insight into the theme(s) of reporting during the Muslim Holy month — with the remaining two broad periods of coverage (October and a slack mid-period covering November and December)

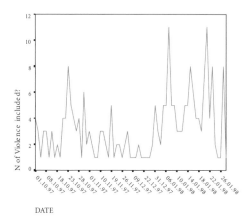

Graph 7.3. Frequency of 'Violence' in Algerian articles, by date

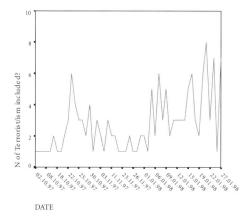

Graph 7.4. Frequency of 'Terrorism' in Algerian articles, by date

also clearly notable. The remainder of this chapter is therefore divided into three sections analysing, in turn, the reporting across these three periods in the broadsheet coverage of Algeria, in order to explore the changes in content which accompanied the changes in journalistic output.

Discourse and intertextuality

Dividing and analysing broadsheet coverage of Algeria separately and chronologically into three periods of coverage in this way is interesting, firstly, from an 'intertextual' or 'dialogical' perspective. Since Bakhtin (1981; 1986), dialogical-ity is regarded as "the idea that any text is a link in a chain, reacting to, drawing in and transforming other [previous] texts" (Fairclough & Wodak, 1997: 262). However, the broadsheet reporting of Algeria during this period was, on first reading, surprisingly anti-dialogical. The argumentative claims of journalists regarding who was responsible for killing civilians switched dramatically be-tween, and *within*, the three time periods in striking ways. With the notable exception of the *Financial Times* (predominantly the reporting of the staff writer Roula Khalaf), all broadsheet newspapers made frequent shifts, changes and *reverses* in identifying the groups they felt were responsible for killing civilians. However, a dominant argumentative position, blaming the civilian deaths on either 'Muslim terrorists' or the Algerian Junta, characterises broadsheet cover-age of Algeria at any point in each of the three periods (October 1997; November — December 1997; January 1998). The periods are not separated by clear junctures however, but rather journalists' dominant argumentation gradually shifts within each period until, eventually, the opposing argument becomes dominant. Thus, in the first half of October 1997, journalists blamed 'Muslim terrorists' for killing civilians — a position which had reversed itself by the second half of October and, until the middle of November 1997, broadsheet journalists predominantly (although not as vociferously) blamed the Algerian Junta for civilian deaths. In the final two weeks of November 1997 however, the original argument of the first period (blaming 'Muslim terrorists') was again ascendant — an argument which, at the onset of Ramadan on 30 December 1997, became both ubiquitous and stridently asserted by broadsheet journalists. But, with the entry of broadsheet journalists into Algeria in the final two weeks of January 1998 to cover the visit of an EU investigative 'troika', dominant argumentation was again reversed and civilian deaths were (again) blamed on the Algerian Junta — using almost identical evidence as journalists had em-ployed in reports printed at the end of October 1997. This is illustrated in Figure 7.1 below:

Figure 7.1. Apportioning blame in the reporting of Algeria

Thus, the coverage of each time period ends with newspapers predominantly adopting the opposite argumentative position than they had its start. Within each period, allegations were made by journalists with a declarative certainty unbefitting the situation, which often belied contradictory claims-to-truth which they had made only days before. Excerpts are numbered throughout in order to facilitate cross referencing.

October 1997: Benthala, Sidi Rais, elections and extremists

In total, 67 articles reporting Algeria were printed during October 1997, the majority of which (n= 49) were printed in the latter half of the month once journalists were allowed to enter Algeria to report the municipal elections. As a result of journalists not being granted access to Algeria, 12 of the 18 articles printed in the first half of October 1997 were by-lined to press agencies. The headlines of reports taken from the start of the month, given below, indicate that these articles were predominantly simplistic, 'single event' reports detailing the (number of) deaths caused by an attack on Algerian civilians:

> **Algerian carnage continues** (*Reuters, Guardian* 1 October)
> **Baby is beheaded in Algerian slaughter** (*AP, Telegraph* 1 October)
> **Baby beheaded in Algerian massacre** (*Reuters, The Times* 1 October)

Each of these reports identify 'Muslims' — either "Muslim rebels", "terrorists" or "extremists" — as the killers of these civilians. The position of the Algerian Junta as the 'identifier' of the killers is backgrounded to an embedded clause, concealed by suggesting that (government backed) Algerian media identified the killers, or else deleted completely. Excerpts are presented in the same order as the reports above:

> (1) Members of the Armed Islamic Group (GIA) killed 40 villagers, including 10 children, on Sunday night in Blida province, South of Algiers, the newspaper El Watan said. (*Guardian*, 1 October)
> (2) Islamic extremists have cut the head off a baby and killed 83 other people [...] in five separate attacks in Algeria. [...] No group has claimed responsibility for the outrages. (*Telegraph*, 1 October)
> (3) Algerian newspapers reported that more than 60 civilians were killed in further massacres in Algeria [...] The massacres were blamed on the extremist Armed Islamic Group (GIA). (*The Times*, 1 October)

These excerpts show first that the violence reported in these articles is part of an ongoing story of violence against civilians — in (3) for example, the 60 civilians were "killed in *further* massacres"; and second that 'Muslims' are blamed, or at the very least suspected, of perpetrating this violence. Even in excerpt (2) where "No group has claimed responsibility", "Islamic extremists" are blamed for the massacres. An editorial printed in *The Times* (**Iron in the Soul: Islam must face and condemn the abomination of Algeria**, 2 October 1997) perfectly summarised these two aspects of reporting, arguing: "The weekend massacre by Islamist terrorists of 40 villagers included atrocities unspeakable even by the standards of the five-year civil war." Here, the newspaper somehow felt empowered to blame "Islamist terrorists" for these massacres, despite their later acknowledgement that due to "censorship amid a swirl of rumour there is little way to uncover what is happening" in Algeria.

This pattern appeared to develop further in the second week of the month, when, perhaps due to the increasingly forceful claims of the Algerian Junta, 'Muslims' began to be identified as killers in the headlines of reports:

> **Algerian rebels kill 12 in shell attack** (*Reuters, Independent* 6 October)
> **Children killed by extremists** (*AFP, Telegraph*, 6 October)
> **FIS split will worsen Algerian violence** (Victoria Britton, *Guardian*, 8 October)
> **Algerian rebels slit throats of 43 on bus** (*AFP The Times*, 14 October)
> **Islamists slip Algerian Army to massacre 54** (*Reuters, Independent*, 15 October)

The headlines above indicate that broadsheet newspapers quite uniformly included such allocation of blame in their headlines — only in the *Guardian* report of 8 October is "Algerian violence" implicitly, as opposed to explicitly, connected with Algerian 'Muslim' groups.

In contrast, the *Financial Times* refrained from making such declarations of 'Muslim guilt' — both in its headlines (for example, **Bus passengers massacred**, 15 October 1997) and in the content of its reports. Whilst the other newspapers were confidently blaming 'Muslims' for the deaths of civilians, the *Financial Times* presented a considerably more measured account. In its first report of October for example, the *Financial Times* quotes Lionel Jospin as saying: "We are confronted with a fanatical and violent opposition fighting against a regime which […] has recourse itself to violence and the power of the state: so we have to be careful [in the allocation of blame]" (**Another 67 die in Algiers**, *AFP* (Algiers), 1 October 1997). In the next report, Roula Khalaf not only further develops the suspected involvement of the Algerian authorities in violence against civilians, but also includes details notably absent from the reporting of other newspapers:

> (4) The FIS is the first to admit that, since its armed wing is not involved in attacks against civilians, it cannot control the violence in the short term. […] Its armed wing, the AIS, is present in the east and west of the country, while massacres of

civilians have been taking place in the centre, the domain of the extremist Islamic group known as the GIA. […] The FIS claims that this group has been infiltrated and manipulated by government forces, as many of the victims today are FIS supporters, a claim dismissed by the government. (**Truce offers scant hope for Algeria**, 3 October 1997)

The relationship between the FIS and the AIS is analogous with the (historic) relationship between Sinn Fein and the IRA — a status acknowledged here in the separation of the FIS and "its armed wing, the AIS" — but the *Financial Times* was the only newspaper during this time which presented the FIS as a political party and not an 'extremist' or 'rebel group'. In presenting the FIS as a political party, and a party whose public support perturbs or perhaps *endangers* the power of the Algerian Junta (earlier, the report acknowledged that "the [Algerian] crisis was sparked by the cancellation of elections the FIS was set to win"), Khalaf is able to imply that the murder of FIS supporters in Benthala is functional to the interests of the Junta. This, in turn, implies that there may be some weight in the claim that the GIA has been "infiltrated and manipulated" by the Junta.

Shifting standpoints

The presentation of the Algerian conflict changed in the second half of October, when, in anticipation of the forthcoming municipal elections and in an effort to promote the 'democratic credentials' of the country, the Algerian authorities started to admit British journalists to Algeria.[2] The first report by-lined to a staff journalist writing from Algeria was published in the *Guardian* (**No squaring the death triangle**, David Hirst, 18 October 1997) and almost immediately the presentation of events offered by the Algerian authorities started to be questioned. For example, the by-line of this first report read: "David Hirst, allowed into Algiers to witness 'democracy' finds the official propaganda hard to reconcile with reality".

The strongest criticisms of Algeria's 'democratic process' came from the pen of Roula Khalaf, writing for the *Financial Times*. On the day of the election, for example, Khalaf wrote: "Today's election will complete the institutional edifice the government is erecting to legitimise its rule" ('**What elections? Everyone in my family is dead**', *Financial Times*, 23 October 1997) The report printed the following day referred to complaints from the "legal opposition parties" ranging "from physical aggression to a candidate by security forces to party observers being prevented from inspecting ballot boxes before the vote

started" (**Turnout low in Algerian election**, *Financial Times*, 24 October 1997).
Although reports in the other papers questioned the particularly dubious
majority by which the pro-government parties won the election[3], Khalaf's
reports contained details regarding the highly questionable *systems* of government erected by General Zeroual:

> (5) The elections were the last step in the army-backed government's plan to
> rebuild elected institutions within a framework that ensures no opposition party
> can challenge its rule. Two-thirds of the upper house created by a constitution
> voted in last year will be drawn from the local and provincial councils with the
> remainder appointed by Liamine Zeroual, the president. The upper chamber will
> thus be overwhelmingly dominated by pro-government parties, which already
> dominate the lower house.

In addition to reporting the 'election', by talking to survivors and surveying the
locations of the massacres, British journalists 'on the ground' in Algeria seemed
suddenly to realise that two significant aspects of the conflict in general, and the
murders of civilians in particular, had not been adequately reported. First, the
possibility that the Army may have been involved in the massacres was bolstered
when reporters saw that Sidi Rais was less than a mile from an army barracks, and
Benthala, site of the largest massacre on 22 September, was barely 500 metres
from an army barracks. In light of this, and echoing the *Financial Times'* report
printed almost three weeks before (excerpt 4), journalists started to ask: "Had
government agents with no wish for a cease-fire infiltrated the ranks of the GIA?"
(**Brutal killers without faces**, *Independent*, 26 October 1997). Second, after
talking to Algerian survivors, the torture and 'disappearances' of significant
numbers of civilians by Algerian police and security forces became a lead feature
of reports. These two 'missed' stories were covered in increasing detail across all
five broadsheets for the remainder of October.

Taking the 'involvement' of the Algerian army first, some reporters, principally Anthony Loyd of *The Times* and Robert Fox of the *Telegraph*, seemed to
find it difficult to believe that the Algerian Army could be actively responsible
for murdering civilians. Loyd's repeated claims to this effect sounded remarkably similar, even when he was 'quoting' a source:

> (6) Though it seems unlikely that the army is perpetrating the bulk of the killings
> themselves, it does little to prevent them. (**Villagers relive terror of night massa-
> cres**, *The Times*, 22 October 1997)
> (7) [quoting an ex-ALN officer] "They [the army] do not perpetrate the atrocities
> themselves, but they do little to stop them" (**Zeroual's zombies can't vote**, *The
> Times*, 24 October 1997)

This inability to believe — or perhaps the inability to *write* — that the army would be actively involved in murdering civilians was also present in the *Guardian*'s reporting, but here the undoubtedly 'functional' nature of the murders of 'Islamists' to the Junta were foregrounded to a much greater extent:[4]

> (8) The rest of the world is beginning to ask the same sinister question that Algerians have been asking themselves for years: *who* is behind these atrocities? Is it simply, according to the regime, religious fanatics, bandits or psychopaths? Or do they enjoy the complicity of others — perhaps of some die-hard faction of the regime itself ('**This is where they shot my wife. Here they killed my daughter with an axe**', Hirst, *Guardian*, 20 October 1997)
>
> (9) [...] does this willingness [of the military] to tolerate a massacre almost under their noses suggest a political agenda in which the excesses of extremism strengthen the hand of military hardliners? (**The killing suburbs of Algiers. Unanswered question: why is the military simply standing by?** *Guardian* Editorial, 21 October 1997)

Whilst Robert Fisk, in his reports for the *Independent*, pushed the envelope a little further:

> (10) Why *didn't* the army venture across the fields? [...] And who are the so-called 'Islamists' performing these acts of unparalleled butchery? Why should Islamists murder the very same villagers who voted *en masse* for the Islamic Salvation Front (FIS) [...] and who have traditionally opposed the Algerian government? ('**I felt the knife at my neck. My wife was so brave. She tried to help. So they cut her throat in front of me**', *Independent*, 22 October 1997)

Alongside these 'editorialising' reports there also stood more traditionally structured news reporting. These news reports appeared to support the implications of Algerian government involvement, which the broadsheets' 'star reporters' were making in their reports written in the field. Or perhaps the events they reported simply *seemed* a great deal more sinister viewed in the light of the implications in the larger reports — for example:

> (11) Gunmen yesterday shot dead a candidate for an Islamist-leaning party running in local elections, party sources said. Three supporters of the Movement for a Peaceful Society (MPS) [the only *legal* Islamist party] also died in the shooting inside a mosque (**Four murdered in mosque**, *The Times*, 22 October 1997)

In light of the questions and allegations of the longer, more editorialised reports — principally, why is it that only Islamists are being killed, so close to the municipal elections? — the killing of four politically active 'Islamists' appeared particularly dubious, fuelling journalists' criticisms of the Algerian Junta's 'democratic process' even further.

Civilian 'disappearances' and 'extra-judicial executions'

Similarly powerful political and humanitarian questions were also being asked in articles which chose to report the torture and 'disappearances' of Algerian civilians. Although much fewer in number (n= 6), articles in which such allegations *did* appear often dedicated the whole report to recounting the stories of torture victims and their families. The *Independent*, for example, printed three lengthy articles on the subject on one day alone (30 October 1997), the first of which was printed on the front-page and included testimony from Algerian Security personnel to support the argument of 'official involvement' in the death of civilians (**Lost souls of the Algerian night: now their torturers tell the truth**). After presenting the personal cases of four 'missing' Algerian women pictured above the article, and quoting members of the Algerian army who "spoke of watching officers torture suspected 'Islamist' prisoners by boring holes in their legs — and in one case, stomach — with electric drills", Fisk argues that

> (12) [...] the first hand evidence from its own former security force personnel of torture and secret executions provides unequivocal testimony that the Algerian government has gone beyond the pale of civilised standards of warfare in fighting its enemies.

Aside from the oxymoron "civilised standards of warfare", Fisk's report stands as damning evidence of the regime's brutality. Lower down, the article cites the same Army source again, adding more inferential evidence of the Army's suspected involvement in the reported 'massacres' of civilians:

> (13) [...] he had found a false beard amid the clothing of soldiers who had returned from a raid on a village where 28 civilians were later found beheaded; the soldier suspects that his comrades had dressed up as Muslim rebels to carry out the atrocity.

The writing of Roula Khalaf on the torture and 'disappearance' of civilians was as insightful as in her previous reports. Khalaf's first article (**Protesters seek news of missing men of Algeria**, *Financial Times*, 21 October 1997) is located at a public demonstration — a rhetorical setting which enables it to simultaneously represent the political will and action of Algerian women (the over-headline reads: 'Women accuse police of abducting sons and husbands from homes and workplaces') as well as the repression of the Algerian police. Just as these articulate and highly motivated women — significantly different from the fatigued and emotionally paralysed women of Fisk's reporting[5] — were retelling their stories, "the police arrived to break up the protest". Second, in criticising the Junta, Khalaf cites the opinions of informed and authoritative sources, who are not directly and *personally* involved in the reported action. The opinions of these sources, and the manner in which Khalaf uses them, draws an implicit comparison between the activities of the 'terrorists' and the Algerian government. For example, Khalaf argues that: "Human rights organisations have [both] condemned Islamist killings and accused the government of responsibility for torture, disappearances and extrajudicial executions". And third, Khalaf takes this comparison a little further, implying (as Fisk did in excerpts 12 and 13) the involvement of Algerian officials in the deaths of civilians. "El Houass Diabi" for example, is quoted as saying "Our children were not taken by terrorists, they were taken by police". In using the double plural — 'our children' — the article seems to open up the implication of officially sanctioned disappearance and murder to include, not only the personal experiences of these protesting women, but the conflict as a whole: "Our [Algeria's] children".

In summary, during the first half of October, 'massacres' of civilians dominated the reporting of Algeria. In all newspapers, except the *Financial Times*, these murders were blamed on 'Muslim' terror groups despite the lack of evidence supporting such confident allocation of blame. The Algerian Junta was, for the most part, completely absent from the reported action. This version of events changed with the entry of five broadsheet journalists into Algeria to report the forthcoming municipal elections. Not only did the confidence in blaming 'Islamist extremists' falter, but reports became dominated by suspicions of Algerian Army involvement in the 'massacres', and the involvement of the Algerian police in the torture and murder (usually reported as the more euphemistic 'extrajudicial executions') of civilians. Robert Fisk, in a report printed after his stay in Algeria, summarised the reporting of the conflict in the following way:

> (14) [...] never before have members of the security forces provided the compelling evidence to prove the brutality of the Algerian regime. And with documentary evidence that thousands — some say as many as 12,000–men and women have been 'disappeared' by a government that claim to be fighting 'international terrorism', *Algeria's military-backed government will find it hard ever again to win sympathy in the West.* (**Lost souls of the Algerian night...** 30 October 1997; emphasis added)

This summarising passage, particularly the final italicised section, should be borne in mind throughout the next two sections of this chapter.

November – December 1997: Shifting blame

Following the Algerian municipal elections, the reporting of the Algerian conflict moved into a decline. In total, 51 Algerian articles were published during November and December 1997: 60.8 per cent (n= 31) of which were published in November; 39.2 per cent (n= 20) printed during December. These articles were split almost equally between staff journalists (n= 26) and press agencies (n= 22), suggesting two characteristics. First that the reporting of Algeria was returning to a stage similar to that witnessed at the start of October, with journalists' access to Algeria being more restricted; and second, that the conflict in Algeria was becoming increasingly less newsworthy. These conclusions are given greater weight by the fact that the vast majority of articles by-lined to staff journalists were printed during November (n= 22; 84.6% of staff written articles).

The articles printed during the first week of November (n= 7) were all written by staff journalists and continued the themes developed during the previous month: the suspected role of the military in the deaths of civilians; torture; and, in the case of the *Financial Times*, the civilian protests sparked by the contrived election results. These themes are clearly observable in the following headlines:

> **Post-mortem Algeria authorities dread**
> (Hirst, *Guardian* 1 November 1997)
> **Conscript tells of Algeria's torture chambers**
> (Fisk, *Independent* 3 November 1997)
> **Algerian MP's demonstration is broken up**
> (Khalaf, *Financial Times* 5 November 1997)
> **No, Algeria, it's not an internal affair**
> (Fisk (column), *Independent* 6 November 1997)

These articles suggest that the by-lined journalists felt either a degree of re-sponsibility — or 'Attachment' (Bell, 1998) — towards the affected Algerian civilians, or at least felt that the Junta's dirty war in Algeria needed to be reported. This is especially apparent in Robert Fisk's articles, where the sources he used in the reports of 1 and 3 November 1997 were recycled from reports printed in October.[6] The messy and contested nature of the conflict — particu-larly in the apportioning of 'blame' — is still very clearly foregrounded in reports printed during the first week of November 1997, as is the need for an external investigation into the massacres of Algerian civilians:

(15) "This government has constructed an entirely false schema for the outside world, that of a democratic, secular state doing battle with terrorists. But the real problem is not the GIA [...but] a system of government basically unchanged since independence, which has failed on all levels, abuses human rights no less than the terrorists themselves and uses every conceivable artifice, including the exploitation of these terrible massacres, to stay in power." (Algerian Human Rights lawyer, in *Guardian*, 1 November 1997)

(16) "We were on a roadblock, stopping anyone we suspected of being a terrorist. If a man had a face like a terrorist, if he had a big beard, he was shot." (Reda, an Algerian army conscript, in *Independent*, 3 November 1997)

Dictated intertextuality

An article printed during this first week of November, was interesting for its portrayal of the reporting constraints which the Algerian press operates under (**Prized place in history for free spirit who dares to be defiant**, *Independent* (*Eye* tabloid supplement) 3 November 1997). Using the journalist Salima Ghezali's acceptance of the Sakharov Prize for Freedom of Thought as a springboard, Robert Fisk presents ways in which the Algerian Junta covertly and overtly manipulates the Algerian press.[7] Despite the award, Ghezali had not had any of her work published in Algeria for almost a year, after the newspaper she edited — *La Nation* — was closed by the Algerian authorities. Acknowledging this irony, she wryly states "I am certainly the only journalist who has won an award without a newspaper", and, in explaining why *La Nation* was closed, illustrates the control which the Algerian authorities exert over information in the public sphere:

> (17) "We do have a debt to the [government-owned] printing plant, but there are papers that owe more and which are still printed. [...] We received a fax that we had to pay our debt of six million Algerian dinars (£100,000) right away [...because] we condemned the government for *increasing* the conflict rather than stopping 'terrorism'" Salima recalls.

In addition to the censorship of the newspaper, Ghezali suggests that the government attempts to censor her personally, by making threats on her life[8] and debasing her reputation as a journalist: "Every time I win a prize people write to the organisations giving the prizes [...] saying that I am an accomplice of the GIA. These are the vulgar methods of our security authorities."

This article is important, not just because it acts to confirm the Algerian Junta's draconian grip on power, but also because of what it reveals of the Algerian newspapers which are *not* closed by the government. The implication of Fisk's article is that since the remaining Algerian newspapers have not had their debt to the government-owned printing plants 'called in', the Junta doesn't regard the news they print as threatening their continued dominion. This is an important observation to make, given the reliance of (first) the press agencies and (second) British newspapers on information taken from 'reports' first printed in Algerian newspapers, exposing the role which the Algerian Junta plays in relaying such information around the world as 'fact'.

Thus, the intertextuality of reporting Algeria exists on two levels: first, historically, with 'chains of texts' developing across time and in each British newspaper. These are the intertextual chains of 'overhearers', and are riven with inconsistencies and contradictions due to British newspapers receiving the story second or, in some cases, third-hand. Second, there exists a dictated intertextuality, with British newspapers reprinting press agency copy (usually AFP, based in Algiers or Paris) which was culled from Algerian newspapers, which was ultimately sourced with Security agencies within the Algerian Junta. Unfortunately British broadsheets did not make such a connection, and in the second week of November, the reporting of Algeria started to revert back to relying on the Algerian Junta's version of events, as printed in Algerian dailies and wired from press agency sources (italics, emphases added):

> (18) Gunmen cut the throats of six foreigners, apparently Asians, and dumped their bodies in the sewerage system in Algiers, *a newspaper said*. Their bodies were found near a beach in Bab el Oued, a Muslim fundamentalist district. (**Algeria slaughter**, [no source] *Independent*, 24 November 1997)
>
> (19) Attackers blew up a bridge and then penetrated an Algerian village in darkness, slitting the throats of 29 people, hospital sources and *newspapers said* yesterday. (**Algerians slit 29 throats**, [*AP*] *Guardian*, 2 December 1997)
>
> (20) More than 280 Algerians, mainly suspected extremists opposed to the government, have been killed in clashes between the Islamic Salvation Army and the Armed Islamic Group [...] *according to press reports*. (**Rebel shoot-out**, [*Reuters*] *The Times*, 4 December 1997)

The similarities between the schema of these reports and those printed at the start of October are clearly visible. An Algerian news story which was frequently printed in British broadsheets during this period referred to civilians being killed at 'fake roadblocks':

> (21) Attackers disguised as police slit the throats of 28 civilians and then decapitated some of the victims [...] The attackers stopped cars at a fake roadblock, took the victims out of the cars [...] and executed them. (**Slaughter in Algeria**, [*AP*] *Independent*, 10 November 1997)

> (22) Armed Islamic Group men disguised as police killed eight motorists after setting up a roadblock in eastern Algeria [...] A dozen assailants dressed in police uniforms stopped motorists and then slit their throats. (**8 killed in Algeria**, [Agencies] *Guardian*, 19 November 1997)
>
> (23) Ninety-seven Algerians have been killed in massacres at fake roadblocks, in a bomb attack and in raids on remote villages since the weekend the Algerian press reported yesterday. [...] No one has claimed responsibility for the killings, which have yet to be confirmed. (**97 killed in Algerian massacres**, [Susannah Herbert] *Telegraph*, 31 December 1997)

An examination of the reported action in these articles, suggests strong doubts about the veracity of their claims may be appropriate. Why, when the suspicious role of the Algerian Junta had been reported in all broadsheets for a period of about four weeks, were these murders being reported in such a way? How did these broadsheet newspapers *know* that the roadblocks were "fake" (thereby entailing 'Islamist' or 'terrorist' involvement)? How did they *know* that the "dozen assailants dressed in police uniforms" were not actually Algerian policemen, bearing in mind the testimony of torturers repeatedly printed during this time, especially in the *Independent*? In excerpt 23, Susannah Herbert feels able to argue that the roadblocks were "fake", even though "No one has claimed responsibility for the killings *which have yet to be confirmed.*" Finally (and although it should be acknowledged that I am not comparing exact like-for-like) it is baffling why the *Independent* printed an article which unproblematically reported "Attackers disguised as police slit the throats of 28 civilians", when seven days earlier the paper quoted an Algerian Inspector who had participated in a roadblock where police officers had shot anyone who "had a face like a terrorist" (see excerpt 16).

The inconsistent manner in which Algeria was reported was made all the more exasperating by occasional articles, quoting authoritative and credible sources, which should have undermined the factual status of articles such as those quoted in excerpts 18–23. Both the *Independent* and the *Guardian* printed articles based on revelations from the French daily *Le Monde* for example, which quoted senior Algerian officers "accus[ing] Algerian security services of being responsible for the massacre in September of 200 villagers at Beni Messous" (**Algeria's dirty secret**, *Independent*, 11 November 1997), and alleged that other massacres "had been carried out by the secret services but blamed on Islamic groups to discredit the opposition" (**Algerian agent verifies atrocities**, *Guardian*, 11 November 1997). The Algerian officers' allegations were presented as 'fact' in both headline and text of these two reports, yet the allegations appear to have been forgotten by their respective papers when they printed the wired reports of Algiers-based press agencies days later.

Backgrounding capitalist interests

The role of actors and interests outside of Algeria were almost completely absent from this period of reporting. Robert Fisk, in an article printed before the shift to 'Muslim-blaming argumentation' became predominant once again (**No, Algeria, it's not an internal affair**, *Independent*, 6 November 1997), argued that "Soon — very soon — the West is going to have to link the purchase of Algerian oil and gas exports to human rights improvements", but appeared oblivious to the fact that Algerian oil and human rights were *already* linked, but in a relationship opposite to that which he suggested. Algeria's proximity to Europe makes it especially important in satisfying Europe's need for oil, gas and petroleum. A *Reuters* report, admittedly wired after Fisk's above article (**Foreign oil firms unmoved in strife-torn Algeria**, Sara el-Gammal, 12 January 1998), explicitly linked the economic power of Algerian oil to European governmental apparent apathy towards the deaths of Algerian civilians:

> (24) "Algeria's importance to the West is its trump card. Its gas supplies to southern Europe are crucial, and Europe can't afford to isolate Algeria" said Martin Stone at London-based Control Risks, a political and economic risk assessment company. Spain depends on Algeria for around 60 per cent of its gas imports while Italy relies on it for around 40 per cent of its gas.

Therefore, although Algeria relies on oil and gas exports for around 95 per cent of its foreign earnings and could therefore conceivably be brought to task for the continuing violence, el-Gammal (1998) shows that "there has been no indication of any plans among oil firms to pull out of the country" — quite the reverse in fact:

> (25) " [...] what would we achieve by pulling out? Would it solve Algeria's political problem? A diplomatic solution is what is needed [...] There's a lot at stake in Algeria, huge investments. Companies would not have made them if they didn't think there was a future in Algeria" [said an oil company official]. (el-Gammal, 1998: 1–2)

Of the sampled broadsheets, only Roula Khalaf in the *Financial Times* reported the conflict in a revelatory way which showed how the business of oil continued unabated in Algeria, despite civilian massacres. On 17 December for example, Khalaf reported that both the World Bank and the International

Monetary Fund were giving their economic and political support to establishing three banks — Citibank, Société Générale and the Arab Banking Corp. — in Algeria (**Three foreign banks to set up in Algeria**, *Financial Times*). Quoting Mr Kelada-Antoun, the World Bank representative for North Africa, Khalaf shows that "the explosion in violence in recent months had not delayed plans for the new banks". Later in the article Khalaf reports, with characteristic detraction, that "The World Bank and the International monetary Fund [are] strong supporters of economic reforms in Algeria, despite criticism that financial aid has only helped to bolster the army-backed government". Here, that most flexible euphemism, "economic reform", is knowingly used in order to draw attention to the wholly ideological agenda of both the IMF and World Bank to open up Algeria and her resources to corporate oil prospectors. The limited nature of Algerian "economic reform" is illustrated lower down the article where Khalaf states that "only the oil and gas sector, sheltered in the well-guarded southern desert, has received significant amounts of foreign investment".

In a later especially denunciatory article (**Opportunities in Algeria for cynical traders**, *Financial Times*, 22 December 1997), Khalaf goes even further, exposing how the interests of capitalists were continually maintained and served whilst — or perhaps *because* — Algerian civilians were dying. The opening paragraph of the article argues that when the violence

> (26) [...] reaches new highs, traders say some European and Japanese institutions holding Algerian paper tend to dump the bonds, depressing prices. Others — for example several US hedge funds, some of the biggest holders of the [traded commercial] debt — are buyers. They take the view that Algeria's army-backed government is here to stay, whatever the level of violence.

Here Khalaf shows that, despite Fisk's optimistic prediction, the deaths of Algerian civilians do not appear to impede the accumulation of capital based on speculating on Algeria — quite the reverse in fact, with some companies specifically targeting the depreciated prices caused by the massacres of Algerian civilians. Lower down, the article quotes a trader who expresses, with remarkable clarity, the opportunities for profit which the massacres of Algerian civilians offer: "The hedge funds buy Algeria because it's high yield paper. *If there were no massacres, the spread would narrow and they would stop buying*" (emphasis added).

No newspaper other than the *Financial Times* reported the material benefits which the conflict brought to individuals and companies outside of Algeria. By not reporting such information, as both background and explanation to the conflict in Algeria, the readers' understanding of the conflict is limited to a superficial level — a level where the version of events presented by the Algerian Junta (a 'fledgling democracy' fighting 'terrorism') becomes plausible. Although the dubious status of the Junta's version was questioned, both implicitly (excerpt 16) and explicitly (excerpt 15) in articles printed at the start of this mid-period in reporting Algeria, by December only the *Financial Times* had maintained a critical reading of the reported events. The remaining broadsheets, relying predominantly on press agency reports, had returned to reporting (numbers of) civilian deaths from a position which implicated 'extremist' involvement (*'fake* roadblocks') and elided the mediating role of the Algerian Junta (*'newspapers* said').

January 1998: Reallocating blame during Ramadan

Broadsheet newspapers had been implying that 'Muslims' and 'Muslim terrorists' were responsible for the deaths of Algerian civilians since the second week of November 1997. By the first week of January 1998, which corresponded closely with the first week of Ramadan[9], the identification of 'Muslims' and 'Muslim terror groups' as the agents responsible for the massacres of civilians in Algeria was *explicit*, even vociferous, in the majority of British broadsheets:

> (27) **After prayers, the slaughter**. As Islamist militants carry out their biggest massacre, Algeria's army looks increasingly unable to cope, David Hirst reports [...] An upsurge in terrorist violence in Ramadan has become a tradition (*Guardian*, 5 January 1998)
>
> (28) The carnage coincided with the first day of Ramadan. [...] Up to 600 civilians have died during the fasting month of Ramadan for the past five years when Muslim guerrillas have stepped up attacks in their "holy war". (**Terrorists murder 78 in Algeria as Ramadan begins**, *Telegraph*, 1 January 1998)
>
> (29) [The violence represented:] the worst slaughter yet by fundamentalist terrorists, coinciding with the start of Islam's holy month of Ramadan. (**Survivors tell of Ramadan massacre**, *The Times*, 5 January 1998)

In excerpt 27, after the *Guardian* placed obviously juxtaposed imagery of the sacred ("prayers") and profane ("slaughter") in the conspicuous position of the article's headline, David Hirst suggests that Ramadan bodes ill for Algeria since it usually brings an *"upsurge* of terrorist violence" — a noun which presupposes a background level of terrorist violence from which an increase is possible. This presupposition is also present in excerpt 27 (which is taken from the article's lengthy by-line), where the deaths on the first night of Ramadan are described as the "*biggest* massacre" carried out by "Islamic militants", as well as in the remaining excerpts given above: "Muslim guerrillas have *stepped up* attacks" (28); and "*the worst slaughter yet* by fundamentalist terrorists" (29). These reports therefore not only return to confidently placing blame on 'Muslim' terrorists, but also locate the reported action within a continuum of slaughter/attacks/massacres for which these 'Muslims' are responsible — a schema identical to that of the first week of October 1997.

The summarising reports of Sunday newspapers printed in this first week were especially liable to such reallocation of blame, particularly the *Independent on Sunday*, which printed a report by-lined to an *Associated Press* journalist named Rachid Khiari (emphases added):

> (30) Gangs armed with knives, axes, hoes and shovels methodically slaughtered more than 400 peasants in four poor villages in western Algeria, *the worst massacre in six years of Muslim fundamentalist insurgency*. [...] Until dawn the next morning *the militants slit people's throats* (**Survivors tell of worst Algeria massacre**, *IoS*, 4 January 1998)

In excerpt 30, the reported violence of 30 December 1997 is presupposed to be part of a "Muslim fundamentalist insurgency". Khiari believes that it was 'Muslim' "militants" who "slit people's throats" (despite disclosing that "No one has claimed responsibility for the attacks") and offers three argumentative supports to substantiate his claim:

- – the murders occurred on "the first night of the Muslim holy month of Ramadan";
- – "Villagers said the gangs wore baggy grey Afghan-style trousers — the sign of the most violent insurgents";
- – and the "militants", specifically the GIA, are "the most militant opponents of President Liamine Zeroual's military-backed government" (with the added presupposition that the murders were motivated by such an opposition to the government).

Argumentation which *counters* the above conclusion of "militant" involvement was available in articles previously printed in the *Independent* as well as within Khiari's article itself. If it is assumed, for the sake of argument, that the murders *were* perpetrated by the Junta — a regime with an almost pathological fear of Islamism and the FIS — then it would be an entirely logical that the 'best time' to murder Muslims would be when they were collected in large groups — for example when "the inhabitants of the hamlets around the town of Relizane

[…] were breaking their daily Ramadan fast at sunset" (Khiari, *IoS*, 4 January 1998). There were similarly large groups of fast-breaking Muslims and, unfortunately, similarly large massacres of Muslims for the remainder of Ramadan.

Second, given that an earlier article written by Robert Fisk contained an Algerian soldier's allegation that he had found a false beard amongst one of his comrade's belongings (excerpt 13), the observation that "the gangs wore baggy grey Afghan-style trousers" should by no means be taken as unequivocal evidence of 'Muslim' involvement. Khiari, working for *AP*, could not be expected to have known about either this article or its revelations, but the *Independent should* have known about this article and should therefore have judged Khiari's claim accordingly.

Third, the murdered Algerians were supporters of the FIS, and many of the survivors, Khiari claims, were now planning "to move to the nearby port of Oran" because of this massacre. Unfortunately Khiari does not explain the significance of this planned move of rural peasants nor its benefit to the Junta: by displacing and relocating the (potential) opposition to the city of Oran, FIS supporters are easier monitor, or, in the words of the army, 'easier to protect'.[10] In addition, the plain of Relizane is an area earmarked as a potential oil field which *BP*, amongst others, had been desperate to explore since investing in Algeria in 1995 (el-Gammal, 1998). The depopulation of the area would mean that such exploration could finally go ahead — obviously important to the Algerian Junta, due to the monopoly held by the state-owned oil company Sonatrach and the reliance of the country on oil revenue.[11] These three readily available counter arguments throw doubt on the certitude of Khiari's conclusion of 'Muslim' involvement in the massacre.

Alternatively, the massacres *could* have been committed by 'Islamist' guerrillas — the AIS or more probably the GIA since, as Robert Fisk points out, "The villagers at Ouled Sahnine, Kheraba, El Abadel and Ouled Tayeb were themselves Islamists and had voted [for the FIS] in the 1991 elections for the Islamic Salvation Front (FIS)" (**Algeria terror touches the world**, *Independent*, 7 January 1998). In addition, the affected hamlets were located particularly close to the oil refinery at Arzew, in an area hitherto untouched by violence on this scale: these villages could therefore have been chosen in order to cause maximum disturbance to the regime through its reliance on oil. However, any evidence 'proving' the involvement of 'Islamists' is just as circumstantial as that 'proving' the involvement of the Junta and can be questioned by interpreting the presented evidence from a different ontological position — one which assumes the guilt of the Junta as opposed to the guilt of the 'Islamists'.

Should the relocation of blame in broadsheets' news reports not have influenced their readers' recollection of the Algerian conflict — which had been reported with such circumspect and hedged accusations of the Junta's culpability only six weeks previously — then the confident and often *strident* accusations of editorials printed during the first week of Ramadan certainly may have done:

> 31) Each year, terrorists have chosen the period of fasting to intensify their "holy war" against the regime. [...] The Western world breathed a sigh of relief when the FIS bid for power was scotched. Six years on it is faced with a country a short distance across the Mediterranean whose instability threatens an exodus of refugees to Europe. (**Holy Terror**, *Telegraph*, 5 January 1998)

> (32) [...] in Algeria, Ramadan has acquired a new, terrible and alien identity as the season in which armed terror strikes most forcibly. Murdering in the name of Allah by methods of unspeakable deliberate cruelty, the fanatical Algerian Armed Islamic Group (GIA) — the group behind most if not all Algerian atrocities — has butchered as many as 850 people in the week since Ramadan began. (**Algeria's great fear**, *The Times*, 5 January 1998)

These articles, better than any others printed at this time, illustrate the explanation of the Algerian massacres which the newspapers (as opposed to journalists or the cited sources) felt most accurate. The *Telegraph* editorial is full of vitriol and hyperbole so immediately abhorrent that no further analysis is needed. Lower down they call the GIA "a canker", whose justification of terror "makes a mockery of a book [the Qur'an] that begins by invoking a merciful and compassionate God" (emphasis added), making their position quite clear. The reference to "an exodus of [Algerian] refugees" was revisited in later reporting, as discussed below.

The editorial in *The Times* is much more interesting, since the newspaper felt able to open with ringing declarations of 'Muslim' guilt despite acknowledging further down the article that "the killings continue amid uncertainty about who is behind all of them". In addition, despite making one of the few references during Ramadan of suspected army involvement in the massacres,[12] both excerpt 32 and the conclusion of the editorial — "The GIA is the most murderous fanatical force the world has seen since Pol Pot's Khmer Rouge; it must be stopped" — make it abundantly clear that *The Times* believes the GIA were to blame for the killings. In order to make their argument appear more plausible in the face of as much (or as *little*) evidence suggesting the involvement of the army, the newspaper employs emotive words and phrases — "fanatical"; butchers (from "butchered"); "terror"; and "unspeakable deliberate cruelty" — in order to draw a *rhetorical* (i.e. not evidential) association between the massacres of Algerian civilians, the GIA, Ramadan and finally Islam.

The honesty of the Financial Times

By way of contrast, the *Financial Times* printed three articles during the first week of Ramadan — a news report; a news feature; and an editorial. The topics reported and argumentation employed reveals the same, 'alternative' view of the conflict which the *Financial Times* presented throughout the sample. In the news article, printed on 5 January 1998, Roula Khalaf was the first journalist to report a governmental call for an independent investigation into the massacres in Algeria, and what's more, to properly identify the initiative as originating with Germany (**Germany calls on EU to act over Algerian killings**; see below for further analysis). This German proposal called for "a diplomatic effort to help end the killings" — killings, which Khalaf illustrates, continued to be a matter of much debate, due to their close proximity to army barracks.

The news feature continued the topic of the proposed EU involvement in Algeria further, and in doing so exposed: the protected and privileged position enjoyed by international oil and gas companies in Algeria; and these same companies' worries that the increased interest in the deaths of Algerian civilians "risks disturbing the isolated existence" (**Algerian killings fuel oil groups concern**, Roula Khalaf & Robert Corzine, *Financial Times*, 6 January 1998). With the increase in violence, "confusion over why the killings occur, and lack of independent information, comes criticism of the army-backed government's human rights record" and concern, from both human rights organisations and others, that oil companies should not be investing in, and therefore supporting, such a regime. The profitable investment opportunities which the massacres in Algeria provide (see 24–26) are drawn out again by Khalaf and Corzine, with a view to criticising the mercenary attitude of the executives and corporations involved:

> (33) "The big money is in countries whose names end in 'ia' or 'stan' [...] places other people don't want to go", said a senior executive of a US oil engineering group active in Algeria.

Another "European oil company executive" is quoted as saying: "It is a concern. There is a feeling opposition groups might be able to capitalise on human rights concerns". This quote alone makes it immediately apparent where 'concerns' of these capitalists lie: in *profit* and not *human life*.

The *Financial Times'* editorial (**Algerian horrors**, 6 January 1998), printed on the same day as the news feature discussed above, is a rare and remarkable piece of journalism: objective without being indifferent; exegetical without tripping over itself in an attempt to apportion blame; and critical in the truest sense of the word. In response to the question central to the reporting of Algeria — 'who are killing civilians?' — the *Financial Times* was honest and measured: they simply did not know:

> (34) No one is sure who to blame, what to demand, or what action to take if demands are ignored. No one wants to reward or encourage such activities by reacting as the perpetrators wish, but even that is hard to avoid so long as it is unclear who the perpetrators really are.

The version offered by the Junta — that the "massacres are the work of Islamic extremist terrorists" — is described as having "the merit of being clear, but is so self-serving that few believe it to be the whole truth". An alternative explanation — that "the regime itself must have a hand in the violence [with the GIA...] widely assumed to have been infiltrated, if not created by the regime's security apparatus" — is "not fully convincing either" since the massacres "make nonsense of its claim to have achieved stability".

In light of the uncertain identification of murderers in Algeria, the editorial argues that the Junta needs to "accede to the growing demand, [...] for impartial external investigators to be given full access so that responsibility for the massacres can be established as clearly as possible". By coincidence, although clearly in response to the German request for a "diplomatic effort to help end the killings" (*Financial Times*, 5 January 1998), both the topic of an independent investigation and the *Financial Times'* line of argumentation were adopted by the remaining broadsheets the following day when the final 'rolling story' of the sample started to develop: the EU announced its intention to send a diplomatic mission to Algeria.

The European Union: Exonerating the Junta

The exact intended purpose of the proposed mission was none too clear from the initial reports, with a "European Official" involved in the formation of the plan appearing as uninformed and pessimistic as the journalists: "We don't know what to do, so we will send a few ministers there and give money to victims, but it will not solve the problem" (**EU ponders Algeria stance**, *Financial Times*, 8 January 1998). British broadsheets tended to place Robin Cook 'centre stage' in these reports, suggesting that the diplomatic mission was his and not the German Foreign Minister, Klaus Kinkel's, plan:

> (35) Britain is leading a European Union attempt to intervene in Algeria after reports that hundreds of civilians were killed last weekend (**Cook steers plan to send EU mission to Algiers**, *Guardian*, 7 January 1998)

> (36) Robin Cook, the Foreign Secretary, yesterday said that the European Union was considering sending a delegation of senior officials to Algeria to discuss the situation with the military government [...] Mr Cook said: "I want to record the shock and horror that we are feeling about the reports of the appalling atrocities in Algeria" (**Cook says EU plans to send mission**, *The Times*, 7 January 1998)

A *Telegraph* editorial which discussed the planned mission (**Terror in Algeria**, 9 January 1998) managed to completely *reverse* the paper's earlier representation of the conflict in Algeria (which was itself a reversal of course), in order to maintain its usual antagonistic position towards the European Union. "The EU", the newspaper argued

> (37) [...] will not address the heart of the problem, which is *the theft of the 1992 elections* by the generals and their subsequent refusal to enter into serious dialogue with *moderate members of the Islamic Salvation Front* (FIS). [emphasis added]

The theft of the election in 1992 was an event which the *Telegraph* previously had little complaint about — in fact, as excerpt 31 shows (printed 5 January 1998), they "breathed a sigh of relief when the FIS bid for power was scotched". Within this reversal of argument there remained — indeed the argument was *based* upon — the presupposed civilising influence of 'the West' and the assumed right of 'the West' (seeming, in this case to mean only Britain) to manage the affairs of other nations:

> (38) The West should now be urging the government in Algiers to reopen dialogue with the FIS leaders [...] The West's acquiescence in the curtailing of the electoral process six years ago has been cowardly and inconsistent with democratic principle. [...] It is time for a change, and *the West should say so*. [emphasis added]

The arrogance of excerpt 38 is accompanied by the somewhat remarkable ability of the *Telegraph* to implicitly exclude itself from "The West's acquiescence", despite the support they gave to the "cowardly and inconsistent" curtailing of democratic principle in their editorial printed only four days beforehand.

Noticeably underplayed in the reporting of the EU mission to Algeria, was the recognition that the diplomatic initiative had originated in Germany.

Following the initial report in the *Financial Times*, the mission was over-whelmingly represented as either Robin Cook's, or an otherwise British, initia-tive. That Britain would take the baton from Germany in this way is to some extent understandable given that Britain occupied the EU presidency during this time. However, the reports of British journalists showed the relish which they also took in the 'historic opportunity' that Britain appeared to have been given to solve the 'problem of Algeria':

> (39) Europe is awakening late to this terrible story. Babies with their throats cut, women raped, entire families massacred by bands of bearded men [...] outrage and revulsion at 1,000 killings over the past fortnight now need to be translated into action. (**We need to save lives** [column, Ian Black], *Guardian*, 16 January 1998)

> (40) The anguish and revulsion are universal, but *nowhere more deeply felt than in Europe*, linked by history and geography to the lands of North Africa [...] Some-thing must be done, the world demands. The question is, what? (**If Algeria cannot be helped, at least let the UN gather the facts**, [editorial] *Independent*, 7 January 1998; emphasis added)

From the representation of the conflict in excerpt 39, it is immediately appar-ent who Ian Black is implying are responsible for the killings with his reference to "bands of bearded men". Other reports employed similar imagery: Thierry Oberlé and John Phillips, writing for *The Sunday Times* for example, blamed the massacres on "men with heavy beards and kohled eyes" (**Algeria sees 1,000 die in holy month**, 11 January 1998). Elsewhere reports contained suggestions that throat slitting may be an especially 'Islamic' way of killing.[13]

In excerpt 40, the *Independent's* claim appears to be based on the presup-position that 'We' in Europe are somehow more 'civilised', more 'caring' than the rest of the World. How else could the paper claim that Europe feels "anguish and revulsion" "more deeply" than anywhere else, based on its prox-imity to and colonial 'history' (nicely obfuscatory) shared with Algeria? Any country in Northern Africa is similarly linked by 'geography', but in addition, may also have social, cultural, linguistic, religious and often *familial* ties to the tragedy in Algeria, therefore making a complete nonsense of the *Independent's* argumentative supports.

Protecting 'fortress Europe'

Running alongside this discourse of Algerian salvation, but in a distinctly backgrounded position to it, other far less noble reasons why Britain and the

EU may have a vested interest in 'solving' the 'problem of Algeria' were being reported: Muslim terrorism and Muslim refugees:

> (41) [Robin Cook:] "We have learned too often in the past that if we allow terrorism to *take root* in any one country, it can all too quickly be exported to other countries." (**Cook seeks to satisfy Algerians after snub**, *Guardian*, 15 January 1998; emphasis added)

> (42) [...] the Austrian Foreign Minister, Wolfgang Schussel, warned: "We believe this is a European problem and that if we don't try to stop the killings now, at some point in the future there will be *huge waves of refugees* coming to Europe." (**Algeria mission saved as EU reacts to snub**, *Guardian*, 16 January 1998; emphasis added)

The schematic nature of these prejudicial themes and 'force of nature' metaphors are well-known and hardly need further discussion here. But consider this: if counteracting the 'threat' of "huge waves" of Algerian refugees *was* a motivating factor in dispatching the EU diplomatic mission, as the quotes above seem to suggest it was, then all the EU would have to do in order to stem this threatened 'tide' would be to confirm that the murders were being committed by 'Islamist terrorists' rather than the Algerian Junta. The EU guidelines on asylum operating at this time "took a 'restrictive approach' by recognising as refugees only people who feared persecution *at the hands of a state*" (no headline [*Reuters*], *The Times*, 21 January 1998; emphasis added). Sure enough, following the 24 hour visit of the 'troika' of EU diplomats, various reports were printed declaring the EU's belief in the complete innocence of the Junta:

> (43) "My personal feeling is that there is no involvement on the part of the government vis-à-vis what is happening; no responsibility at all", Manuel Marin, responsible for EU relations with the southern Mediterranean and Middle East said in Brussels. (**EU official rules out Algiers link to killings**, *Sunday Times*, 17 January 1998)

> (44) Mr Fatchett said no evidence existed to support the perception of government implication in the violence. (**Faint hopes as Algeria mission ends**, *Financial Times*, 22 January 1998)

These conclusions were clearly disappointing but wholly understandable given that the EU delegation: were not allowed to visit any of the massacre sites; were not allowed to speak to either members of the opposition nor the Algerian public; and, if the statements of Robin Cook to the EU Parliament are anything to go by, had already decided who was the innocent party *before they had left*:

> (45) [Robin Cook:] *We have seen no evidence to support allegations of involvement by the Algerian Security Authorities* [...] It is in the interests of the Algerian

> authorities to let the press see for themselves what is going on in their country and who is responsible *for the terrorism.* (*Reuters* Press Release, 14th January 1998; emphasis added)

In addition, the Algerian press were harassed and threatened to keep quiet during the visit of EU delegates, to the extent that several massacres of civilians were not reported by even the larger newspapers. Commenting on this harassment, the editor of Liberté said: "it was hard to report yet another atrocity that seemed to show the state is incapable of protecting its citizens" (**Press holed up in no man's land**, *Guardian*, 23 January 1998). Further, several opposition leaders were arrested on trumped up or non-existent charges either immediately previous to or during the visit itself: AbdelKader Hachani (FIS), for example, was arrested "for giving interviews to two French newspapers" in which he requested the intervention of the UN in Algeria (**Algeria relents over visit from EU team**, *Independent*, 16 January 1998; also reported in **Leader of banned activists arrested**, *The Times*, 15 January 1998). With such suppression of material contesting the Junta's version of events, the EU delegation found itself quite able to announce they had "come up with no evidence to support allegations of direct government complicity" (**EU uses rights as weapons against Algeria**, *IoS*, 25 January 1998).

The continuing complication of counter-evidence

Contrary to the EU's assessment, evidence was in fact mounting against the Algerian Junta. Many of the reports wired from Ian Black (*Guardian*), who had been allowed into Algiers to cover the EU visit, contained accusations of military complicity in civilian massacres *identical* in style and content to those printed at the end of October 1997. Perhaps more damning however, was the testimony of former Algerian security personnel to Anne Clwyd's all-party Parliamentary human rights group:

> (46) Captain 'Joseph' Harnoun, described as a former member of the Algerian secret service, told the Commons all-party Parliamentary human rights group that his former colleagues were implicated in "dirty jobs, including the killing of journalists, officers and children" [...] He also claimed that the militant GIA had been infiltrated by the Algerian security forces. This charge was also made by Rashid Messaudi, an Algerian-born journalist (**Security service linked to killings**, *Guardian*, 23 January 1998)

The Times' report of this same story was even more declarative, placing accusations of the Algerian army's involvement in the first clause of the first sentence of the article, thereby facilitating a 'factual reading':

> (47) Algeria's state authorities are behind the torture and murder of civilians, a former member of the Algerian secret service alleged to an all-party group of MPs and peers. (**Zeroual secret agents accused of massacres**, *The Times*, 23 January 1998)

Notice in excerpt 47 the declaration of 'fact' in "are", whilst the 'alleger', the "former member of the Algerian secret service", is placed in a subordinate clause.

Even Tim Butcher, the *Telegraph's* Defence Correspondent, started to seriously doubt the official version of the massacres after he was allowed into Algiers to cover the visit of the EU delegation.[14] After talking to "half a dozen" survivors of a massacre at Sidi Hamed, on the outskirts of Algiers, Butcher wrote:

> (48) [...] It appears that a group of men dressed in army uniforms knocked on some of the doors and told the villagers to be quiet. Others in baggy clothes, described as "Afghan-style Mudjahideen" then surrounded the hamlet. There was an army outpost about 300 yards away but the survivors said that the soldiers did not emerge until the attack was complete (**EU unable to end the nightmare of Algeria**, *Telegraph*, 21 January 1998)

Although the report does not state as such, the implication again appears to be that since the army "did not emerge until the attack was complete", they had conspired with the killers — perhaps the first group of men *were* the army whilst the "Afghan-style Mudjahideen" were the army wearing disguises. Such an account of the massacre was also implied by the article written from Sidi Hamed by Ian Black[15] (**Blood runs cold in Algeria**, *Guardian*, 21 January 1998); although Anthony Loyd's article in *The Times* (**Algeria massacre village barred to EU visitors**, 21 January 1998) took the opposite view — that the first group were militants disguised in army uniforms — illustrating the possibilities for different interpretations, even amongst journalists working side-by-side, in the same location (Algiers), at the same time. In the absence of 'informed, authoritative and credible' sources it appears that the interpretation of journalists working 'on the ground' is all we are left with.

Coda

The reporting of Algeria between October 1997 and January 1998 is characterised by conflicting and contradictory shifts in broadsheet newspapers' 'claims-to-truth' — specifically regarding their identification of who is 'to blame' for the deaths of Algerian civilians. In general, during the periods in which broadsheets relied upon the reporting of press agencies based in Algeria, 'Muslims' were blamed for the violence. Needless to say the influential hand of the Junta in the production of such claims, whereby information is "first produced by the security services in Algeria, passed through the Algeria press and the *AFP*, then reproduced in the Western media" (Slisli, 2000: 53) was backgrounded or deleted in these reports. Broadsheet journalists were only allowed to enter Algeria at such time as an opportunity arose to promote the Junta's preferred image of a 'fledgling democracy' — during the municipal elections and later during the visit of the EU delegation. That journalists allowed into Algeria did not represent the country in such a way is testament to the availability of evidence which contradicts the explanation of the Junta.

It could therefore be argued that the improved detail and critical analysis of Algerian reporting during the periods in which broadsheets had sent staff journalists to Algeria, illustrates the importance of having journalists 'at the scene' of the events being reported. This is unquestionably true, although it is not the most significant argument of this chapter. Both following and, on occasion, *during* the periods in which staff journalists were in Algeria, broadsheet newspapers reverted back to the simplicity and clarity of blaming 'Muslims' for murdering (other Muslim) Algerian civilians, despite the veracity of such claims being repeatedly and comprehensively brought into question. The origin of such reports can be traced back to the Algerian Ministry of Internal Affairs — the only source in Algeria allowed to divulge 'security information', and a propaganda arm of the Junta which intended to build, "on the basis of western stereotypes, a deliberate campaign of misinformation" (Slisli, 2000: 49). How and why such transparently falsifiable claims were repeatedly printed — especially following the detailed and circumspect reports of staff journalists 'in the field' — is mystifying. Roula Khalaf, critical as ever, quoted a French diplomat whose view on Algeria is quite instructive:

> (49) "It has always been that policymakers convinced themselves of the goodwill of the regime, insisting that *it was close to our values and it couldn't be totally negative*", says a French diplomat. "This made our policy rational. The worst fear has always been Islamic fundamentalism and the spread of terrorism to France." (**EU ponders Algeria stance**, *Financial Times*, 8 January 1998)

It appears that a similar perspective ruled the coverage of Algeria in the British broadsheet press: this was, after all, a secular 'government' fighting a war with

'Muslims'. Faced with massacres in a Muslim country; given the 'choice' between apportioning blame for such crimes to 'Muslims' or a military-backed government (Junta by any other name); given that the evidence pointing to the connivance or complicity of the army in such killings was only circumstantial, albeit increasingly persuasive; broadsheet newspapers found the racist stereotypes and misinformation provided by the Algerian Junta were much more convenient to print than the messy and uncomfortable reality: they *did not know* what the truth was. This, combined with the fear of European governments that any meaningful intervention may result in a 'flood of *Muslim* refugees' and the potential estrangement of their local petroleum provider, has since contributed to the deaths of countless more men, women and children in Algeria.

Conclusion

Throughout this book I have applied a context-sensitive theoretical model of discourse, defined as 'language in use'. That is, journalism should be approached as the inseparable combination of social practices, discursive practices and texts themselves, with (critical) discourse analysis aiming to expose the meanings — implicit and explicit, transparent and opaque — of and within journalistic texts. In taking such an approach, I have been able to illuminate the social and ideological meanings which journalistic texts variously presuppose, draw upon, imply and therefore (implicitly and/or explicitly) support. More specifically, adopting a critical discourse analytic framework (re)*contextualises* journalistic practice within its historic, political, economic, social, cultural and professional circumstance(s), thereby enabling a critical and precise examination of the salient features of the sampled items of journalistic coverage. This grounded, critical approach supports inferential conclusions as to how the above contexts exert an influence upon and during the production of journalistic discourse, and how the analysed texts may, in turn, affect these (social, cultural, professional etc.) contexts, particularly in their ability to produce and reproduce racism.

In accordance with such a pragmatic focus, a central assumption of the book has been that journalism is argumentative and should be studied as an argumentative discourse genre. Echoing such a perspective, Keiran (1998) argues that "a journalist's news report should aim to persuade the audience that his or her description and interpretation is the rational and appropriate one" (p. 27). However, given that 'definite demonstration' (or the establishment of the ultimate veracity of a journalist's version of events via irrefutable evidence) is unattainable, journalists are left with rhetorical strategies aimed "at persuading others to adopt [their] same point of view" (Thomson, 1996: 6). This is not to suggest that journalism is mere *rhetoric* (in a more pejorative sense of the word) of course, but rather, that journalism represents "opinion statements [...] embedded in argumentation that makes them more or less defensible, reasonable, justifiable or legitimate as conclusions" (van Dijk, 1996: 24). The three strategic rhetorical manoeuvres which van Eemeren and Houtlosser (1999; 2002a; 2002b) suggest are employed to advance the standpoint of the protagonist — the exploitation of the topical potential, adapting to audience (ideological) demand and the use of presentational devices which frame "their contribution in the most effective wordings" (van Eemeren & Houtlosser, 1999: 484) — were all found in abundance in these broadsheet reports.

Further, in the same way that dialectic argumentative forms perform a 'laundering' function for rhetorical argument (lending the appearance of fairness and 'even-handedness') so journalism's conventions of objectivity operate in order to ward off negative inferences regarding the protagonists. In making such a point we need to distinguish between argumentative *processes* (journal*ism*) and argumentative *products* (journalistic *texts*). Thus, while journal*ists* aim to persuade or convince the readers of the acceptability of their version of events with "the aim of securing agreement in views" (van Eemeren et al., 1997: 208), this is achieved via journal*ism's* 'standards of reasonableness' — the primary example of which is the ideal of 'objectivity'. To be 'objective' journalists need to distance themselves from the truth-claims of their reports. As suggested earlier, Tuchman (1972) offers four strategies employed in realising this goal of objectivity in reporting: First, the use of sources in the verbalisation of (competing) truth-claims; second, the presentation of supporting evidence; third, the use of quotation marks to distance themselves from (very often *their own*) truth claims and assumptions; and finally, to use the structure of news reporting *itself* (primarily the episodic structuring of information in an 'inverted pyramid' of decreasing importance) to simultaneously present and yet background conflicting, uncomfortable or alternative 'facts' (Tuchman, 1972). Each of these strategies helps conceal the very active role of the journalist as the argumentative protagonist.

Therefore, this book concludes that journalists employ argumentative strategies to:

- first, make their version of the reported action appear persuasive;
- second, to simultaneously distance themselves from these very claims
- which, third, is clearly highly functional to appearing reasonable, justifiable or legitimate and maintaining the facade of objectivity.

Hence, journalism is a genre in which journalists attempt to promote the acceptance of their arguments in the eyes of an audience and hence persuade this audience of the adequacy of their point of view.

Further issues regarding the audience cannot be overlooked in (critical) discourse analysis of journalism. Newspapers 'sell' their readers, as commodities, to advertisers, and newspapers that attract rich, over-consuming readers can charge advertising agencies a greater amount for advertising space than newspapers with poorer readers. Consequently, readership demographics are inherently — indeed *directly* — connected with the profitability of newspapers, particularly in deregulated 'free market' economies like the UK. As in the rest of Western Europe (and indeed the world), 'race' and class are intimately connected in the UK, with British Pakistani and British Bangladeshi Muslims (as the most populous British Muslim communities) significantly over-represented in the impoverished and ill-educated social strata. Broadsheet newspapers do not want to become identified with impoverished readers like these since advertising revenue would drop; hence, they do not 'waste' their resources attempting to appeal to them. As such, the readers of the British broadsheet newspapers sampled for this study are not only the middle and upper class élite, they are also predominantly White and non-Muslim. To retain this readership, broadsheet newspapers adopt a White outlook in their reporting, imagining and positioning their readers as White readers and talking to them *about* Muslims rather than assuming that they are talking *to* Muslims. This tone inevitably distances 'Them' from 'Us', since 'Them Muslims' are written about in the third person.

Clearly therefore, some of the omissions as well as the constituents of coverage are a result of structural characteristics of capitalism and the drive for profit in particular. We need to bear in mind that these broadsheet newspapers are, first and foremost, businesses that compete with each other to attract and retain a portion of the rich 20% of the population who read broadsheet newspapers.[1] This daily competition is subsidised by other corporations via advertising — a pressure which demands that at least one editorial eye is trained on ensuring that these corporate backers remain satisfied with coverage. In the words of Sparks (1999), newspapers "do not exist to report the news, to act as watchdogs for the public, to be a check on the doings of government, to defend the ordinary citizen against abuses of power, to unearth scandals or to do any of the other fine and noble things that are sometimes claimed for the press. They exist to make money, just as any other business does. To the extent that they discharge of any of their public functions, they do so in order to succeed as businesses" (pp. 45–6). These systematic failings of journalism — cited here because I believe that newspapers *should* exist to fulfil these public functions — will continue so long as newspapers are left at the mercy of corporations and readers are valued in terms of their buying power. Instead, the readers of newspapers should be viewed as *citizens* (see Husband,

2000): when readers are viewed as citizens, they gain *rights* to information and certain reasonable *expectations* about the content and tone of the news they receive, irrespective of their capacity to consume. This may seem a little idealistic (and at the moment I guess it is) but such an approach to news is actually enshrined in the ideals of Public Service Broadcasting: we should all be *served* by journalism in order to enable us to act as better citizens in our countries and in the world.

In the presentation and discussion my results, I attempted to foreground the dialectic characteristic of discourse, to show that journalistic texts should be understood as being both socially determined and socially constitutive and, therefore, that journalistic discourse plays a crucial role in the enactment as well as in the reproduction of racist social systems. As I illustrated, 47.4% (n= 1205) of these sampled broadsheet newspaper articles about Muslim individuals, organisations and nations, did not refer to or draw upon 'Islam' to explain or contextualise the reported action. In these articles, in stark contrast to items which *did* invoke 'Islam', the Runnymede Trust's 'open' and 'closed' representations of Muslims were barely present. Thus, the more 'everyday' actions of Muslims, and the more 'ordinary' political decisions of 'Muslim nations' are neither reported nor understood in relation to their 'Islamic-ness', either via open/positive or closed/negative argumentative approaches. It is difficult to account or explain this pattern, other than via the resilience of primary stereotypes which shape (journalist) perceptions of Muslim social (inter-)action. When (people who happen to be) Muslims engage in negative social activities — particularly activities which are threatening, or violent, or sexist, or otherwise intolerant or repressive — it seems to activate within journalists a reservoir of ideas, or core images about 'Muslims', "from which specific statements can be generated" (Ivie, 1980, cited in Karim, 1997: 153). The educational qualifications of both the journalists and readers of élite, broadsheet newspapers (who are disproportionately University, and indeed, 'Oxbridge' educated), make it *more* rather than *less* likely that contemporary actions of Muslims will be placed into a (distorted and partial) historic continuum of 'Western/Christian' vs. 'Eastern/Islamic' antagonism and conflict. These ideas or images, which are drawn from what Connerton (1989) labels the 'collective cultural memory', are repeatedly reiterated in reporting, thereby reinforcing these and other stereotypical images of 'the Muslim' and increasing the possibility of their future reactivation. In the case of Islam, these *topoi* revolve around a central dominant idea that Muslims are essentially barbarians in need of (Our) civilisation — the long and rich history of such ideas are partially documented in Chapter 1. Hence, actions by (people who happen to be) Muslims which diverge or differ from these negative *topoi*, or stereotypical key images, activate neither negative or positive collective cultural memories and, as such, are reported outside of a 'Muslim representational frame'. As Malik has argued, this is precisely how obdurate ideas about racial, cultural and religious 'difference' are maintained: "through the dual strategies of stereotyping and exclusion, or what James Snead, in his study of Black representation in film termed, *marking* and *omission* (Snead, 1994)" (Malik, 2002: 176). Thus, in less negative reporting contexts, the 'Muslim-ness' of Muslim social action is *omitted* — the reported activities of Muslims are not recognised as 'things which Muslims do/are' and hence they are not picked up on or contextualised in relation to (religious, 'ethnic') difference. Conversely, in negative reporting contexts or in moments of social crisis or antagonism, Muslims are *marked out* and rhetorically 'Other-ed'.

These articles which 'mark out' Islam and Muslims are dominated by a rhetorical process of textual exclusion. Martín-Rojo (1995) suggests that this textual exclusion is articulated on two axes. First: DIVIDING, that is, establishing the referents — the *us* and *them*. An archetypal and pervasive approach to such a division is in the use of a noun phrase: 'the Muslim world'; the referential ambiguity, fuzziness and indeterminacy of this phrase paradoxically *adding* to its utility, its breadth and its power. The belief that British Muslims represent some form of fifth columnist relies to a certain extent on such a notion — that they are allied with 'Them in the Muslim world' and not 'Us in the West'. Second: "REJECTING, that is, segregating, marginalizing, creating a negative image" (1995: 50). At this point, the terms of reference change from 'us *and* them' to 'us *vs.* them', or 'us *over* them' — a distancing and confrontational schema often captured in terms of normality vs. abnormality. Of course this twin process can occur *implicitly* and together, since words are not value neutral: the way in which 'asylum seeker' has become a term of derogation in itself is a testament to this; and evidence provided in the chapters above seems to suggest that 'Muslim' is being similarly used, as a term of derogation in itself, used to identify negative social actions and negative social actors (actors are labelled 'Asian', or 'of Middle Eastern descent' when acting lawfully or otherwise legitimately).

These British broadsheets divide and reject Muslims via a three part process: first they identify a 'space' — which can be social or mental or physical (etc.) — and rhetorically separate it from 'Our own' space; second, they explain the workings or composition of this space in contrast to 'Our own'; and third British broadsheet newspapers place a (negative) social value on both this space and its composition. These are, in turn, processes of: *separation*; *differentiation*; and *negativisation*. Again, these 'stages' often occur simultaneously given that it is impossible to separate without differentiating (how do you demarcate that which is to be separated?..) and that value judgements are often implicit in the very process of naming and describing. At the time of the study, the key implicit approach used to place negative value onto 'Muslim social spaces' drew on notions of: civility; modernity; a linear and universal notion of 'social progress'; and the inferior position of the identified 'Muslim space' in comparison to 'Ours'. This strategy has increased in usage dramatically following the attacks on America on September 11, 2001. More specifically, broadsheet representations of Islam and Muslims predominantly argue that Muslims are 'homogenous', 'separate', 'inferior', 'the enemy', (etc.) and can therefore, by the Runnymede Trust's (1997) suggested binary oppositions, be regarded as 'Islamophobic'. Accordingly, British broadsheet newspapers predominantly reframe Muslim cultural *difference* as cultural *deviance* and, increasingly it seems, as cultural *threat*.

However, in keeping with the theoretical model adopted, the exact forms which such 'Islamophobic' and racist discourses take varies between different reporting contexts and across different reporting topics. In Chapter 3 I identified four archetypal prejudicial strategies, or *topoi*, which are predominantly used across the sampled texts to derogate Muslims: the military threat 'They' pose to other countries; the terrorist or extremist threat 'They' pose; the threat 'They' pose to the democratic stability of 'Their' own countries; and the threat 'They' pose to women — both Muslim and non-Muslim. Different national reporting contexts and different reporting topics draw differently on these four prejudicial discourses. Thus, the reporting of Iran focuses predominantly on the 'military threat' Iran poses to other countries, the threat 'Islam' poses to the democratic stability of Iran and, to a lesser extent, on Iranian gender inequality. The reporting of Palestine on the other hand focuses almost exclusively on the 'terrorist or extremist threat' of Muslims and, to a lesser extent, suggested that Palestinian Muslims pose a military threat to 'other countries' — in this case Israel.

The findings of this book therefore emphasise the need for any future research on broadsheet journalism to adopt a context-sensitive analytic position, and take into account not merely the product(s) of reporting, but also the ideological, the contextual and the structural controls on reporting (specific stories and in general). In embracing such an approach, future research will not only foreground broadsheet newspapers' location *in* the social and political world, but should also illustrate the way journalists are marshalled by capitalism, manipulated by powerful social/political élites and the manner in which journalism is used to maintain racist global inequalities.

Notes

Notes to the Introduction

1. This percentage was lower than much of the remaining member states. For example: 83 per cent of Danish respondents identified themselves as 'racist'; as did 82 per cent of Belgians; 75 per cent of the French; 74 per cent of Austrians; 77 per cent of the Dutch; and 68 of German respondents.

Notes to Chapter 1

1. I do not want to misrepresent Anthias' argument here. In much of the article, the intertwined relations of biological 'scientific' racisms and cultural 'new' racisms are explicitly drawn out. Indeed the article as a whole is a dedicated investigation of "the demise of old deterministic and unitary conceptions of race phenomena and their related axes of exclusion and subordination" (p.279), "the plurality of racisms as opposed to some unitary system of representations and practices" (Ibid.) and the somewhat paradoxical need for "a core of *racism* [which] must lie in any definition of racisms in order for the term to be meaningful" (p.280; emphasis added).

2. This is not true, of course, of British anti-semitism which, particularly at certain junctures in British history, has been both significant and conspicuous. However, like all racism, British anti-semitism is constituted by both 'thought' and 'deed': constituted by the belief in the innate inferiority of Jews and also in the active discrimination, exclusion, and (often, ultimately) extermination of Jews. These practices are only made possible with the actual, or often only the '*threatened*' existence of Jews in Britain - a presence which anti-Semites oppose of course. Therefore, British anti-semitism also fits with the general model of racism proposed: racism, be that against Jews, Muslims, blacks, etc., involves *contact*, or the maintenance of social policy (for example immigration policies) which both regulates and acts as a *proxy* contact, with (the variously inferiorised) 'Others'; short of this contact, 'prejudice' certainly exists, but not racism by the definition which this book adopts.

3. See Sardar (1999) for detailed, critical and enlightening analyses of films including David Cronenburg's *M. Butterfly* (1993), Disney's *Aladdin* (1992); popular fiction by writers such as John Updike and Frederick Forsyth; and the work of contemporary Orientalists such as Kenneth Cragg, Daniel Pipes and Patricia Crone.

4. The introduction and justification of the concept are discussed at greater length in Halliday's (1996) publication, *Islam and the myth of confrontation*.

5. Here 'transforms', and 'transformation', are being used in Bourdieu's (1991) sense of 'modifying power relations in other social fields'.

6. A 'low income household' is defined as having 60% less disposable income (total income minus deductions for income tax, local taxes, & pension & NI contributions) than the national median income (statistics from www.statistics.gov.uk/cci/nugget.asp?ID=269&Pos=3&ColRank=2&Rank=160, consulted 31 March 2003).

7. Between April and July 2000 for example, Humberside Police, in the North of England, dealt with 35 "racial [*sic*] incidents", the majority of which were attacks on asylum seekers, ranging from: verbal harassment in the street; a 26 year-old Kosovan who was blinded in one eye after he answered a knock at his door and someone threw a rock in his face; two Afghanis who were seriously attacked in the street by three men, one brandishing a knife and another with 'knuckle-dusters'; and the activities of Mr Simon Sheppard of Ella Street, recently jailed for inciting racial hatred after admitting to distributing leaflets throughout the middle class 'Avenues' area of the City which referred to a "foreign invasion" and to people of mixed ethnicity being a "mongrel race" who ought to be removed (Kurdistan Report, Winter 2000: 83; previously reported in the *Independent*, 15 August 2000).

8. From hrw.org/wr2k2/europe21.html (consulted 31 March 2003).

Notes to Chapter 2

1. This average daily rate is calculated through averaging annual figures obtained in the *Bulletin of the World Health Organisation* (1994: 447-80), cited in van Ginneken (1998: 24).

2. Nor by much of the theoretical discussion outside of Critical Discourse Analysis in other social scientific disciplines. An in-depth discussion of the literature on and around 'Ideology' is neither the intention nor a realisable goal of this current work. For excellent introductions and historical summaries of ideology, see Billig (1982; 1991; 1995) Eagleton (1991), Larrain (1979) and Zizek (Ed.) (1994).

3. The other analytical categories listed are: 'categorisation', 'specification', 'genericisation', 'assimilation', and 'objectivation' (Reisigl & Wodak, 2001: 46-7).

4. Examples of such valid forms of argumentation are: *Modus ponens* (If A, then B; A; therefore B); *Modus Tolens* (If A then B; not B; therefore not A); *Hypothetical Syllogism* (If A then B; If B then C; therefore, if A then C); *Disjunctive Syllogism* (Either A or B; not A; therefore B).

5. Examples of such violations are the *fallacies*, a particularly strong criticism, suggesting that an argument contains "systematically deceptive strategies of argumentation, based on an underlying, systematic error of reasoned dialogue" (Walton, 1989: 16). Classically fallacious arguments involve *post hoc ergo propter hoc* errors, involving an unwarranted move from a relation of correlation to a relation of causality.

Notes to Chapter 3

1. This chapter summarises a sample of reports located in countries other than Britain, Iraq and Algeria, given that these countries form the focus of latter chapters. Here I focus predominantly on reports from Palestine, Israel, Iran, Turkey and Pakistan, and draw occasionally on reports from Afghanistan, Saudi Arabia, Jordan and Egypt, in order to analyse the reporting of nations located both inside and outside of 'the Middle East'.

2. Ironically, this letter was written in response to a column (**The shifting sands**, David Gardner, *Financial Times*, 19 November 1997) in which, Lord Stone suggests, David Gardner had chosen "a convenient cast of villains to blame for US policy 'failures' in the Middle East".

3. The 'repression of Muslim women' is also reflected in two photographs which accompany this article which will not be analysed in this study. However, I feel they ought to be mentioned here in order to present a more comprehensive account of the article. In the first photo, an attractive South Asian woman (no conclusive evidence she is Muslim) wearing 'Westernised' dress and full make-up looks directly into the camera (and therefore directly at the viewer). She is wide eyed, smiling and confident; the camera has a direct angle, level with the model's face, connoting an equal relation between subject and viewer. In contrast the second photograph shows three conspicuously Muslim women wearing the *hijab* and holding veils across their faces so that only their eyes and the fringe of one woman are visible. They are all looking away from the camera, eyes to the ground; the expression of their eyes is not exactly 'inviting' or friendly, in as much it is non-expressive; the camera is angled down on them, connoting an elevated and therefore empowered (perhaps male) gaze. The contrast between the photographs is striking: the liberated, attractive and seemingly happy Westernised Asian woman vs. the deferential, unhappy and repressed Muslim women. The juxtaposed meaning of the photos is also reflected in the punning photocaption: "Restricted viewing: toiletry adverts showing women smiling seductively have been banned as growing fundamentalism demands only the modestly dressed can be portrayed".

Articles which use 'sexism' and 'the repression of women' in derogating Islam are analysed in more detail in a later section of this chapter.

4. My code sheet recorded the presence and textual location of 27 words and phrases, nine of which were recorded with their antonyms. For some words it was particularly difficult to think of an antonym, and therefore the words eventually chosen may appear a little strange — particularly 'ambassador/ial' as the antonym for 'terrorist'. This choice was based on finding a term opposite to the definition which I had adopted of a terrorist — 'one who brings terror'. 'Ambassador' seemed to capture a sense of 'one who attempts to make peace' in addition to its use as a complementary adjective: 'ambassadorial'.

5. This power is not merely symbolic - *every* democratically elected government since 1986 has been dismissed in such a way. The then-President Farooq Leghari had used it to dismiss Benazir Bhutto, the leader of the Pakistan People's Party and Prime Minister immediately prior to Sharif's term in office.

6. Should Sharif have been found guilty of this charge — which was brought following his alleged criticism of the Chief Justice at a press conference — he would have had to stand down from office with no right of appeal.

7. Surprisingly, the *Independent* did not report the political stand-off *at all*. The *Guardian* reported the 'events' of the dispute infrequently and with very little editorial commentary. On only one occasion did the *Guardian* express a position - in a weekly news summary (6 December 1997) where it stated the army has "thankfully" maintained that it is not interested in political power.

Notes to Chapter 4

1. It is interesting to speculate on whether the use of the determiner "conservative" is intended to elliptically suggest that Khatami, in opposition, is "a moderate [cleric]"; or to simply provide a slightly pejorative modifier to the head noun "clerics". On balance, it appears that the *Telegraph* is using 'moderate', not as an adjective determining the elliptical noun "cleric", but as a noun in itself: 'Khatami is a moderate; he is one of the moderates'. With this choice, "a moderate" can be positioned in opposition to 'a cleric', (with, in this case, the added adjective "conservative _") implying that clerics are *per se* non-moderate.

2. A *hojatol-eslam* is a junior shi'a Muslim cleric, subordinate to the higher ranking Ayatollahs and Grand Ayatollahs (*Ayatollah-ol-ozma*). They are not qualified to practice *ijtihad*, as Ayatollahs are, but have to spend a number of years in religious training in order to qualify - the exact amount depends on their ability and energy. In addition to being *hojatol-eslam*, Khatami also has an MA equivalency in Islamic Theology from Tehran University.

3. At time of writing, the end of 2002, this schematic representation of Israel/Palestine has undergone a partial shift. Newspapers' positioning Israel as 'We' has become problematic due to the seeming 'shoot to kill' policy of the Israeli army and, particularly, the growing number of Palestinian children killed by Israeli troops. There is, however, a residual level of identification in the press (in the sense of 'identifying oneself with') illustrated by journalists representing the violence as Palestinian *action* (however ineffectual) and resulting Israeli *re*action. Although this does represent a significant shift from the framing of the conflict as 'Palestinians/Muslims attack; Israelis defend' shown in this sample, it still provides a defence (however tenuous) for Israeli violence and ignores the ongoing proactive and provocative policies of, amongst other things, humiliation, intimidation, incarceration, house demolition and torture practised by Israel in the occupied territories.

4. Despite Yatom's long and close friendship with Binyamin 'Bibi' Netanyahu, Ephraim Halevi replaced him as the Head of Mossad in 1998.

5. Israel unleashes its death squads, Queensland Newspapers, 18 January 2003, cited on *Indymedia* (www.indymedia.org.il/imc/israel/webcast/47449.html) consulted 25 March 2003.

6. Quoted in: **Insights into new Mossad chief Meir Dagan**, *Israeli Press Review* (www.lebanonwire.com/0209/02091717DS.asp) consulted 25 March 2003.

Notes to Chapter 5

1. This chapter analyses and discusses broadsheet newspapers' reporting of British Islam and British Muslims. An article was considered 'domestic' if it was: geographically located in the UK; or all actors cited were identified as, or else could be construed as being 'British'; or else all reported action was located within the domestic sphere. All domestic articles (n= 276) were temporarily separated from the remainder of the data-set (n= 2264) in order to facilitate this analysis.

2. Labour MP correspondence, written to Clement Atlee on the day the Empire Windrush landed (PRO HO 213/244, 22 June 1948), cited in Alibhai-Brown (2000: 56.).

3. In Toynbee's column, Islam and Muslims are represented as separate; inferior; the enemy; and manipulative; criticisms of 'the West' by Muslim sources are not considered; 'Islam' and 'the West' are regarded as incompatible, and in conflict; and Islamophobia is, as the title suggests, defended.

4. These and other offences were covered by the introduction of the Terrorism Act (2000). See Fekete (2002b) for evidence of the ways which this legislation is being used and abused by British Police, Immigration and Security forces post- 11 September 2001.

5. The photograph — of a pretty Muslim girl, wearing a veil and playing what appears to be a 'ring-of-roses' with her school friends — was also used by the *Telegraph* and *The Times* reports of the same day. In addition, the column written by Trevor Phillips in the *Independent* and the news reports in the *Guardian* were also accompanied by two other, different photographs of Muslim girls wearing the veil. Although I regard this as significant, the content and implications of these photographs are not discussed any further in this study, due to the focus of analysis on *lexical* representation.

6. These conclusions exist side-by-side with a parallel argument suggesting that such schools don't really matter that much anyway since most Muslims want to attend 'mainstream' schools: "Those who prize the clear religious and moral ethos of a faith-oriented school — as very many Catholic parents do — [...] will continue to press for more State support. The majority, however, will continue to want their children to be taught in mainstream classrooms." Here, the granting of funding for those Muslims who desire it still appears to be approved of, through the Muslim schooling being described as "moral" and the rhetorical use of "Catholic parents" in the argument.

7. Yusuf Islam was even the 'star' of one of the *Guardian*'s ongoing 'pass notes' columns (27 January 1998).

8. For example, see the Robert Fisk article '**Religion - the fundamental problem**' (*Independent*, 3 December 1997).

9. Of the 37 articles which argued 'Islam vs. the West' is 'problematic' or 'erroneous': 15 were 'letters to the editor'; 8 were 'news reports'; 7 were 'columns'; 4 were 'features'; 2 were 'obituaries'; and 1 was a 'review'.

10. **Muslims should change radically**' (*Daily Telegraph*, 25 October 1997). See Richardson (2001a) for a detailed critique of the content and implications of this letter.

Notes to Chapter 6

1. This chapter explores broadsheet newspaper reporting of Iraq across the sampled four month period. I explore the assumptions and arguments of these newspaper articles, dominated as they were by a single story: the UNSCOM weapons inspections and resulting 'stand-off' between Iraq, the UN and the US.

2. The seeming concordance of views between the head of UNSCOM and the US drew criticism from some quarters. Eric Rouleau (French Ambassador to Turkey, 1988–1992) for example, said that Richard Butler was at that time acting "less like an official observing proper diplomatic discretion than a spokesman for US views" — views which he "spread […] about in public meetings and the media in alarmist terms which were not borne out in his reports to the Security Council" (*Le Monde Diplomatique* (English Ed.) 23 March 1998). These criticisms became more widespread later in the UNSCOM crisis. After the American bombing of Iraq on 16 December 1998, representatives from the Russian Federation attacked Richard Butler, claiming that he had "artificially created" the crisis which preceded the bombings (UN Security Council Press Release SC/6611, 3955th meeting (night) 16 December 1998). Going further, the Russian representative claimed that "Richard Butler had presented a distorted picture of what was taking place in the country", that he had "grossly abused his authority" and that "his actions led to the sharp deterioration of the situation in the country" (Ibid.). The content of Russian (and to a lesser extent Chinese) criticisms were not published in the press.

3. In 1996 for example, during Madeleine Albright's time as US Ambassador to the UN she appeared on the American programme '60 Minutes' and was asked about the child deaths in Iraq. Asked what she felt about the effects which the sanctions were having on Iraq she replied, "I think this is very hard choice, but the price we think is worth it" (quoted in *Washington Post* 17 December 1998). For the record, infant mortality was estimated to have increased six-fold since the onset of sanctions (WHO, March 1996) due in part to "one out of every four Iraqi infants [being] malnourished. […] Chronic malnutrition among [Iraqi] children under five has reached 27.5 per cent" (UNICEF, May 1997). I do not think it unwarranted to presume that Albright would be party to statistics such as these.

4. This rhetorical strategy in which everyday objects were used to 'illustrate' the threat posed by Saddam Hussein, specifically the ease with which he would apparently be able to kill large numbers of 'Us', reached a peak in the now infamous articles published by the British tabloid newspaper the *Sun* on and around 18 March 1998. The *Sun* reported that the Home Office had given an all-ports warning, claiming that "Iraq may launch chemical and biological attack using material disguised as harmless fluids. Could officers therefore be alert for any items which might contain harmful substances". According to the *Sun*, Iraq planned to target Britain in revenge for any military strikes. Possible containers in which such "harmful substances" could be found were "duty free goods including spirits, cosmetics, cigarette lighters and perfume sprays". The following week however, the alternative news agency *South News* quoted "former UN weapons inspector Col. Terry Taylor" as saying: "If it were really being sent in like this, in bottles, it's quite difficult to keep alive and to get it out in a form that might actually kill somebody. […] It would only affect the person

opening the bottle and possibly people nearby. It's not something that would kill hundreds of thousands of people". (*South News* Commentary, 23 March 1998).

5. In a remarkable denial of US chemical, biological and nuclear weaponry, William Cohen put Iraq's chemical and biological weapons proliferation down to a "rogue regime" seeking "unconventional ways of countering the vast US preponderance of *conventional* arms". Here, the term "rogue *regime*" is presumably used to indicate a stronger dislike than the usually preferred "rogue *state*". Cohen continues his deception when the Iraqi "rogue regime" is expanded to include North Korea, a country which he describes as being an "unpredictable and increasingly desperate regime armed with a very large chemical arsenal". The fact that America used bubonic plague against North Korea in the 1950s (see *South News* Commentary, 23 March 1998), an episode which would have provided a little context to the article, is absent from his criticisms.

6. This refusal is possibly due to the criticism which the United States drew from the General Assembly (1968–69) on their use of "defoliants", "non-lethal tear gases" and "other chemical agents" in the Vietnam conflict (see Shearer, 1994: 509).

7. That Clinton chooses to use the Tokyo sarin gas attack as an analogy is also interesting, since Japan was another member of the Security Council during the UNSCOM crisis that were less than eager to launch military attacks at Iraq.

Notes to Chapter 7

1. This chapter explores broadsheet newspaper reporting of Algeria between October 1997 and January 1998, with 'Algerian articles' (n= 242) temporarily separated from the remainder of the data-set (n= 2278) in order to facilitate this analysis.

2. All the British broadsheet dailies sent a journalist to Algeria to cover the municipal elections. In alphabetical order: the *Financial Times* sent Roula Khalaf; the *Guardian* sent David Hirst; the *Independent* sent Robert Fisk; the *Telegraph* sent Robert Fox; and *The Times* sent Anthony Loyd.

3. For example: in '**Claims of fraud as ruling party wins Algeria poll**' (*Telegraph*, 25 October 1997) Robert Fox wrote that "During the campaign, 10 [opposition] candidates were murdered, allegedly by the GIA." Robert Fisk was a little more polemical, and in '**Algerian election results beggar belief**' (*Independent*, 27 October 1997) he wrote that "last week's election results in Algeria suggest that the people's voice was distorted beyond recognition to produce a fraudulent victory for the two pro-government parties [...] an incredible - a truly incredible - 70 per cent of Algerians voted for these two parties."

4. Although the reports printed in the *Guardian* did not explicitly allege that the Algerian army were actively involved in killing civilians, the implication that the Army were *culpable* for the deaths of civilians was clear - as evidenced by the angry response their articles provoked from Ahmed Benyamina, Algeria's Ambassador to the United Kingdom. In one letter Mr Benyamina argued: "only the terrorists benefit from your articles: not only do they commit these massacres, for which they have claimed responsibility [...] but they are assured, thanks to the leniency shown by articles such as yours, that at least part of the responsibility for their acts is pushed onto the shoulders of the government." (**Murder and conspiracy in Algeria**, *Guardian*, 23 October 1997)

5. See Fisk's report '**Women who wait for lost souls to come home**' (31 October 1997) and compare his representation of Algerian women with that of a male lawyer in his report '**One man's heroic fight against a regime with a taste for torture**' (30 October 1997). Obviously in contrasting Fisk's representation of (Algerian) gender in these reports we are not comparing like for like: active, educated, emotionally detached male lawyer; and passive, uneducated, female relations of victims. But Roula Khalaf's reporting illustrates a wealth of contrasting (Algerian) female experience and political *activity*, which neither Fisk nor (to be fair) any other reporter mentioned or appeared to notice when reporting the torture and murder of civilians by the Algerian Army and Security forces.

6. The "exiled witness" of Fisk's 1 November report was also used (albeit not centrally) in **Witness from the front line of a police force bent on brutality** (*Independent*, 30 October 1997); whilst the "Conscript" in his 3 November report was the same conscript quoted in excerpt 13 (**Lost souls of the Algerian night: now their torturers tell the truth**, *Independent*, 30 October 1997). These sources are used by Fisk in order to state and restate his argument regarding the brutality of the Algerian regime.

7. Further: in January 1997 Salima Ghezali and the Algerian human rights lawyer Abdennour Ali Yahia were awarded the Oscar Romero Award from the Rothko Chapel in Houston, Texas, presented every alternate year to organisations or persons who distinguish themselves by their courage and dignity; and in March 1997, Ghezali was named "international editor of the year" by the World Press Review.

8. These threats occur "whenever she writes freelance articles for the European press. 'I've never been called in by the authorities', she says. 'It's very perverse — friends of friends are told by 'someone' that I talk too much, that my body will one day be found in a ditch with my throat slashed'."

9. Ramadan actually started on the 30 December 1997 but, due to a 'time-lag', presumably caused by the New Year and British newspapers printing the reports of Algerian or French newspapers (who had in turn reprinted Algerian newspaper articles), the murder of Algerian civilians on the first night of Ramadan was not reported until 1 January 1998.

10. General Kamel Abderahman, the military commander for western Algeria, had earlier warned that "People must either arm or take refuge in the towns. The state does not have the means to put a soldier outside every front door" (**Algeria terror touches the world**, *Independent*, 7 January 1998).

11. This depopulation of the Relizane province — by murder and the subsequent exodus of surviving villagers — continued over the next week, and was reported mainly in small 'news reviews': "Further massacres in Algeria's western province of Relizane have cost the lives of 62 civilians and left 48 wounded, according to state-run radio [...] Hundreds of civilians fled the remote mountainous region after a massacre a week ago and the exodus continued after gunmen attacked two more villages at the weekend" (**Algerian terrorists add to death toll**, *The Times*, 8 January 1998).

12. The editorial states: "even where army garrisons are close by, troops mysteriously almost never arrive until the killing squads have gone. The army […] has armed semi-official militias, some of which are themselves suspected of participating in the killings".

13. For example, two articles reported that Brigitte Bardot had been taken to court (again) for making racist comments — more specifically, she had "made an explicit connection between the slaughter of animals in Islamic rituals and the slaughter of people by funda-mentalist groups in Algeria" (**Racist slur puts Brigitte Bardot in court again**, *Independent on Sunday*, 18 January 1998). The 'slur' was made in an article Bardot had written for *Paris Match*, who did not appear to have been reprimanded in any way for printing such bigoted nonsense. Contrary to the triumphalism with which her conviction was treated in a follow-up report (**Bardot guilty of race hate**, *Independent*, 21 January 1998), the allegedly 'Islamic' character of throat slitting was implied in a great many articles reporting civilian massacres.

14. Previous to visiting Algeria, Tim Butcher (*Telegraph*, Defence Correspondent) blamed 'Muslims' and 'Islamist groups' for the massacres of civilians. Take, for example, the presentation of the Algerian conflict in his report '**EU considers sending mission to Algeria**' (7 January 1998): "When the war began in 1992 these [Islamist] groups attacked police stations, post offices and other totems of the state, but their violence was soon extended to a holy war against any person perceived not to be sufficiently Muslim."

15. Ian Black did not, however, appear to realise the ideological significance of referring to a massacre at "a *fake roadblock* set up by *militants disguised as police*" two days beforehand (**British minister urges candour from Algeria**, *Guardian*, 19 January 1998; emphasis added).

Note to the Conclusion

1. Of course since "none of the players has much to gain from driving down prices" (Sparks, 1999: 49), this competition between broadsheets exists in a relatively stable oligopolistic financial environment, relying on 'product differentiation' rather than making their prod-ucts cheaper. The exception to this rule was the aggressive price war initiated by Rupert Murdoch, of News International (owner of *The Times*), whose refusal to 'play the game' - targeted, as it was, at reducing the profits and threatening the continued existence of his competitors more than increasing his own market share - infuriated the other editorial and executive players on Fleet Street.

Bibliography

Ainley, Beulah 1998. *Black Journalists, White Media*. Oakhill: Trentham Books.

Alibhai-Brown, Yasmin 2000. *Who do We Think We Are?* London: Penguin Press.

Allan, Stuart. 1999. *News Culture*. Buckingham: Open University Press.

Alloula, Malek 1986. *The Colonial Harem*, trans. Myrna Godzich & Wlad Godzich. Minneapolis: University of Minnesota Press.

Allport, Gordon W. 1954. *The Nature of Prejudice*. Cambridge, Ma.: Addison-Wesley.

Althusser, Louis 1971. *Lenin and Philosophy*. New York: Monthly Review Press.

Ankomar, Baffour 2001. Is coverage of Africa racist? (conference paper) *Freedom Forum* (London, 16 May 2001), see www.reportingtheworld.org/clients/rtwhome.nsf/lkseminars/seminar_three.

Antaki, C. & Wetherell, M. 1999. Show Concessions. *Discourse Studies*, 1 (1): 7–27.

Anthias, Floya & Yuval-Davies, Nira 1992. *Racialised Boundaries: Race, Nation, Gender, Colour and Class and the Anti-Racist Struggle*. London: Routledge.

Anthias, Floya 1995. Cultural Racism or Racist Culture? *Economy and Society*, 24 (2): 279–301.

Anthias, Floya 1998, Rethinking social divisions: some notes towards a theoretical framework. *Sociological Review*, 46 (3): 505–535.

Asad, Talal 1993. *Genealogies of Religion: Disciplines and Reasons of Power in Christianity and Islam*. Baltimore: John Hopkins University Press.

Atkin, Albert 2000. Punishment and the Arsenault Case, *Sheffield Online Papers*, 1 (1), URL: www.shef.ac.uk/uni/academic/R-Z/socst/Shop/atkin.htm, (consulted 21 September 2000).

Austin, John L. 1962. *How to do things with words*. Oxford: Clarendon Press.

Azmeh, Aziz al 1993. *Islams and Modernities* (2nd edition). London: Verso.

Badawi, Zeinab 1988. Reflections on recent TV coverage of Africa, in *The Black and White Media Book*. J. Twitchin (ed.) Stoke-on-Trent: Trentham Books.

Bagdikian, Ben 1987. *The Media Monopoly*, (2nd edition). Boston, Ma.: Beacon Press.

Bakhtin, Mikhail 1981. *The Dialogical Imagination*. Austin, Tx.: University of Texas Press.

Bakhtin, Mikhail 1986. *Speech Genres and Other Late Essays*. Austin, Tx.: University of Texas Press.

Barakat, Halim 1990. Beyond the Always and the Never: A Critique of Social Psychological Interpretations of Arab Society and Culture, in *Theory, Politics and the Arab World*: Critical Responses, H. Shirabi (Ed.) 132–159. London: Routledge.

Barker, Martin 1981. *The New Racism*. London: Junction Books.

Beinin, Joel & Stork, Joe 1997. On the Modernity, Historical Specificity and International Context of Political Islam, in *Political Islam: Essays from Middle East Report*, J. Beinin & J. Stork (Eds.) 3–28. London: I. B. Tauris.

Bell, Allan 1991. *The Language of News Media*. Oxford: Blackwell.

Bell, Martin 1998. The Journalism of Attachment, in *Media Ethics*, M. Kieran (Ed.) 15–22. London: Routledge.

Billig, Michael 1982. *Ideology and Social Psychology*. Oxford: Blackwell.

Billig, Michael 1991. *Ideology and Opinions: Studies in Rhetorical Psychology*. London: Sage.

Billig, Michael 1995. *Banal Nationalism*. London: Sage.

Bitzer, Lloyd F. 1959. Aristotle's enthymeme revisited, *Quarterly Journal of Speech*, 45: 399–408.

Blommaert, Jan & Verschueren, Jef 1998. *Debating Diversity: Analysing the discourse of tolerance*. London: Routledge.

Boroumand, Ladan & Boroumand, Roya 2000. Illusion and Reality of Civil Society in Iran: an Ideological Debate, *Social Research*, 67 (2): 303–344.

Bourdieu, Pierre 1991. *Language and Symbolic Power*, edited by J. B. Thompson, translated by G. Raymond. London: Polity Press.

Braham, Peter 1982. How the media report race, in *Culture, society and the media*, M. Gurevitch, T. Bennett, J. Curran & J. Woolacott (Eds.) 268–286. London: Routledge.

Brown, Gillian & Yule, George 1983. *Discourse Analysis*. Cambridge: Cambridge University Press.

Burton, Graeme 1990. *More Than Meets the Eye: An Introduction to Media Studies*. Sevenoaks: Arnold.

Cameron, Deborah 1996. Style policy and style politics: a neglected aspect of the language of the news, *Media, Culture and Society* 18: 315–333.

Campbell, Christopher P. 1995. *Race, Myth and the News*. Thousand Oaks, Ca.: Sage.

Carapico, Sheila 1997. Introduction to Part One, in *Political Islam: Essays from Middle East Report*, J. Beinin & J. Stork (eds.) 29–32. London: I. B. Tauris.

Chomsky, Noam 1999. *The New Military Humanism: Lessons from Kosovo*. Monroe, ME: Common Courage Press.

Chomsky, Noam 2000. *A New Generation Draws the Line: Kosovo, East Timor and the Standards of the West*. London: Verso.

Commission for Racial Equality 1996. '*We Regret to Inform You…*'

Conley, Thomas M. 1984. The enthymeme in perspective. *Quarterly Journal of Speech*, 70: 168–187.

Connerton, P. 1989. *How Societies Remember*. Cambridge: Cambridge University Press.

Cottle, Simon 1998. Making Ethnic Minority Programmes inside the BBC: Professional Pragmatics and Cultural Containment, *Media, Culture and Society* 20(2): 295–317.

Cottle, Simon 1999. Ethnic Minorities in the British News Media: Explaining (Mis)Representation, in *The Media in Britain: Current Debates and Developments*, J. Stokes & A. Reading (Eds.) 191–200. Houndsmills, Hamps: Macmillan Press Ltd.

Cottle, Simon 2000a. Media Research and Ethnic Minorities: Mapping the Field, in *Ethnic Minorities and the Media: Changing Cultural Boundaries*, S. Cottle (Ed.) 1–30. Buckingham: Open University Press.

Cottle, Simon 2000b. A Rock and a Hard Place: Making Ethnic Minority Television, in *Ethnic Minorities and the Media: Changing Cultural Boundaries*, S. Cottle (Ed.) 100–117. Buckingham: Open University Press.

Curran, James & Seaton, Jean 1997. *Power without Responsibility: The Press and Broadcasting in Britain*. London: Methuen.

Daniel, Norman A. 1960. *Islam and the West: The Making of an Image*. Edinburgh: Edinburgh University Press.

Daniels, Jessie 1997. *White Lies: Race, Class, Gender and Sexuality in White Supremacist Discourse*. New York: Routledge.

Delano, Anthony & Hennington, John 1995. *The News Breed: British Journalists in the 1990s*. London: The London Institute.

Department or Education and Employment 1999. *Jobs for All*.

Dijk, Teun A. van 1984. *Prejudice in Discourse*. Amsterdam: Benjamins.

Dijk, Teun A. van 1987. *Communicating Racism: Ethnic Prejudice in Thought and Talk*. Newbury Park: Sage.

Dijk, Teun A. van 1988. *News as Discourse*. Hillsdale, NJ: Lawrence Erlbaum.

Dijk, Teun A. van 1991. *Racism and the Press*. London: Routledge.

Dijk, Teun A. van 1992. Discourse and the denial of racism, *Discourse and Society*, 3(1): 87–118.

Dijk, Teun A. van 1993. *Élite Discourse and Racism*. Newbury Park, Ca.: Sage.

Dijk, Teun A. van 1996. Discourse, power and access, in *Texts and Practices: Readings in Critical Discourse Analysis*, C. R. Caldas-Coulthard & M. Coulthard (Eds.) 84–104. London: Routledge.

Dijk, Teun A. van 1997. Political Discourse and Racism, in *The Language and Politics of Exclusion: Others in Discourse*, S. H. Riggins (Ed.) 31–64. Thousand Oaks, Ca.: Sage.

Dijk, Teun A. van 1998a. *Ideology: A Multidisciplinary Approach*. London: Sage.

Dijk, Teun A. van 1998b. Critical Discourse Analysis, unpublished article. URL: http://www.let.uva.ul/~teun/cda.2, (consulted 20 April 1998).

Dijk, Teun A. van 1999. Discourse and Racism, unpublished article. URL: www.hum.uva.nl/teun/dis-rac.htm, (consulted 31 January 2000).

Dijk, Teun A. van 2000. New(s) Racism: A Discourse Analytical Approach, in *Ethnic Minorities and the Media: Changing Cultural Boundaries*, S. Cottle (Ed.) 33–49. Buckingham: Open University Press.

Dijk, Teun A. van 2003. Élite discourse and racism in Spain (conference paper), *A new research agenda in (Critical) Discourse Analysis: Theory and Interdisciplinarity*. DPI, Vienna (6–8 March, 2003).

Dijk, Teun A. van, Ting-Toomey, Stella, Smitherman, Geneva, Troutman, Denise 1997. Discourse, Ethnicity, Culture and Racism, in *Discourse Studies: A Multidisciplinary Introduction, Vol 2*, T. A van Dijk (Ed.) 144–180. London: Sage.

Donald, James & Rattansi, Ali 1992. Introduction, in '*Race', Culture and Difference*, J. Donald & A. Rattansi (Eds.) 1–9. London: Sage.

Donnan, H. & Stokes, M. 2002. Interpreting interpretations of Islam, in *Interpreting Islam*, H. Donnan, (ed.) 1–19. London: Sage.

Eagleton, Terry 1991. *Ideology: An Introduction*. London: Verso.

Eemeren, Frans H. van & Grootendorst, Rob 1992. *Argumentation, Communication and Fallacies: A Pragma-Dialectical Perspective*. Hillsdale, NJ: Lawrence Erlbaum.

Eemeren, Frans H. van & Grootendorst, Rob (eds.) 1994. *Studies in Pragma-Dialectics*. Amsterdam: Sic Sat.

Eemeren, Frans H. van and Houtlosser, Peter 1999. Strategic manoeuvring in argumentative discourse, *Discourse Studies*, 1(4): 479–497.

Eemeren, Frans H. van and Houtlosser, Peter 2002a. Strategic manoeuvring with the Burden of Proof, in *Advances in Pragma-Dialectics*, Frans H. van Eemeren (ed.) 13–28. Amsterdam: Sic Sat.

Eemeren, Frans H. van and Houtlosser, Peter 2002b. Strategic Manoeuvring: Maintaining a delicate balance, in *Dialectic and Rhetoric: The Warp and Whoof of Argumentation Analysis*, Frans H. van Eemeren & P. Houtlosser (eds.) 131–159. Dordrecht & Boston: Kluwer Academic Publishers.

Eemeren, Frans H. van, Grootendorst, Rob, Jackson, Sally, and Jacobs, Scott 1993. *Reconstructing Argumentative Discourse*. London: University of Alabama Press.

Eemeren, Frans H. van, Grootendorst, Rob, Jackson, Sally, and Jacobs, Scott 1997. Argumentation, in *Discourse Studies: A Multidisciplinary Introduction Vol 1*, T. A. van Dijk (ed.) 208–229. London: Sage.

Eemeren, Frans H. van, Grootendorst, Rob, Snoeck Henkemans, Francisca, Blair, J. Anthony, Johnson, Ralph H., Krabbe, Erik C. W., Plantin, Christian, Walton, Douglas N., Willard, Charles A., Woods, John and Zarefsky, David 1996. *Fundamentals of Argumentation Theory: A Handbook of Historical Backgrounds and Contemporary Developments*. Mahwah, NJ: Lawrence Erlbaum Associates.

Eliasoph, Nina 1988. Routines and the making of Oppositional News, in *Social Meanings of News: A Text-Reader*, D. Berkowitz (Ed.) (1997) 230–253. Thousand Oaks, Ca: Sage.

Eliasoph, Nina 1990. Political Culture and the Representation of a Political Self', *Theory and Society*, 19 (4): 465–494.

Ellul, Jacques 1965. *Propaganda: The Formation of Men's Attitudes*. New York: Random House Inc.

Entman, Robert E. 1990. Modern Racism and the images of Blacks in local television news, *Critical Studies in Mass Communication*, 7 (4): 332–45.

Esposito, John L. 1998. *Islam: The Straight Path* (3rd edition). New York: Oxford University Press.

Essed, Philomena J. M. 1991. *Understanding Everyday Racism: An Interdisciplinary Approach*. Newbury Park, CA: Sage.

Ettema, James S., Whitney, D. Charles & Wackman, Daniel B. 1987. Professional Mass Communicators, in *Social Meanings of News: A Text-Reader*, D. Berkowitz (Ed.) (1997) 31–50. Thousand Oaks, Ca: Sage.

Fairclough, Norman & Wodak, Ruth 1997. Critical Discourse Analysis: an overview, in *Discourse Studies: A Multidisciplinary Introduction, Vol 2*, T. A. van Dijk (Ed.) 67–97. London: Sage.

Fairclough, Norman 1989. *Language and Power*. London: Longman.

Fairclough, Norman 1992. *Discourse and Social Change*. Cambridge: Polity Press.

Fairclough, Norman 1995a. *Media Discourse*. London: Arnold.

Fairclough, Norman 1995b. *Critical Discourse Analysis: The Critical Study of Language*. London: Longman.

Fairclough, Norman 2000. *New Labour, New Language?* London: Routledge.

Fekete, Liz 2002a. The Emergence of Xeno-Racism. *Institute of Race Relations* (www.irr.org. uk/xenoracism/index.htm) (consulted 28 August 2002).

Fekete, Liz 2002b. Racism: the hidden cost of September 11. *European Race Bulletin*, 40. London: Institute of Race Relations.

Ferguson, Robert 1998. *Representing 'Race': Ideology, identity and the media*. London: Edward Arnold.

Ferrara, Abel 1985. Pragmatics, in *Handbook of Discourse Analysis, Vol 2: Dimensions of Discourse*, T. A. van Dijk (ed.) 137–158. London: Academic Press.

Fowler, Roger 1991. *Language in the News: Discourse and Ideology in the Press*. London: Routledge.

Fowler, Roger 1996. 'On Critical Linguistics', in *Texts and Practices: Readings in Critical Discourse Analysis*, C. R. Caldas-Coulthard, & M. Coulthard (Eds.) 3–14. Routledge: London.

Fowler, Roger, Hodge, Robert, Kress, Gunther & Trew, Tony 1979. *Language and Control*. London: Routledge and Kegan Paul.

Fradgley, Kimberley E. & Niebauer Jnr, Walter E. 1995. London's 'Quality' Newspapers: newspaper ownership and reporting patterns. *Journalism and Mass Communication Quarterly* 72 (4): 902–912.

Francis, Joy 2002. BBC still showing its 'hideously white' face. *Guardian* (13 May, 2002).

Franklin, Bob 1997. *Newszak and the news media*. London: Arnold.

Franklin, Bob 1998. *Tough on Soundbites, tough on the causes of soundbites*. London: The Catalyst Trust.

Gabriel, John 1994. *Racism, Culture, Markets*. London: Routledge.

Galtung, Johan & Ruge, Mari 1965. Structuring and Selecting News, in *The Manufacture of News: Social problems, deviance and the news media*, S. Cohen & J. Young (Eds.) (1973) 62–72. London: Constable.

Gandy, Oscar H. Jnr 2000. Race, Ethnicity and the Segmentation of Media Markets, in *Mass Media and Society, 3rd edition*, J. Curran & M. Gurevitch (eds.) 44–69. London: Arnold.

Gellner, Ernest 1993. The mightier pen? *Times Literary Supplement* (19 Februrary, 1993).

Gerbner, George 1958. On Content Analysis and Critical Research in Mass Communication, in *People, Society and Mass Communications*, L. A. Dexter & D. Manning (Eds.) (1964) 476–500. New York: Free Press.

Gill, Ann M. & Whedbee, Karen 1997. Rhetoric, in *Discourse Studies: A Multidisciplinary Introduction Vol 1*, T. A. van Dijk (Ed.) 157–184. London: Sage.

Gilman, Sander 1986. Black Bodies, White Bodies: Toward an Iconography of Female Sexuality in Late Nineteenth-Century Art, Medicine and Literature, '*Race', Writing and Difference*, in H. L. Gates Jnr (Ed.) 223–261. Chicago: Chicago University Press.

Ginneken, Jaap van 1998. *Understanding Global News: A Critical Introduction*. London: Sage.

Goffman, Erving 1986. *Frame Analysis: An Essay on the Organisation of Experience*. Boston, Ma.: Northeastern University Press.

Golding, Peter & Murdock, Graham 2000. Culture, Communications and Political Economy, in *Mass Media and Society*, J. Curran & M. Gurevitch (eds.) 70–92. London: Arnold.

Gramsci, Antonio 1971. *Selections from the Prison Notebooks*, trans Q. Hoare & G. N. Smith. London: Lawrence & Wishart.

Haddad, Yvonne Yazbeck & Esposito, John L. (Eds.) 1998. *Islam, Gender and Social Change*. New York: Oxford University Press.

Haddad, Yvonne Yazbeck 1998. Islam and Gender: Dilemmas in the Changing Arab World, in *Islam, Gender and Social Change*, Y. Y. Haddad & J. L. Esposito (Eds.) 3–29. New York: Oxford University Press.

Hage, Ghassan 1998. *White Nation: fantasies of white supremacy in a multicultural society*. Annandale, Australia: Pluto Press.

Hall, Stuart 1973. The Determination of News Photographs, in *The Manufacture of News: Social problems, deviance and the news media*, S. Cohen & J. Young (Eds.) (1973) 176–190. London: Constable.

Hall, Stuart 1980. Encoding and Decoding, in *Culture, Media and Language*, S. Hall, D. Hobson, A. Lowe & P. Willis (Eds.) 128–38. London: Unwin Hyman.

Hall, Stuart 1990. The Whites of Their Eyes: Racist Ideologies and the Media, in *The Media Reader*, J. O. Thompson (Ed.) London: British Film Institute.

Hall, Stuart 1997. *Representation: Cultural Representations and Signifying Practices*. London: Sage.

Halliday, Fred 1996. *Islam and the Myth of Confrontation*. London: I. B. Tauris.

Halliday, Fred 1997. 'Islam is in danger': Islam, Rushdie and the Struggle for the Migrant Soul, in *The Next Threat: Western Perceptions of Islam*, J. Hippler & A. Leug (Eds.) 71–81. London: Pluto Press.

Halliday, Fred 1999. 'Islamophobia reconsidered', *Ethnic and Racial Studies*, 22(5): 892–902.

Halloran, James D. 1977. Introduction, in *Ethnicity and the Media: An analysis of media reporting in the United Kingdom*, Canada and Ireland, J. D. Halloran (Ed.) 9–24. Vendome: UNESCO.

Hammond, Phillip 2000. Reporting 'Humanitarian' Warfare: propaganda, moralism and Nato's Kosovo War, *Journalism Studies*, 1 (3): 365–386.

Hammond, Phillip, & Stirner, Paul 1997. Fear and Loathing in the British Press, in *Cultural Difference, Media Memories: Anglo-American Images of Japan*, P. Hammond (Ed) 85–114. London: Cassel.

Hardy, Roger 1999. Islamophobia, lecture at *Symposium on Images of Islam in the Media*, Al-Khoei Foundation and The Islamic Educational, Scientific and Cultural Organisation (ISESCO), 25 October 1999.

Harrison, Paul & Palmer, Robin 1986. *News out of Africa: Biafra to Band Aid*. London: Hilary Shipman.

Hartley, John & Montgomery, Martin 1985. Representations and Relations: Ideology and Power in Press and TV News, in *Discourse and Communication*, T. A. van Dijk (ed.) 233–269. Berlin: Mouton de Gruyter.

Hartley, John 1992. *The Politics of Pictures: The Creation of the Public in the Age of Public Media*. London: Routledge.

Hartmann, Paul & Husband, Charles 1973. The Mass Media and Racial Conflict, in *The Manufacture of News: Social problems, deviance and the news media*, S. Cohen & J. Young (Eds.) 270–283. London: Constable.

Hartmann, Paul & Husband, Charles 1974. *Racism and the Mass Media: A study of the role of the Mass Media in the formation of white beliefs and attitudes in Britain*. London: Davis-Poynter.

Hartmann, Paul, Husband, Charles & Clark, Jean 1974. Race as News, in *Race as News*. J. D. Halloran (Ed.) Paris: UNESCO.

Hastings, Max 2002. *Editor: An Inside Story of Newspapers*. London: Macmillan.

Heider, Don 2000. *White News: Why Local News Programs Don't Cover People of Color*. Mahwah, NJ: LEA Publishers.

Henwood, Karen & Phoenix, Ann 1999. 'Race' in psychology: teaching the subject, in *Ethnic and Racial Studies Today*, M. Bulmer & J. Solomos (Eds.) 98–114. London: Routledge.

Herman, Edward S. & Chomsky, Noam 1994. *Manufacturing Consent*. London: Vintage.

Herman, Edward S. 1992. *Beyond Hypocrisy: Decoding the News in an age of Propaganda*. Boston, Ma.: South End Press.

Herman, Edward S. 1995a. Media In the US Political Economy, in *Questioning the Media: A Critical Introduction*. J. Downing, A. Mohammadi & A. Sreberny-Mohammadi, (Eds.) Thousand Oaks, Ca: Sage.

Herman, Edward S. 1995b. *Triumph of the Market: Essays on Economics, Politics and the Media*. Boston, Ma.: South End Press.

Hicks, Wynford 1998. *English for Journalists* (2nd edition). London: Routledge.

Hijab, Nadia 1998. Islam, Social Change and the Reality of Arab Women's Lives, *Islam, Gender and Social Change*, in Y. Y. Haddad & J. L. Esposito (Eds.) 45–55. New York: Oxford University Press.

Hodge, Robert & Kress, Gunther 1993. *Language as Ideology* (2nd edition). London: Routledge.

Hodgson, Jessica 2002. Institutional racism in print? *Guardian* (20 May 2002).

Huffschmid, Jorg 1983. Economic power and the freedom of the press, *Media, Culture and Society*, 5 (1): 29–37.

Huntington, Samuel P. 1993. The Clash of Civilisations? *Foreign Affairs* (Summer, 1993): 22–49.

Huntington, Samuel P. 1996. *The Clash of Civilisations and the Remaking of World Order*. New York: Simon & Schuster.

Husband, Charles (Ed.) 1987. *'Race' in Britain: Continuity and Change*. London: Hutchinson.

Jhally, Sut & Lewis, Justin 1992. *Enlightened Racism: The Cosby Show, Audiences and the Myth of the American Dream*. Boulder, Co.: Westview Press.

Jowett, Garth, S. & O'Donnell, Victoria 1992. *Propaganda and Persuasion*. London: Sage.

Jucker, Andreas. H. 1992. *Social Stylistics: Syntactic Variation in British Newspapers*. Berlin: Mouton de Gruyter.

Kabbani, Rana 1986. *Europe's Myths of Orient*. Bloomington: Indiana University Press.

Karim, Karim H. 1997. The Historical Resilience of Primary Stereotypes: Core Images of the Muslim Other, in *The Language and Politics of Exclusion: Others in Discourse*, S. H. Riggins (Ed.) 153–182. Thousand Oaks, California: Sage.

Karmi, Ghada 1999. Images of Islam and the Arab World, lecture at *Symposium on Images of Islam in the Media*, Al-Khoei Foundation and The Islamic Educational, Scientific and Cultural Organisation (ISESCO), 25 October 1999.

Keddie, Nikki 2000. Women in Iran since 1979, *Social Research*, 67 (2): 405–438.

Keeble, Richard 1997. *Secret State, Silent Press: New Militarism, the Gulf and the modern image of warfare*. Luton: University of Luton Press.

Keeble, Richard 2001. *Ethics for Journalists*. London: Routledge.

Kieran, Matthew 1998. Objectivity, Impartiality and good Journalism, in *Media Ethics*, M. Kieran, (Ed.) 23–36. London: Routledge.

Klaidman, Stephen & Beauchamp, Tom L. 1987. *The Virtuous Journalist*. New York: Oxford University Press.

Kleiner, Brian 1998. The modern racist ideology and its reproduction in 'pseudo-argument', *Discourse and Society*, 9 (2): 187–216.

Knightly, Phillip 2000. *The First Casualty: The war correspondent as hero and myth-maker from the Crimea to Kosovo*. London: Prion.

Kopperschmidt, Josef 1985, An analysis of argumentation, in *Handbook of Discourse Analysis, Vol. 2: Dimensions of Discourse*, T. A. van Dijk (Ed.) 159–168. London: Academic Press.

Kress, Gunther 1983. Linguistic and Ideological transformations in News Reporting, in *Language, Image and Media*, H. Davis & P. Walton (Eds.) 120–138. Oxford: Basil Blackwell.

Kress, Gunther 1994. Text and Grammar as Explanation, in *Text, Discourse and Context: Representations of Poverty in Britain*, U. H. Meinhoff & K. Richardson (Eds.) 24–46. London: Longman.

Lakoff, George & Johnson, Mark 1980. *Metaphors We Live By*. Chicago: University of Chicago Press.

Larrain, Jorge (1979) *The Concept of Ideology*. London: Hutchinson.

Law, Ian 2002. *Race in the News*. Houndmills: Palgrave.

Lawrence, Errol 1982. Just plain common sense: the 'roots' of racism, in *The Empire Strikes Back: Race and racism in 70s Britain*, Centre for Contemporary Cultural Studies (Eds.) 47–94. London: Hutchinson.

Leeuwen, Theo van 1995. Representing social-action, *Discourse and Society*, 6 (1): 81–106.

Leeuwen, Theo van 1996. The Representation of Social Actors, in *Texts and Practices: Readings in Critical Discourse Analysis*, C. R. Caldas-Coulthard & M. Coulthard (Eds.) 32–70. London: Routledge.

Leug, Andrea 1995. The Perceptions of Islam in Western Debate, in *The Next Threat: Western Perceptions of Islam*, J. Hippler & A. Leug (Eds.) 7–31. London: Pluto Press.

Lewis, Bernard 1964. *The Middle East and the West*. New York: Harper Torchbooks.

Lewis, Bernard 1990. The Roots of Muslim Rage, *The Atlantic Monthly*, 266.

Lewis, Bernard 1993. *Islam and the West*. Oxford: Oxford University Press.

Lewis, Philip 1994. *Islamic Britain: Religion, Politics and Identity among British Muslims*. London: I. B. Tauris.

Lewis, Philip 1997. The Bradford Council for Mosques and the Search for Muslim Unity, in *Islam in Europe: The Politics of Religion and Community*, S. Vertovec & C. Peach (Eds.) 103–128. New York: St Martin's Press.

Lewis, Reina 1996. *Gendering Orientalism: Race, Femininity and Representation*. London: Routledge.

Lule, Jack 1995. The Rape of Mike Tyson: Race, the Press and Symbolic Types, in *The Social Meanings of News: A Text-Reader*, D. Berkowitz (Ed.) (1997) 376–397. Thousand Oaks, Ca.: Sage.

Macfie, A. L. 2002. *Orientalism*. London: Longman.

MacKenzie, John M. 1995. *Orientalism: History, Theory and the Arts*. Manchester: Manchester University Press.

Malik, Kenan 1996. *The Meaning of Race: Race, History and Culture in Western Society*. Houndsmill: Macmillan.

Malik, S. 2002. *Representing Black Britain: Black and Asian Images on Television*. London: Sage.

Manning, Paul 2001. *News Sources: A critical introduction*. London: Routledge.

Martín-Rojo, Luisa & van Dijk, Teun A. 1997. "There was a problem and it was solved!": legitimating the expulsion of 'illegal' migrants in Spanish parliamentary discourse, *Discourse and Society*, 8 (4): 523–566.

Martín-Rojo, Luisa 1995. Division and Rejection: from the personification of the Gulf Conflict to the demonisation of Saddam Hussein, *Discourse and Society* 6(1): 49–80.

Mernissi, Fatima 1991. *The Veil and the Male Élite: A Feminist Interpretation of Women's Rights in Islam*, trans. Mary Jo Lakeland. Reading, Ma.: Addison-Wesley Publishing Co.

Meyer, Thomas 2001. *Identity Mania: Fundamentalism and the Politicisation of Cultural Differences*. London: Zed Books.

Miller, Judith 1993. The Challenge of Radical Islam, *Foreign Affairs*, Spring: 201–15.

Mills, Sara 1991. *Discourses of Difference: An Analysis of Women's Travel Writing and Colonialism*. London: Routledge.

Modood, Tariq & Berthoud, Richard et al. 1997. *Ethnic Minorities in Britain: diversity and disadvantage*. Policy Studies Institute.

Modood, Tariq 1990. British Asian Muslims and the Rushdie Affair, in *'Race', Culture and Difference*, J. Donald & A. Rattansi (Eds.) (1992) 260–271. London: Sage Publications.

Modood, Tariq 1994. *Racial Equality: Colour, Culture and Justice*. Institute for Public Policy Research.

Modood, Tariq 1997. 'Difference', Cultural Racism and Anti-Racism, *Debating Cultural Hybridity: Multi-Cultural Identities and the Politics of Anti-Racism*, in P. Werbner & T. Modood (Eds.) 154–172. London: Zed Books.

Modood, Tariq 1998. Anti-essentialism, Multiculturalism and the 'Recognition' of Religious groups, *The Journal of Political Philosophy* 6 (4): 378–399.

Mohanty, Chandra Talpade 1988. Under Western Eyes: Feminist Scholarship and Colonial Discourses. *Feminist Review*, 30 (Autumn).

Mortimer, Edward 1999. Concluding Remarks: Islam in the Media, lecture at *Symposium on Images of Islam in the Media*, Al-Khoei Foundation and The Islamic Educational, Scientific and Cultural Organisation (ISESCO), 25 October 1999.

Mowlana, Hamid, Gerbner, George & Schiller, Herbert I. (Eds.) 1992. *Triumph of the Image: The Media's War in the Persian Gulf — a Global Perspective*. Boulder, Colorado: Westview Press.

Murdock, Graham 2000. Reconstructing the Ruined Tower: Contemporary Communications and Questions of Class, in *Mass Media and Society*, J. Curran & M. Gurevitch (eds.) 7–26. London: Arnold.

Nahdi, Fuad 1997. No more Muslim apartheid, *New Statesman*, 31 October 1997, pp.18–19.

Negrine, Ralph (1994) *Politics and the Mass Media in Britain* (2nd edition). London: Routledge.

Nohrstedt, Stig A., Kaitatzi-Whitlock, Sophia, Ottosen, Rune & Riegert, Kristina 2000. From the Persian Gulf to Kosovo: War Journalism and Propaganda. *European Journal of Communication*, 15 (3): 383–404.

Orbe, Mark P., Warren, Kiesha T. & Cornwell, Nancy C. 2001. Negotiating Societal Stereotypes: Analysing The Real World Discourse by and About African American Men, in *Constituting Cultural Difference through Discourse*, M. J. Collier (Ed.) 107–134. Thousand Oaks, Ca.: Sage.

Parker-Jenkins, Marie 1995. *Children of Islam: A teacher's guide to meeting the needs of Muslim Pupils*. Stoke-on-Trent: Trentham Books Ltd.

Pêcheux, Michel 1982. *Language, Semantics and Ideology*. London: Macmillan.

Perelman, Chaim and Olbrechts-Tyteca, Lucie 1969. *The New Rhetoric: A Treatise on Argumentation*, translated by J. Wilkinson and P. Weaver. Notre Dame: University of Notre Dame Press.

Perelman, Chaim 1979. *The New Rhetoric and the Humanities*. Dordrecht: Reidel.

Perelman, Chaim 1982. *The Realm of Rhetoric*. Notre Dame: University of Notre Dame Press.

Philo, Greg 2002. Hard News from Israel: media coverage of the Israeli/Palestinian conflict (consulted 19 June 2002). Available at: www.gla.ac.uk/Acad/Sociology/Israel.pdf.

Philo, Greg (Ed.) 1999. *Message Received: Glasgow Media Group Research 1993–1999*. London: Longman.

Poole, Elizabeth 1999. Framing Islam: An Analysis of Newspaper coverage of Islam in the British Press, in *Islam and The West: Fragmented Images in a Globalised World*, K. Hafez (Ed). Cresskill, NJ: Hampton Press.

Poole, Elizabeth 2000. Media Representation and British Muslims, *Dialogue*, April 2000: 4–5.

Poole, Elizabeth 2002. *Reporting Islam: Media representations of British Muslims*. London: I. B. Tauris.

Reinhart, Tanya. 2003. Israel/Palestine: How to end the war of 1948. New York: Seven Stories Press.

Reisigl, Martin & Wodak, Ruth 2001. *Discourse and Discrimination: Rhetorics of Racism and Anti-Semitism*. London: Routledge.

Rex, John 1996. *Ethnic Minorities in the Modern Nation State: Working Papers in the Theory of Multiculturalism and Political Integration*. New York: St Martin's Press.

Richardson, John E. 2001a. 'Now is the time to put an end to all this' Argumentative discourse theory and letters to the editor, *Discourse and Society*, 12(2): 143–168.

Richardson, John E. 2001b. British Muslims in the Broadsheet Press: a challenge to cultural hegemony?, *Journalism Studies*, 2(2): 221–242.

Riggins, Stephen H. 1997 (Ed.) *The Language and Politics of Exclusion: Others in Discourse*. Thousand Oaks, California: Sage.

Rodinson, Maxime 1979. *Marxism and the Muslim World*. London: Zed Press.

Runnymede Trust 1997. *Islamophobia: A Challenge for Us All*. London: Runnymede Trust.

Runnymede Trust 2000. *The Future of Multi-Ethnic Britain: The Parekh Report*. London: Runnymede Trust.

Sadowski, Yahya 1997. The New Orientalism and the Democracy Debate, in *Political Islam: Essays from Middle East Report*, Beinin & Stork (eds.) 33–50. London: I B Tauris.

Said, Edward W. 1978. *Orientalism: Western Conceptions of the Orient*. London: Penguin Books.

Said, Edward W. 1997. *Covering Islam: How the Media and the Experts Determine How We See the Rest of the World*. London: Vintage.

Sardar, Ziauddin 1999. *Orientalism*. Buckingham: Open University Press.

Sayyid, Bobby S. 1997. *A Fundamental Fear: Eurocentrism and the Emergence of Islamism*. London: Zed Books.

Schiffrin, Deborah 1987. *Discourse Markers*. Cambridge: Cambridge University Press.

Schiffrin, Deborah 1994. *Approaches to Discourse*. Oxford: Blackwells.

Searle, Chris 1989. *Your Daily Dose: Racism and The Sun*. London: Campaign for Press and Broadcasting Freedom.

Searle, John 1969. *Speech Acts: An Essay in the Philosophy of Language*. Cambridge: Cambridge University Press.

Searle, John 1979. *Expression and Meaning*. Cambridge: Cambridge University Press.

Sedlak, Maria 1999. You really do make an unrespectable foreigner policy… Discourse on Ethnic Issues in Austrian Parliament. URL (consulted 16 January 2001): www.oeaw.ac.at/wittgenstein/racism/sedlakAustriaTOC.htm.

Shahak, Israel 1997. *Open Secrets: Israeli Nuclear and Foreign Policies*. London: Pluto Press.

Shearer, I. A. 1994. *Starke's International Law* (11th edition). London: Butterworths.

Simon, Roger 1982. *Gramsci's Political Thought: An Introduction*. London: Lawrence & Wishart.

Slisli, Fouzi (2000) The western media and the Algerian crisis, *Race and Class*, 41 (3): 43–57.

Sparks, Colin 1999. The Press, in *The Media in Britain: Current Debates and Developments*, J. Stokes & A. Reading (Eds.) 41–60. Houndsmills: Macmillan.

Spivak, Gayatri Chakravorty 1986, Three Women's Texts and a Critique of Imperialism, in H. L. Gates (Ed.) *'Race', Writing and Difference*. Chicago: University of Chicago Press.

Spivak, Gayatri Chakravorty 1988. Can the Subaltern Speak?, in *Marxism and the Interpretation of Culture*, C. Nelson & L. Grossberg (Eds.) Urbana: University of Illinois Press.

Statham, Paul 1999. Political mobilisation by minorities in Britain: negative feedback of 'race relations'? *Journal of Ethnic and Migration Studies* 25(4): 597–626.

Thomson, Anne 1996. *Critical Reasoning: A Practical Introduction*. London: Routledge.

Titscher, Stefan, Meyer, Michael, Wodak, Ruth & Vetter, Eva 2000. *Methods of Text and Discourse Analysis*. London: Sage.

Trades Union Congress (TUC) 2002. *Black and Underpaid*. TUC.

Trew, Tony 1979. 'What the papers say': linguistic variation and ideological difference, in *Language and Control*. R. Fowler, B. Hodge, G. Kress & T. Trew, (Eds.) London: Routledge and Kegan Paul.

Trinh, T. Minh-ha 1986–7. Introduction, *Discourse*, 8 (Winter).

Troyna, Barry 1987. Reported Racism: the 'British way of life' observed, in C. Husband (Ed.) *'Race' in Britain: Continuity and Change*, 275–291. London: Hutchinson.

Tuchman, Gaye 1972. Objectivity as Strategic Ritual, in *American Journal of Sociology*, 77: 660–679.

Turner, Bryan S. 1994. *Orientalism, Postmodernism and Globalism*. London: Routledge.

Turner, Bryan S. 2002. Orientalism, or the politics of the text, in *Interpreting Islam*, H. Donnan (ed.) 20–31. London: Sage.

Twitchin, John (Ed.) 1992. *The Black and White Media Book: Handbook for the Study of Racism and Television*. Stoke-on-Trent: Trentham Books Ltd.

Vertovec, Steven 1996. Muslims, the State, and the Public Sphere in Britain, in *Muslim Communities in the New Europe*, G. Nonneman, T. Niblock & B. Szajkowski (Eds.) 169–186. London: Ithaca Press.

Walsh, Jeremy (Ed.) 1995. *The Gulf War Did Not Happen: Politics, Culture and Warfare Post-Vietnam*. Aldershot: Arena.

Walton, Douglas N. 1989. *Informal Logic: A Handbook for Critical Argumentation*, Cambridge: Cambridge University Press.

Wieviorka, Michel 1995. *The Arena of Racism*. London: Sage.

Wilson, Clint C. & Gutierrez, Felix 1995. *Race, Multiculturalism and the Media: From Mass to Class Communication*, (2nd edition). Thousand Oaks, Ca.: Sage.

Wilson, Clint C. 2000. The paradox of African American Journalists, in *Ethnic Minorities and the Media: Changing Cultural Boundaries*, S. Cottle (Ed.) 85–99. Buckingham: Open University Press.

Wodak, Ruth 1995. Critical Linguistics and Critical Discourse Analysis, in *Handbook of Pragmatics*, J. Verschueren, J-O Ostman & J. Blommaert (Eds.) 204–210. Amsterdam: John Benjamins Publishing Co.

Wodak, Ruth 1996. *Disorders of Discourse*. London: Longman.

Wodak, Ruth, de Cillia, Rudolf, Reisigl, Martin, Liebhart, Karin 1999. *The Discursive Construction of National Identity*, trans A. Hirsch & R. Mitten. Edinburgh: Edinburgh University Press.

Worcester, Robert, M. 1998. Demographics and Values: What the British public reads and what it thinks about its newspapers, in *Sex, Lies and Democracy*, M. Bromley & H. Stephenson (Eds.) 39–48. London: Longman.

Wrench, John & Modood, Tariq 2000. *The Effectiveness of Integration Policies towards Immigrants and Ethnic Minorities in the UK*. International Labour Office.

Wykes, Maggie 2001. *News, Crime and Culture*. London: Pluto Press.

Yeğenoğlu, Meyda 1998. *Colonial Fantasies: Towards a feminist reading of Orientalism*. Cambridge: Cambridge *University Press*.

Zizek, Slavoj (Ed.) 1994. *Mapping* Ideology. London: Verso.

Zokaei, M. Saeed n.d. *Solidarity and Inclusion among British Muslims: Empirical application of social differentiation theory* (unpublished article).

Zoonen, Liesbet van 1994. *Feminist Media Studies*. London: Sage.

Zubaida, Sami 1970. Introduction, in *Race and Racialism*, S. Zubaida (Ed.) 1–16. London: Tavistock Publications.

Index of names

Index of subjects

In the series *Discourse Approaches to Politics, Society and Culture* the following titles have been published thus far or are scheduled for publication:

32   **RAMSAY, Guy:** Shaping Minds. A discourse analysis of Chinese-language community mental health literature. 2008. ix, 149 pp.

31   **JOHNSTONE, Barbara and Christopher EISENHART (eds.):** Rhetoric in Detail. Discourse analyses of rhetorical talk and text. 2008. viii, 330 pp.

30   **POWERS, John H. and Xiaosui XIAO (eds.):** The Social Construction of SARS. Studies of a health communication crisis. 2008. vi, 242 pp.

29   **ACHUGAR, Mariana:** What We Remember. The construction of memory in military discourse. 2008. x, 246 pp.

28   **DOLÓN, Rosana and Júlia TODOLÍ (eds.):** Analysing Identities in Discourse. 2008. xi, 204 pp.

27   **VERDOOLAEGE, Annelies:** Reconciliation Discourse. The case of the Truth and Reconciliation Commission. 2008. xiii, 238 pp.

26   **MILLAR, Sharon and John WILSON (eds.):** The Discourse of Europe. Talk and text in everyday life. 2007. viii, 200 pp.

25   **AZUELOS-ATIAS, Sol:** A Pragmatic Analysis of Legal Proofs of Criminal Intent. 2007. x, 180 pp.

24   **HODGES, Adam and Chad NILEP (eds.):** Discourse, War and Terrorism. 2007. x, 248 pp.

23   **GOATLY, Andrew:** Washing the Brain – Metaphor and Hidden Ideology. 2007. xvii, 431 pp.

22   **LE, Elisabeth:** The Spiral of 'Anti-Other Rhetoric'. Discourses of identity and the international media echo. 2006. xii, 280 pp.

21   **MYHILL, John:** Language, Religion and National Identity in Europe and the Middle East. A historical study. 2006. ix, 300 pp.

20   **OMONIYI, Tope and Joshua A. FISHMAN (eds.):** Explorations in the Sociology of Language and Religion. 2006. viii, 347 pp.

19   **HAUSENDORF, Heiko and Alfons BORA (eds.):** Analysing Citizenship Talk. Social positioning in political and legal decision-making processes. 2006. viii, 368 pp.

18   **LASSEN, Inger, Jeanne STRUNCK and Torben VESTERGAARD (eds.):** Mediating Ideology in Text and Image. Ten critical studies. 2006. xii, 254 pp.

17   **SAUSSURE, Louis de and Peter SCHULZ (eds.):** Manipulation and Ideologies in the Twentieth Century. Discourse, language, mind. 2005. xvi, 312 pp.

16   **ERREYGERS, Guido and Geert JACOBS (eds.):** Language, Communication and the Economy. 2005. viii, 239 pp.

15   **BLACKLEDGE, Adrian:** Discourse and Power in a Multilingual World. 2005. x, 252 pp.

14   **DIJK, Teun A. van:** Racism and Discourse in Spain and Latin America. 2005. xii, 198 pp.

13   **WODAK, Ruth and Paul CHILTON (eds.):** A New Agenda in (Critical) Discourse Analysis. Theory, methodology and interdisciplinarity. 2005. xviii, 320 pp.

12   **GRILLO, Eric (ed.):** Power Without Domination. Dialogism and the empowering property of communication. 2005. xviii, 247 pp.

11   **MUNTIGL, Peter:** Narrative Counselling. Social and linguistic processes of change. 2004. x, 347 pp.

10   **BAYLEY, Paul (ed.):** Cross-Cultural Perspectives on Parliamentary Discourse. 2004. vi, 385 pp.

9   **RICHARDSON, John E.:** (Mis)Representing Islam. The racism and rhetoric of British broadsheet newspapers. 2004. xxiii, 262 pp.

8   **MARTIN, J.R. and Ruth WODAK (eds.):** Re/reading the past. Critical and functional perspectives on time and value. 2003. vi, 277 pp.

7   **ENSINK, Titus and Christoph SAUER (eds.):** The Art of Commemoration. Fifty years after the Warsaw Uprising. 2003. xii, 246 pp.

6   **DUNNE, Michele Durocher:** Democracy in Contemporary Egyptian Political Discourse. 2003. xii, 179 pp.

5   **THIESMEYER, Lynn (ed.):** Discourse and Silencing. Representation and the language of displacement. 2003. x, 316 pp.

4   **CHILTON, Paul and Christina SCHÄFFNER (eds.):** Politics as Text and Talk. Analytic approaches to political discourse. 2002. x, 246 pp.

3   **CHNG, Huang Hoon:** Separate and Unequal. Judicial rhetoric and women's rights. 2002. viii, 157 pp.

2   **LITOSSELITI, Lia and Jane SUNDERLAND (eds.):** Gender Identity and Discourse Analysis. 2002. viii, 336 pp.

1   **GELBER, Katharine:** Speaking Back. The free speech versus hate speech debate. 2002. xiv, 177 pp.